Innovation Strategies in Interdependent States

NEW HORIZONS IN THE ECONOMICS OF INNOVATION

Founding Editor: Christopher Freeman, *Emeritus Professor of Science Policy, SPRU – Science and Technology Policy Research, University of Sussex, UK*

Technical innovation is vital to the competitive performance of firms and of nations and for the sustained growth of the world economy. The economics of innovation is an area that has expanded dramatically in recent years and this major series, edited by one of the most distinguished scholars in the field, contributes to the debate and advances in research in this most important area.

The main emphasis is on the development and application of new ideas. The series provides a forum for original research in technology, innovation systems and management, industrial organization, technological collaboration, knowledge and innovation, research and development, evolutionary theory and industrial strategy. International in its approach, the series includes some of the best theoretical and empirical work from both well-established researchers and the new generation of scholars.

Titles in the series include:

Technological Systems and Intersectoral Innovation Flows
Riccardo Leoncini and Sandro Montresor

Inside the Virtual Product
How Organisations Create Knowledge Through Software
Luciana D'Adderio

Embracing the Knowledge Economy
The Dynamic Transformation of the Finnish Innovation System
Edited by Gerd Schienstock

The Dynamics of Innovation in Eastern Europe
Lessons from Estonia
Per Högselius

Technology and the Decline in Demand for Unskilled Labour
A Theoretical Analysis of the US and European Labour Markets
Mark Sanders

Innovation and Institutions
A Multidisciplinary Review of the Study of Innovation Systems
Edited by Steven Casper and Frans van Waarden

Innovation Strategies in Interdependent States
Essays on Smaller Nations, Regions and Cities in a Globalized World
John de la Mothe

Internationalizing the Internet
The Co-evolution of Influence and Technology
Byung-Keun Kim

Asia's Innovation Systems in Transition
Edited by Bengt-Åke Lundvall, Patarapong Intarakumnerd and Jan Vang-Lauridsen

National Innovation, Indicators and Policy
Edited by Louise Earl and Fred Gault

Innovation Strategies in Interdependent States

Essays on Smaller Nations, Regions and Cities in a Globalized World

John de la Mothe

University of Ottawa, Canada and University College London, UK

NEW HORIZONS IN THE ECONOMICS OF INNOVATION

Edward Elgar
Cheltenham, UK • Northampton, MA, USA

Published by
Edward Elgar Publishing Limited
Glensanda House
Montpellier Parade
Cheltenham
Glos GL50 1UA
UK

Edward Elgar Publishing, Inc.
136 West Street
Suite 202
Northampton
Massachusetts 01060
USA

A catalogue record for this book
is available from the British Library

Library of Congress Cataloging in Publication Data
De la Mothe, John.
    Innovation strategies in interdependent states : essays on smaller nations, regions, and cities / John de la Mothe.
    p. cm. — (New horizons in the economics of innovation)
    Includes bibliographical references.
    1. Technological innovations—Economic aspects. 2. States, Small. 3. Economic growth. I. Title. II. Series.

    HC79.T4D442 2005
    338'.064—dc22   2005049819

ISBN-13: 978 1 84376 927 9
ISBN-10: 1 84376 927 1

Printed and bound in Great Britain by MPG Books Ltd, Bodmin, Cornwall

Contents

Acknowledgements   *viii*

1. Introduction: Innovation in an Age of Interdependence   1

PART ONE   THE TEXTURE OF THE NEW ECONOMY

2. The New Competition   12
3. Some Economic Consequences of Knowledge   36
4. Technology, Trade and Investment in Interdependent Economies   51
5. Innovation, Institutions and International Development   66
6. The Institutional Governance of Innovation   92
7. Capacities and Priorities in Innovation   107

PART TWO   CONSTRUCTING ADVANTAGE IN THE NEW
            ECONOMY

8. Interdependence and National Systems of Innovation   125
9. Transitional Systems of Innovation   138
10. Learning in Local Systems of Innovation   152
11. Constructing Advantage in Smaller Regions   166
12. Constructing Advantage in Cities   171
13. Lessons From Cities and Smaller Nations   177

PART THREE CULTURES OF THE NEW ECONOMY

14. Innovation, Globalization and the Challenges to Science
    and Technology Policy   188
15. Innovation, Science and Priorities in Open Societies   201
16. Innovation and Interdependence in the New Republic of
    Knowledge   209
17. Conclusion: The Embedded Culture of Innovation   222

Bibliography   233
Index   243

'A Man's reach must exceed his grasp, or what's a heaven for?'
Robert Browning

To the memory of a friend

D. Allan Bromley
1926–2005

Acknowledgements

This collection of essays was written over a period of time and was never initially intended to culminate in a single volume. Nevertheless, after much work on innovation in smaller nations, regions and cities, these papers seem to come together. Please read them as individual contributions though, with a macro thread on the changing nature of innovation and interdependence. Each chapter raises issues for smaller nations. These pieces originally emerged at the behest of various government agencies: In Canada, Industry Canada, the Department of Finance, Natural Resources Canada, the House of Commons, and the Department of Foreign Affairs and International Trade. Internationally, questions were asked by CONACYT in Mexico, APEC, the Organization of American States (OAS), the OECD, industry agencies in Norway and the Netherlands, as well as such industry associations and NGOs as the Canada Advanced Technology Association Alliance (CATA) and the Ottawa Center for Research and Innovation (OCRI). The financial assistance of the Social Sciences and Humanities Research Council of Canada was enormously important throughout. The intellectual collaborations of Geoff Mallory, Hollis Whitehead and Paul Dufour are appreciated and acknowledged – friends all. Discussions of these topics with members of the Innovation Systems Research Network (ISRN), of which I am a member, has been most stimulating, as have conversations with my colleagues in the Department of Science and Technology Studies at the University College London (UCL) – particularly Beck Hurst, Jon Turney and Brian Balmer and my friend Phil Cooke in Cardiff. Interactions with the 'Friday Night Irregulars' also contributed in surprising ways – thus thanks to Anthony Griffith and Anastasia Vakos, Mark Henderson, Joy Senack, Sandra Matthews, Barry Gander, Jerome and Mel (of Regents Park), and the red-wrapped plinth of Lord Napier in his generous and salubrious accommodation in South Kensington for inspiration. Technical support from Natasha Guiller, Amy Harrington, Graham Vickery and Andrew Evans was indispensable.

JdlM
London, Maida Vale, June 2005

1. Introduction: Innovation in an Age of Interdependence

Innovation and interdependence. These are two central elements not only of advanced economies but, indeed, of human culture and societies. They are predicated on ideas (mostly the result of creativity, research, development, science and technology – or the new production of knowledge), reflected in the institutions we choose to design, and result in the standards of living that we achieve. This implies of course a form of competition. But remember that the term 'competition' means 'to seek together'.

Innovation comes in myriad forms. However those who still view it in a singular way – in terms of scientific and technical 'breakthroughs' – are caught in a Popperian illusion. Thomas Kuhn, in his *The Structure of Scientific Revolutions*, bolstered by the work of Derek de Solla Price, recognized that the vast majority of innovators and research scientists alive today work in 'everyday jobs' as professors or industrial researchers (normal science). Their work is incremental, not revolutionary. Only rarely do they have the privilege of truly and radically changing the world – as for example the late Sir Francis Crick and his colleague James Watson did in fathoming the structure of DNA. That day, in 1953,[1] truly *was* a Popperian event.[2] But they are rare. Innovations, upon which capitalist economies rely (especially for what has been called 'exuberant growth'), are in fact rather small incremental improvements in products or processes in which genuine novelty and imitation shade imperceptibly into one another.

Of course, to take the full realm of meaning from Schumpeter, we can certainly expand the practical notion of innovation into the realms of institutions and social organization (for example, the nineteenth century British Post Office, the application in industry of Taylor's scientific management, the development of Ford's assembly lines, and the creative culture of Apple's workplace are all testimony to that). And we can accept the benefits of the opening up of new markets as well as the discovery and development of new materials (for example,

1

replacing hard steel in car manufacturing with new composite materials involving carbon fibers, graphite and aluminum which were lighter – thus resulting in greater fuel efficiencies as well as enhanced safety for those traveling within the passenger cage). The creation of national labs in the early twentieth century, such as the Department of Scientific and Industrial Research in Britain and the National Research Council in Canada, have fueled and supported an impressive array of innovations to the benefit of their respective countries – and world science.

Interdependence too comes in myriad forms, and not just the incoherent 'bloc' mentality of the globalization/anti-globalization debate. It is much more subtle and historical. At the same time, the growth of interdependence cannot, of course, simply be traced to the growing importance of science, technology and innovation. It can be seen as a product of many developments: rapid industrialization worldwide, reduction of trade barriers, population growth and migration, increased specialization and division of labor amongst nations, and others. In some eyes, the hegemony of nations has lost its hegemon, especially under George W. Bush. The importance of knowledge and technology, in and of themselves, have become a focus and, as a result, technology transfer between multinationals has become central to understanding interdependence. SNC-Lavalin, for example, has offices in 30 countries and works in 100, Seimens has operations in 175 countries, both in a variety of related businesses. Interdependence can also be seen in corporate alliances, in the value added supply chain, in distribution channels, in international markets, in trade and foreign direct investment. It can, in other words, be seen in relationships – from the familial (such as parents and child), to the marital, to the scholastic (as between a mentor and the student), to 'tribal' ties which traverse time and which are often bound by language. It can certainly be seen in international relations, as fluid though they may be. Canada and Mexico are inexorably linked to the United States. But their European origins can never be lost. Similar ties can assuredly be found in Europe, Asia and the Americas.

Learning too, is central to both innovation and interdependence. Kenneth Arrow and others, in the 1950s and 1960s, discussed different types of learning: by doing, knowing who, knowing what, knowing where, and so on. Michael Polanyi, in the same period, differentiated codified knowledge (things you could write down, as in a blueprint, patent or code that could then be replicated *in abstentia*) and tacit knowledge. But to pursue the primary notion, we might reflect on the observation that much learning, in the innovative and interdependent context, is not passive. Learning is active is several respects. First, learning is an analytic construct. People interpret contexts through their own assumptions and worldviews. As Barbara Levitt and James March conclude, what an actor learns may be influenced 'less by history than by the frames applied to that history'. Second, actors actively search for the information they believe is necessary for action.

However, much of the importance of innovation is lost in the often inarticulate noise regarding sovereignty in an age of globalization and movements of anti-globalization. Borders in truth no longer define identity. Identity implies association, not geographical separation or distance. How many of us have changed jobs to different 'countries', or studied abroad only to make life-long friends? To be a citizen of ancient Athens was to be a member of a select club, not an inclusive one. In the United States today, after waves of immigration, the principle source of new citizens is Latin America. In Canada, it was Europe but is now Asia. Most nations, especially those with imperial pasts, are wonderfully diversified. In fact, the commercial world is one made of association – firms, negotiated standards and regulations, free trade agreements, diversity.... i.e. interdependence.

The crossover effects of innovation should be clear. Knowledge crosses borders. Students cross borders to gain post-graduate training and credentials, and return. Faculty cross borders, and return, as do industrial researchers. Italians and Canadians go to English universities – as they do in France, Sweden, Australia or Japan. Technically this is even more true. Who could think of medicine without chemistry, health care diagnosis without information and communications technologies, or air travel without a knowledge of fluid dynamics. The list of cross overs is endless and is striking when expanded and pondered upon since university curricula are too often siloed 'disciplines' when in fact it is the *interaction* between knowledge fields and their *interdependence* that produces innovations and that fuels economic growth and social progress. Only government bureaucrats really think that borders create identity.

In many authentic ways, innovation is a microeconomic activity, intimately operating at the level of the firm. Differences are striking when one compares sectors, firm sizes, supply chains, multinational organizations, histories or transitions and so on. But this book will not focus on the micro, although – as some of the chapters will make clear – the firm or organization is never far away from the surface of discussion. Indeed, firm innovation absolutely requires stable political and market environments. This may seem clear, but, as Martin Wolf of the *Financial Times* has argued,[3] the most important fact about our world is the inequality of states. By this he means not the gap in scale – Singapore and many other smaller nations compete quite well in the world economy – but instead he worries about the gulf in *effectiveness*. '[M]any of the world's states are incapable of providing…a dynamic market economy.' States provide the institutions upon which complex market economies depend. They also decide the policies that determine how well private agents are able to identify and exploit economic opportunities. The collection of essays that follow are centrally interested in this idea.

As a result, one must also be focally aware of the important impacts that regulatory regimes, intellectual property rights, copyright and trade laws, investment policies, educational systems that ensure high literacy and math competencies,[4] public universities, national laboratories, and so on have on the performance and potential of a nation's growth prospects, including job creation and retention. As I write, the outsourcing of jobs is high in the rhetoric of American politics and media attention. (This is wrong-headed.) In Canada, we do not talk of 'Brain Drain' but of 'Brain Circulation' (science is, after all, an international – but not always a public – good). And this is a good thing. At the macro level, graduates in computing science from Waterloo University are heavily hired by Microsoft in California, but they never leave Ontario. In 2002, Hewlett Packard had a six week rotation out of San Francisco to Dresden to help ramp-up the Fab-Lab of Infineon. Germany's Siemens (which started more than a century ago with manufacturing facilities in London and St. Petersburg) today has tens of thousands of employees in the US. Still, the TV program '60 Minutes' has fueled American populist fears about foot loose call centers in India[5] without noticing the low pay of such jobs (between US$3000-US$5000 per annum) which many Americans would not wish to hold and without noticing the low impact such jobs have on innovation-led economic growth. Indeed, once a technological innovation becomes routine within a firm or a sector, it is common to see these routines exported, thus freeing the firm and knowledge-based labor force to pursue new technical challenges, what some call a strategy of 'exuberant growth'.[6]

However, smaller nations, regions and cities have, in many cases, recognized innovation as a key to the future, have not fully understood what they could and could not do about it, and have reviewed their spending, capacity and incentive activities, and many have tried to create innovation strategies. South Korea, Canada, South Africa, Scotland and Ireland immediately come to mind. Many have tried to measure and construct innovation clusters, such as Dresden and Ottawa. But a major difference must be made evident.

During the 1980s, much discussion around the macroeconomic innovative performance of nations focused on the Triad – the US, Japan and Germany (later the European Union) as exemplars. This led to an error by some smaller nations, who did not have the capacity, scale, scope or institutions, to try to emulate the Triad. In broad terms, these large influential countries had adopted strategies that were a blend of being mission oriented or diffusion oriented. The scale and scope of the United States of course allowed it to institutionally adopt the full spectrum, involving both centralized decision-making in the military-industrial complex, but also promoting an entrepreneurial culture at the firm and university spin-off levels. Japan had a long history of being a closed society but it has rapidly evolved, by the mid-twentieth century, through an important phase of reverse engineering and into an innovation strategy posture that has been described by Chalmers Johnson as a form of a 'cartel of the mind'. (Japan has opened up remarkably in the past twenty years in terms of its engagement with the world and its sharing of ideas and research.) South Korea, as a counter example, has in recent years – disrupted by the so-called Asian Contagion which seriously affected all of South-East Asia in the currency collapse – set a GERD/GDP target of 5 percent by 2010. A casual observation of this simple example is that imitation led Japan's innovation post-World War Two evolution while South Korea began to travel down the road of invention and basic research (i.e. the creation of new knowledge) in the belief that research would lead to long-term economic performance. One required reverse engineering whilst the other requires a culture of entrepreneurship.

Now, while smaller economic and demographic nations,[7] such as Canada, Sweden, Australia, Finland and Denmark each show some aspects of these two 'styles' of innovation strategy – mission and diffusion – this can be seen as thoroughly understandable. All abut on the borders or in the close proximity of a key hegemon: Canada with the US, the Nordics with the former Soviet Union and now, more meaningfully with the EU, Ireland with England and Europe, etc. This physical relationship clearly effects behavior. Eighty three percent of Canada's exports go to the US; Sweden trades mostly with Germany, the UK and Norway; Finland trades with Germany and Sweden, and Denmark with Germany.

But this pattern doesn't just mean that proximity matters to smaller nations. This is self-evident in a globalized electronically connected information economy. Three broad elements can be highlighted.

The first is that according to neo-Ricardian trade theory, comparative advantage prevails. Wealth and value-added is based on what you *have*. Canada, in this theory (which continues to have considerable explanatory power) would continue to export resource-related products – from mining, forestry and energy – but today employment is 26 percent in agriculture and industry while high value-added services represent 74 percent. In Portugal, which in neo-Ricardian terms is well recognized for example for its excellent wines and olive oil, employment is 51 percent in services. Singapore, which in comparative advantage terms should not even exist with only 639 square kilometers and only 8 percent of arable land, has a GDP per head of more than $35,000 (more than the US) and an employment structure that is 71 percent in services (0 percent in agriculture). It also highlights the fact that being smaller means that ideas – the basis of innovation – need to be shared. The meaning of value-added has therefore shifted to what you *do*. To achieve this, an entrepreneurial culture needs to be nurtured and institutions need to be (and have been) created not only to generate new knowledge so that the state, region or city can be part of the global economy, but also that they can contribute (there are no 'free rides'), can have the talent to develop, attract and retain creative people, and can identify and apply new knowledge that is being produced domestically.

A second element can be superimposed on this trade perspective, and that is neo-Porterian 'competitive advantage' in which the size and scope of a domestic market mattered. Harvard Business School's Michael Porter called this approach 'the Diamond' in which a combination of factors of production combined to generate a powerful innovation engine that included research and development, access to infrastructure and risk-accepting finance,[8] and managerial leadership.

A third approach, which is closely related to the neo-Porterian identification of necessary attributes but which works at the decision-makers' level in cities, smaller states and regions has been called 'constructed advantage'.[9] This new work, which is also being developed by scholars in Wales, the Netherlands, Scotland, Denmark, Jamaica, Australia, amongst others, as well as city mayors in Canada, builds on the notion of local and regional systems of innovation, and on 'clusters'. By the combination of local leadership, the availability of smart *and* physical infrastructure, access to the full range of capital, and technological capacity, areas that were not traditionally thought of in terms of serious growth and high value added standards of living have been created.

This third stratagem is pregnant with possibility insofar as it allows analysts and decision-makers to understand innovation at the level of location and exchange. Marshall did this by looking at industrial districts. But since the work of Moses Abramovitz and Robert Solow in the late 1950s and early 1960s on growth theory, since the work of James Kendrick on total factor productivity, and since Wassily Leontief identified the paradox of labor and capital-intensive exports in the face of Ricardo, a number of no longer stylized facts can be identified. One is that, in growth accounting, technological innovation was finally recognized as being responsible for the rapid post-1970s rise in investment and knowledge-based activity (even though the majority of economics textbooks – such as those by Harvard's N. Gregory Mankiew – and academic media commentators – such as Princeton's Paul Krugman – continue to largely ignore endogenous growth theory (i.e. technological change). Another is that productivity since the 1970s did not initially show the impacts of the introduction of computing into the private sectors (largely due to a major transition phase from manual to automated office services).[10] The impact of informatics in a broad range of sectors has, I think, been demonstrated since. A final cursory observation is that, as Leontief noted, labor-intensive nations would be expected to export labor-intensive products (like China) and capital or technology-intensive nations would show a capital/technology export profile. However, by the late 1970s, Germany and the US were both trading power tools. The difference was that one (the US) was shipping do it yourself (DIY) tools whilst Germany was shipping high construction quality tools. In other words, the difference was in the application or technical performance specifications of the products. DIYs were weekend amateur handy-men fixing their kitchen cupboards while the industrial firms were needing tools that could be used at serious construction sites. So despite the simplified models of trade theorists, dynamic economies could indeed trade in *both* labor and technology/knowledge/capital-intensive areas. The dramatic shift in employment patterns towards knowledge-based services in both OECD countries (in many cases to over 70 percent) and dynamic emerging economies since the 1960s is testimony to that.

The above broad and cursory sketch has allowed us to highlight a number of vistas that readers can look for in the chapters that follow.

We live in an age of intense, compressed and increased complexity. Over the last three decades, innovation and interdependence have changed the world in which we live. Now, for both corporate managers and policy strategists, they are recognizing that they have to work in a challenging environment in which they *do not* have a detailed understanding of the innovation horizon.

We live in an age of networks, an age of access and an age of association. This can be seen in the way that firms, community and industry associations interact with their particular milieux. Interactive innovation, collective learning and associative practices are key analytic tools in regional and corporate economic performance.

Smaller states, regions and cities are where we will learn. There are now more than 300 'city-states' around the world with populations of greater than one million. They are expanding rapidly and many of them are growing through innovation and knowledge-based services. The Westphalian view is being redefined. The processes of global economic integration and accelerated urban growth and concentration are making traditional policies and strategies antiquated.

In the spirit of the above sketched notions, this book will focus mostly on smaller states, regions and cities in the global economy. It will end with some historical and cultural observations, because innovation and interdependence are very human activities.

NOTES

1. During the academic year, 1953-54, Crick was on leave of absence at the Brooklyn Polytechnic in New York. However the work began as a doctoral research project at the Strangeways Laboratory at Cambridge (1947) with Arthur Hughes, and in 1949 in the Medical Research Unit at the Cavendish Laboratory where he met James Watson. The first announcement of their achievement was made at The Eagle pub on Benet Street in Cambridge on February 28, 1953. Thanks to Donia Stick and Kristian Barber for this. Of course, by 1952, much was known about DNA, including its exclusive role as genetic material - the sole substance capable of storing all the information needed to create a living being. What was not yet known was what the elusive DNA molecule looked like, or how it performed this amazing hereditary function. This would change within a year. The now familiar double helical structure of DNA, and the base-pairing crucial to its hereditary function, were deciphered in 1953, and the individuals most commonly associated with this remarkable feat are Watson and Crick. Maurice Wilkins played a crucial role as well, and he shared the 1962 Nobel Prize for Physiology and Medicine with Watson and Crick for the discovery. However, another important figure remains, without whom the discovery would not have been possible: the brilliant but short-lived Rosie Franklin. She died, unrecognized, in 1958 at the age of 38.
2. Karl Popper's work on the logic of scientific discovery (in parallel with his work on conjectures and refutations), argued that the work of scientists in the advancement of knowledge was based on the falsification of theories. Thomas Khun on the other hand, and drawing on the observation made by Derek de Solla Price that 95 percent of all the professionally trained scientists and engineers who had ever lived in history were alive and working today, argued that scientists in fact performed 'normal' science in which they worked with the existing theories. For Kuhn, this approach collected extensive support for the dominant framework. It was only when a sizable number of anomalies were noticed that the scientific community would work to explain the anomalies thus resulting in a paradigm shift or a 'scientific revolution'.
3. Martin Wolf, 'Market and State: The Two Faces of Liberal Democracy', *Financial Times*, London, Wednesday July 21 2004 p.13; and his *Why Globalization Works*,

Yale University Press, New Haven, 2004.
4. Canada, Ireland, Sweden, Denmark, the Netherlands, the US, South Korea etc. All have literacy rates of over 97 percent. India's rate is 53.5 percent; Nigeria's is 59 percent.
5. 60 Minutes, CBS, Sunday, July 31, 2004
6. Joseph Schumpeter himself, as early as in *Capitalism, Socialism and Democracy* (Harper and Row, New York, 1942, p. 132) noted that technological change itself is being reduced to routine.
7. Canada has a population of 33 million and a GDP of $950 billion. Sweden has a population of 9.5 million and a GDP of Skr 21 billion. Finland has a population of 5.5 million and a GDP of Fmk 687 billion, and Denmark's population was 5.3 million with a GDP of Dkr 1167 billion.
8. William Baumol, in his *The Free Market Innovation Machine: Analyzing the Growth Miracle of Capitalism* (Princeton University Press, Princeton, 2002) p.11 reminds us of W.C. Fields, who was trying to lure a novice into a card game. The novice asked questions about the 'morality of games of chance' to which Fields hastened to reassure his victim by saying 'Young man, when you play with me, all elements of chance have been removed.'
9. John de la Mothe and Geoffrey Mallory, 'Local Knowledge and the Strategy of Constructing Advantage: The Role of Community Alliances', *International Journal of Technology Management*, Inderscience, Amsterdam, 2004.
10. See the TEMPO (Technology and Employment Opportunities) Project at the Science Policy Research Unit (SPRU), led by Christopher Freeman in the mid-1980s.

PART ONE

The Texture of the New Economy

2. The New Competition

Competition, in an interdependent world, is an obscure – yet politically pregnant – term. It has been called a cliché, 'the C word', and an evangelical pursuit. It has engaged the media, business, NGOs and most citizens. We need only think of the anti-globalization events of Seattle, Whistler or Davos around the WEF, the IMF, the World Bank or the WTO. Competition has been the subject of analysis, polemic, rhetoric and extensive consultation by governments. And yet, the issue of competitiveness – which lies at the very core of our long-term well-being – remains unresolved. It remains a critical but inadequate debate.

What is at stake is nothing less than the livelihoods of our children, the levels of education and health care we will be able to afford, and the kind of environment that will surround us. How competitive we are will depend quite simply on the intellectual abilities and skills of our people, on the kinds of industries we attract and develop, and on the strength of our policies and policy mechanisms.

Unfortunately, the debate about competitiveness has to date been partial and rather lopsided, especially given the rapidly changing nature of the world economy. In part, this is because the meanings of competitiveness are not easily grasped. The new world economy with its emerging, highly interconnected web of companies is far too complex for traditional economic ideas and their derivative policies, which can deal with the new competitiveness only in very limited ways. Too often, the underlying factors of competition – such as research, technology and innovation – are ignored or seen as being non-dynamic, equally accessible features of economies. Compounding all of this, the debate on competitiveness in smaller nations has been notable for an absence of vision and of leadership from governments, business and academia.

This chapter is designed to aid in the debate. It attempts to clarify the linkages between research, technology, innovation, various types of interdependence and competitiveness – to get beyond the traditional ideas that have influenced the debate so far. With such an improved understanding, countries can develop an effective, long-term, wealth-producing position in the new world economy.

COMPETITIVENESS AT THE LEVEL OF THE FIRM

Although the term 'competitiveness' has been used relentlessly in debates since the mid-1980s, no comprehensive, fully realistic, or consistent definition has been given to it. Originally, the notion of competitiveness was born out of firm-level economics. It means 'to seek together'. At this firm level, and in very general terms, a competitive firm was one that regularly created and sold a better product or offered a better service than its rivals. Importantly, the firm generally knew who its rivals were since they were usually in exactly the same business, had similar products to sell, and operated in the same markets. On the strength of its products and services, a competitive company was typically one that made a profit and had a large or healthy share of its markets. A firm's first markets were usually nearby – except in the case of large multinational firms. To be competitive, a firm constantly had to try to improve its products and services. It also had to be as efficient as possible, in terms of cost control, in terms of close supplier linkages, and in terms of production processes. Indeed these were often seen as the principal measures of the quality of a firm's management. The world is no longer so simple. And yet it is undeniably at the level of the firm that notions of competitiveness make real sense – it is here and only here that wealth and jobs are created.

COMPETITIVENESS AT THE LEVEL OF THE SECTOR

It is important to realize that notions of competitiveness that are based on industrial sectors are problematic. Sectors do not compete: only firms do. A sector is little more than a convenient mental construct that is used either by analysts and researchers, or by people within an industry to connote a grouping of firms that tend to have core products, processes, or markets in common.

Having said this, however, one can talk about the general conditions for promoting or retarding the competitiveness of firms within a sector. From a policy point of view, one might call this setting the environment for sectoral competitiveness. While individual firms succeed or fail largely on the basis of their actions and reactions to their specific environments, it is equally true that the conditions that are conducive to the competitiveness of firms within a sector vary significantly from one region or country to another. Such conditions are known to be related to the number of firms in the sector, the mix of different-sized firms in the sector, and the size of the home market. As the number of firms and the size of the home market both increase, the competition within the sector intensifies. Clearly there are advantages to firms if their sector is geographically clustered. For example, it becomes easier to keep informed about one's rivals, there is a common labor pool with the requisite skills, and technologies or ideas can more easily move from firm to firm. In high technology industries, for example, Canada has rather limited geographical clustering. As a result many Canadian firms are competing against distant competitors. This tends to dull their competitive edge, thin out the available labor pool, and provide little stimulus for the development (in size and sophistication) of a home market.

Thus, as interesting as sectorally-based analysis of competitiveness may be, sectoral-level data must be used with great caution because the general observations that may be gleaned from the data tend to have limited applicability for either the individual firm or the analysts wishing to make meaningful comparisons.

COMPETITIVENESS AT THE LEVEL OF THE STATE

At the level of the state – particularly small and medium sized interdependent nations – the idea of competitiveness is also open to interpretative difficulties. For example, what is a competitive country? It is not reasonable to view competitiveness as being simply a matter of the 'average competitiveness' of its firms, but it does make some sense to think of a competitive economy as one with enough competitive firms to keep people employed and prosperous. Moreover, it is not at all clear whether – if one wished to – one could define a nation's firms in terms of the nationality of the firm's ownership – or in terms of whether the firm operates in Canada and thus provides Canadians, Swedes or New Zealanders with jobs, pays taxes, contributes to communities, and so on.

Thus, while there are parallels between the ideas of firm-level, sectoral-level and nation-level competitiveness, the definition of the latter is much more elusive. For example, most analysts would have no difficulty in locating the source of a firm's strategies and decisions in the firm's management. There would be no end of difficulty, however, in trying to locate similar functions at the national economic level, and there would be outright hostility if attempts were made to equate the roles of firm management with the roles of national governments. There are a great many other such difficulties.

COMPARATIVE INDICATORS OF COMPETITIVENESS

The debate has had problems in defining competitiveness in terms of international norms against which nations should be measured. For example, many Canadians wonder: Is it reasonable for us to expect to compete with countries such as the United States, Japan, or Germany, which have much larger workforces, consumer markets, and capital markets? Or: Is it reasonable for us to try to compete with countries such as Mexico, Poland, or Thailand, which have much lower labor costs? What exactly can we expect from our economy when we have a small but extremely well-educated population, a heavy reliance on trade, and a country that is still extremely rich in natural resources?

These types of worries are all legitimate, but they really stem from well-entrenched ideas of the old economic order and do little to advance our understanding of the nature of the new competitiveness. Thus, when discussing the competitiveness of Canada in terms of norms, we rely most frequently on a wide variety of both qualitative and quantitative indicators of our collective and personal standards of living. What is the unemployment rate or the price of groceries this year? Are housing costs taking a higher share of my take-home pay? Can I afford a vacation this year? Do there seem to be more plant closures or homeless people in my city? And so on.

However, there is also a major problem with the use of indicators in the competitiveness debate, as two brief examples will illustrate. Each year, the World Economic Forum publishes *The World Competitiveness Report*. This renowned report has a broad readership but is really of use only to a small number of specialist economists. It has very limited direct applicability to policy-making. For example, the WEF publishes 'scoreboards' on countries that combine seven 'factors of competitiveness' with 330 'criteria of competitiveness.' A complicated and rather subjective methodology was used to weigh each of these indicators. Thus any international rankings that were based on the sum of these 2310 indicators and that compared highly industrialized countries with newly industrializing ones must be interpreted extremely carefully.

While interesting, such measures not only raised the difficult question (mentioned above) of what a competitive nation is, but they also lacked any explicit theory to justify and integrate them. Moreover, the process of being competitive, at the firm, sectoral and national level, is a highly dynamic process that takes place over time: it is more of a motion picture than a snapshot. It is not very helpful, therefore, when newspapers and magazines publish Canada's or Finland's overall ranking each year without any kind of solid theoretical underpinning or preamble. As it turns out, the WEF ranked Canada 11th overall in 1982 but then this rose to 5th in 2002. If one were a trend-watcher, one might easily be convinced that the Canadian economy is improving, but in the recent debate on competitiveness, policy analysts, media analysts and business representatives were all arguing over the meaning of our drop from 4th place the year before. Clearly, such casual indicator watching can be misleading without reference to methodology; it cannot tell us much at all about how well we are really doing, regardless of whether the indicators go up or down.

To take a second example, there has been a great deal of discussion over the past decade about the importance of science and technology to the future of our economy. However, it has become fashionable in some circles to argue in favor of R&D 'targets' at the national aggregate level. Recently, the Canadian federal government has announced that it will move from 15th to 5th in world R&D performance by 2010, and that they will 'create' 10 new technology clusters across the country. (There are 10 provinces, this is suspected as being a political move which has now been dropped.) 'How' is left unexplained. What this will mean for economic performance, education, environment and sustainability (never mind the citizenry) is a question well dodged. It is not uninteresting that, in the 2004 election, none of the federal parties discussed R&D, even though the government had just 'completed' a vacuous 'innovation strategy'.

Research and development expenditures at the national level are often measured, and compared internationally, as a ratio – this being the gross expenditure on R&D (GERD) as a percentage of gross domestic product (GDP). Using this measure, Canada has consistently fluctuated around the 1.3 percent GERD/GDP level for about 20 years (it is now about 1.8 percent and was as low as 0.9 percent in the 1970s). In comparison the US ratio is 2.8 percent, and Britain's is 2.2 percent. The blunt argument in Canada's 'target' debate is simply that we, as a country, need to set a target and a schedule to increase our GERD/GDP ratio to, say, 2.5 percent by the year 2010. The assumption here is that if Canada spends more on science and technology, then Canada will have a 'high technology economy.' If we have a 'high technology economy', then we will be competitive.

Unfortunately, the relationship between GERD/GDP ratios and competitiveness is not quite so easily made – for a vast number of reasons that can be summarized as follows.

If the people of Canada or Australia were to sign a cheque for, say, $1 billion to be spent on science and technology, and if the cheque were to be cashed tomorrow and divided amongst the existing researchers and companies who are already doing R&D, then the real effect on our economy would be minimal. This is because there would be no capacity to effectively or productively use this money. To use such funds for the benefit of the country, and the researchers and firms involved, there has to be infrastructure in place to allow the effective absorption of new investments. For R&D to be productive, university and industrial labs both need 'high-quality' instrumentation and equipment. For research scientists and engineers to be productive, they need assistants with high-quality technical and vocational training as well as good co-researchers with undergraduate and postgraduate training. For firms to turn their R&D investments into new products, services, and profits, they need – among other things – technically literate marketing and administrative staff with a wide range of skills. Moreover, using such macro-indicators as the GERD/GDP ratio as a focus for policy ignores the problems associated with the quality of the research and the source or distribution of the research (be it industry, university, or government) relative to other countries.

TRADITIONAL ANALYTICAL APPROACHES TO COMPETITIVENESS

In the process of analysis, the complexity of competitiveness is too often reduced to single items of concern – the implication being that if we can just fix this one item then a country, or the industrial sector in question, will be competitive. Unfortunately, the identification of lone problem areas, while often important, rarely goes to the heart of the problem of competitiveness. Moreover, by focusing on one or another symptom of competitive decline, traditional analytical approaches have tended to ignore the real dynamics of business and the contributions that research, technology and innovation are making to the changing ways of creating wealth. These traditional foci have included a close attention on prices, costs, exchange rates, productivity, saving, the cost of capital, and investment – or what neo-Ricardian political economics packages as comparative advantage or what neo-Porterian managerial economics characterizes as competitive advantage. Both still have powerful utility, but they need to focus more on the constructed advantage of knowledge and innovation. Let us explain why.

PRICES, COSTS, EXCHANGE RATES AND COMPETITIVENESS

Prices, costs and exchange rates are often cited by business representatives as being at the center of their industry's international competitiveness problems. Undoubtedly these are important elements for firms, especially those firms that compete on the basis of cost instead of product differentiation. But analytical approaches that focus almost exclusively on these factors typically do not accurately reflect the changing competitive experiences of firms. Often these approaches hold that export prices are principally determined by industrial costs – most notably, wages. In terms of economic policy, this view has led to a good deal of importance being placed on wage control and currency devaluation as avenues to competitiveness.

This view has seen something of a revitalization in smaller nations, despite the evidence of Germany, Japan and Switzerland, which have by all accounts been very competitive internationally, while having extremely strong currencies and high-wage workforces. Moreover, highly respected studies have shown that in the United States and Britain, contrary to traditional analytical expectations, drops in the relative unit wage costs and export prices have gone hand in hand with significant losses of world market share in manufacturing. By contrast, in Germany, Japan and Switzerland rises in relative unit wage costs and export prices have occurred at the same time as significant increases in world market share. Thus, relying uniquely on prices, costs and exchange rates is not a trustworthy guide to understanding competitiveness.

There is another misleading aspect of the view that emphasizes labor costs as a negative pressure on the competitiveness of firms. As the now-late Economic Council of Canada had shown, overall hourly wages and salaries in Canada have – when corrected for inflation – remained about constant since 1975. However, US studies have shown that the average Canadian chief executive officer makes 12 times more than the average Canadian shop-floor worker. This multiple is higher than that for the CEOs in Germany, Ireland, Japan, Korea, the Netherlands, Sweden and Switzerland. Individual cases that have been cited in the press show that some firms have a salary and compensation package for their senior executives that amounts to more than 1000 times what they pay the average worker. The US study made clear that these executive pay packages were usually not tied to firm performance and thus raises important questions about business leadership. Anderson Consulting and Enron experiences raise of course even deeper questions.

PRODUCTIVITY AND COMPETITIVENESS

If one area of concern is singled out most frequently as a prime determinant of competitiveness, it is productivity. Indeed, Michael Porter's much discussed report on Canada (*Canada at the Crossroads*) – and the recent report by Michael Porter and Roger Martin of the University of Toronto – says exactly this: 'the underpinning of competitiveness, and thus of a country's standard of living, is productivity.' Productivity is extremely important. It is a measure of how efficiently we are using our workers, our machines, and other means of production. In a sense, though, singling out productivity as the pivotal problem of competitiveness may be pointing to something of a truism. After all, along with long-term survival and the continual search for profitability, isn't the goal of every responsible firm or organization to make as productive use of its resources as is possible? In addition, although productivity growth is an important part of the competitiveness equation in both analytical and firm performance terms, it is not an area that government policies can really affect.

Having said this, Canada's basic level of productivity is high, though the growth in productivity has slowed. From 1979 to 1999, Canada's total factor productivity – which measures the productivity of both labor and capital – rose by a mere 0.4 percent per year. This was identical to the American performance. (In the last quarter of 2003, US growth and productivity are said to have soared, although critics argue that this is a short-term phenomenon built on the back of increased deficits and spending associated with the military deployment and homeland security.) However, over the same period, the growth in manufacturing labor productivity in Canada was the lowest of the G-7 countries, averaging only 1.8 percent per year. This is a worrisome situation because, in general, the more a country can produce per unit of labor or capital, the more its products will be able to compete with similar products of other countries (assuming stable exchange rates). Moreover, a high base of productivity and a high rate of productivity growth may not be sufficient to make Canadian industries more competitive than their foreign counterparts. We stand to lose world share, while other smaller countries – such as Ireland, Taiwan and South Korea – are gaining. But this too is misleading, as we will discuss.

There are many well-known ways to improve productivity, such as up-dating equipment and machinery or smoothing production processes. But none of these in and of themselves spell long-term competitiveness. None reflect the fact that much of what is happening in the economy is new. Simply becoming more productive at manufacturing uncompetitive products, (imagine being the world's best buggy whip manufacturer in 1925) or becoming more efficient at performing poor processes, will not give us the edge we are seeking. Meanwhile, the sources of our faltering productivity growth continue to be the focus of much debate among economists. Adding to the complexity of the debate is the fact that most measures of productivity relate to manufacturing and tangible processes (such as the number of tons of pig iron produced per hour), whereas more than 70 percent of Canada's gross domestic product now comes from the service industries and intangible products (such as software). Thus standard productivity measures can give us a distorted picture of what is wrong with our economy. Research, technology development and innovation tend to be such intangible activities. All in all it is difficult to find any solace in approaches based on productivity as a key to competition. Productivity growth remains an important piece of the puzzle, but it is not the whole picture.

SAVINGS, COST OF CAPITAL, INVESTMENT AND COMPETITIVENESS

Two further factors that are important for competitiveness are the rate of savings and the cost of capital, which affect the level of investment. Together these two factors help determine the degree to which we are able to invest and reinvest in the upgrading of our productive systems and resources. Typical examples of investment requirements are for new plant and equipment, new technologies and upgraded skills.

Not surprisingly, there is a close connection between a country's productivity growth and the growth in physical productive stock (the amount of net investment), the speed with which it is modernized (which depends on gross investment), and the way the stock is allocated (the types of investment). All are sensitive to the cost of capital and, in the case of high-risk, high technology operations, the availability of 'patient' capital, including venture capital. In the case of the latter, as Richard Lipsey has said, 'the idea of venture capital in Canada seems to be something of an oxymoron.' That is to say, there is a severe limitation on the amount of capital that is available to firms in smaller nations – particularly small and medium-sized high technology firms – involved in activities that are viewed by the large banks and lending organizations as being 'nontangible intensive' (i.e., having non-securable assets such as knowledge). Instead, a growing portion of new venture funds are being diverted away from small and medium-sized high technology firms towards expansions, mezzanine financing and leveraged buy-outs. From 1985 to 1988, the share of risk capital infusions into high technology companies dropped from 60 percent of all venture capital investments to 32 percent. Today it is 28 percent. Much of the blame for this trend had been placed on professional fund managers – for their lack of expertise in technology ventures – and on the managers of small, technology-intensive firms who, venture fund managers claim, are inept at preparing business plans. We can see similar repeats in the dot.com collapse and in the 'Asian Contagion'.

The cost of capital is the price that a business plans for additional financial assets, whether to investors or lenders, taking into account expected dividends, interest and tax payments. Thus the overall cost of capital depends not only on the sources of funds but also on what the funds are used for – to buy land, buildings, equipment and inventories. The cost of capital is also important for research and development and for other types of knowledge capital. Not only does R&D compete for corporate funds, but the rate at which research results can be put to use depends on how quickly a firm can modernize its plant and equipment to incorporate new products and processes – the effectiveness of R&D in raising productivity is greatly enhanced if the cost of capital is low enough for businesses to undertake, adopt and adapt more R&D. Improvements in human capital through education and training of all kinds (including training in advanced research, language, literacy and numeracy) often depend on access to sufficient quantities of quality, up-to-date equipment. Elementary and secondary education, for example, can benefit from more computers, research and language laboratories, and materials. The availability of any of these forms of capital is sensitive to the cost of capital. However, low savings rate relative to competitors such as Japan, high public debt load, and high dollar or euro valuations have all had the effect of driving the cost of capital up in smaller nations.

Overall, it is true that total investment growth in smaller nations has been quite strong. However, there is a lag behind major competitors in terms of private sector investments that are linked directly with improving productive systems and resources. Between 1980 and 1989, investment in machinery and equipment as a percentage of GDP was lower than that of most other industrialized countries. Similarly, Canadian private sector investment in research and development as a percentage of GDP was the second lowest of the G-7 countries. Canadian business investments in worker training fell well short of the investments made by Germany, Japan, the United States and many other industrialized nations. Moreover, anecdotal evidence suggests that, following an international trend, Canadian investments in nonproductive activities (such as moving funds globally and daily to high-interest deposit accounts) are outpacing investments in productive activities by as much as 250 times.

COMPARATIVE ADVANTAGE, TRADE AND COMPETITIVENESS

Another traditional area for analyzing international competitiveness is a country's comparative advantage, trade levels and trade patterns. By comparative advantage, we mean the relative export strength of a particular sector of the economy compared with the same sector in foreign economies. It is seen as a way for countries to trade with one another in order to benefit from their differences in resources, skills, and so on. It builds on the observation that no country can be competitive in every sector or industry. Thus the underlying industry mix of a country – and the unique mix of resources that a country has – will shape its pattern of international trade. For example, countries with a highly skilled workforce, such as Germany, will tend to export goods that are skill-intensive. Countries that have unique capabilities in niche markets – as Canada has in scientific instrumentation, remote sensing, and telecommunications equipment – will tend to have trade surpluses in those sectors.

While comparative advantage and trade are extremely important elements of the competitiveness debate, traditional analytical approaches to these areas tend to model world trade in terms of a series of static 'factor endowments' that seek 'equilibrium.' Although traditional trade theory does accept that technology and technological capability are potentially important endowments, it tends to assume that technology is unchanging and that the rate of technical change is static. It also tends to assume that the effects of technology in determining comparative advantage and trade can be perfectly substituted by any other factor of production. Clearly such approaches have little to offer government policy since they not only reduce the firm and the nation to mere abstractions, but they cast the highly dynamic worlds of firm competitiveness, trade and the forces of production as being static.

Whether taken individually or collectively, all of the above-noted traditional approaches to understanding competitiveness tend to suffer from theoretical difficulties and from discrepancies with the real experiences of people, firms and nations. For example, in the case of trade, it was thought in the 1960s and 1970s that the production costs and production structures in the various industrialized countries were converging and that the expansion of trade would therefore lead to greater specialization. Consequently, it was widely believed that international trade could grow without precipitating massive dislocations of firms and workers, and that the political costs of expanded trade were low. For example, in the machine-tool industry, Germany would capture a large share of the market for some tools while the United States would increasingly dominate in other areas of the market. Expanded trade would only lead to increased company specialization and produce higher incomes for both trading nations. In the world of growing trade – and for all industrialized participants – there would be only winners.

And yet, as we know, there are circumstances in the new competitiveness in which increased international trade produces real losses. These losses can be in terms of lower standards of living, lost jobs, lost industries, lost purchasing power, lost ability to pay for social security and health systems, eroded educational facilities, and so on. These conditions have created significant adjustment problems for governments, businesses, and individuals alike. Two changes in the world trading system have made this point clear in the past decade. The first is the entrance of producers from newly industrializing countries into the markets of the industrialized nations. The second significant trade change is rooted in the new nature of competition between firms in the advanced countries. Put in its most blunt terms, the Canadian response to the challenge of the newly industrializing nations should not be to panic about competing with the low-wage workers for low value-added activities in Mexico because we do not want a low-wage economy. Citizens in both countries want – and deserve – high-wage jobs in high value-added industries, for it is these industries that will generate the wealth through which we will all be able to afford the health, social security and education systems that we want. The events of 9/11 plus incursions into Iraq and Afghanistan have dramatically raised economic issues of trade, borders and security.

Citizens sense that the new competition is about rivalry – that it is about winners and losers and increasingly about international competition. Moreover, many successful smaller-nation's multinational firms – like Nokia, Nortel and deBeers – know well that the new, long-term competition is increasingly based on intangibles such as research, innovation, knowledge and people – that it has to do with non-price factors such as quality, corporate strategies and attitudes, and organizational patterns. (Though cartel economics cannot be ignored.) These – along with staying near the forefront of research and innovation – are the underlying determinants of competition, not simple productivity or costs per se. The source of our future wealth therefore is latent in our people and in their ideas. The site of our future wealth is to be found in the types of companies and the mix of industries that we can attract and develop. The environment conducive to productive wealth creation can be greatly stimulated and enhanced by government policies. But still the question remains, 'what are the new forms of competing?'

WHAT IS NEW ABOUT INTEGRATED COMPETITION?

Everywhere there are signs of a shift in the nature of competition. Among the more profound shifts – to which smaller countries must respond – are the following:

1. *A fundamental redefinition of the manufacturing company is taking place.* The manufacturing company is traditionally a site for production, and the economist's formulation of production is the production function: that is, the mix of capital and labor that is required to make things. But the new manufacturing firm is beginning to invest more in its research and development of new products and processes than it is in capital. Indeed, in Japan in 1986, R&D investment surpassed capital investment in manufacturing, and the change occurred rapidly. This has continued, but not evenly. Yet it is a signal of fundamental change, for if R&D investment is thought to be more important to the competitive position of a large number of such firms, then they could be said to be changing from being a site for production to a place for thinking.

2. *There are deep changes taking place in the definition of a firm's business.* Today, technological diversification has progressed so much that it is hard to distinguish between a firm's principal and secondary businesses. In Germany, Japan and the Netherlands, for example, the once principal business of many firms has been overtaken by secondary business. Or, in other cases, competitive firms are actively redefining their core businesses;

steel companies, for example, are moving away from steel towards new materials and (in the case of Japan) biotechnology. Thus, competitive firms are finding that their rivals may no longer even be in the same industry as they are. Such businesses are moving from visible to invisible enemies. Less successful firms are seeking corporate diversification through mergers and acquisitions. According to several analyses of North American mergers and acquisitions, however, corporate growth through diversification is surprisingly low, and many attempts at diversification along these lines have ended in failure.

3. *Competitive firms are increasingly evaluating their core strengths, not on the basis of end products but on the basis of core knowledge and competencies.* No longer are top managers in competitive firms being judged on their ability to restructure, unclutter, and de-layer their corporations. Today, they are being judged on their ability to identify and cultivate the core capabilities of the firm. They are, in effect, having to rethink the idea of the distributed corporation itself. A core competency involves the collective learning or knowledge of a firm, especially as it relates to the coordination of diverse production skills and the integration of multiple streams of production technology. It involves the flexible organization of work – so that the isolated cost centre or strategic business unit is no longer seen as the optimal productive organization – and the clear expression of corporate values. Firms that understand their core competencies ensure that technologists, engineers and marketers have a shared understanding of customer needs and the technological possibilities

4. *Competitive multinational firms are moving rapidly towards lean and adaptive, rather than craft or mass production.* Craft producers use skilled workers and simple but flexible tools to make custom designed products one at a time. Mass producers tend to use narrowly skilled professionals to design highly standardized products made by unskilled or semi-skilled workers with expensive single-purpose machines. Jobs are broken down into small, easy-to-master steps, permitting the employment of inexperienced workers. Lean producers are employing teams of multi-skilled workers at all levels of the organization and use highly flexible and increasingly automated machines to produce volumes of products in enormous variety. There is a major implication in the flexible and automated lean production system. It is possible both to attain economies of scale and to offer variety.

5.   *The very concept of value added is changing from what we have to what we do*. No longer are competitive firms adding value simply by working more efficiently with their raw materials – be they wood, silicon, or semi-fabricated components. Instead, these firms are migrating. If their traditional business is in raw materials, then they are moving their product lines up through processing, semi-fabrication, componentry, subsystems and full systems. Staying at the low end of the new value-added chain will only mean increasing competition with firms in low-wage economies. As world resource prices continue to fall and new suppliers continue to enter the market, a firm's ability to pay fair wages, upgrade technology, or to migrate the business, will only be eroded. This is important to realize because smaller nations still depend heavily on resource commodities to generate a trade surplus – which it uses to pay for sophisticated machinery, medical equipment, and so on. Many competitors, having situated their principal businesses at the high value-added end of the chain, are migrating their businesses down the chain and in so doing are both strengthening their own supplier linkages and setting the terms for operation in those downstream activities.

6.   *There are major changes taking place in the technology development process*. In the most advanced technology areas, the key issue for technology policy has become not how to break through technological bottlenecks, but how to access best-practice research and technologies and put them to the best possible use. Accordingly, a day of reckoning is coming for technology policy, which has traditionally concentrated on the supply side of technology (funding of basic research, technology creation, and so on). Increasingly – and rapidly – technology policy will need to deal with the demand side of technology, and in particular with demand articulation. Through this process, the need for specific technologies can manifest itself and the R&D effort can be targeted toward accessing, developing and perfecting them.

7.   *There are major changes taking place in the patterns of technological innovation*. Conventional wisdom holds that technological innovation is achieved by breaking through the performance boundaries of existing technologies. With regard to new fields such as opto-electronics, biologics and mechatronics, however, it would be more appropriate to view leading-edge technological innovation as fusing different types of technology rather than as technical breakthroughs. Canada, Scotland and Portugal,

for example, seem to be more active in the more traditional style of technological innovation.

8. *A final important factor underpinning the new competitiveness has to do with the social innovation associated with technology diffusion.* The widespread generation and utilization of information and communication technologies and services (ICTS) throughout IT and non-IT sectors of the economy is possible only after a period of adaptation in the social organization of firms and social institutions. This adaptation is one that opens the organization to the potential of the new technology. Although technological innovation can happen very rapidly, there is usually a great deal of institutional inertia to overcome. Diffusion relies on a succession of firms identifying, adopting and adapting a technology of potential use.

A FRAMEWORK FOR GROWTH: RESEARCH, TECHNOLOGY AND INNOVATION

Research, technology and innovation are the driving forces underlying competitiveness in high value-added firms and advanced industrial countries. However, there is almost as much confusion about what these terms really mean as there is about competitiveness. For example, innovation is most often thought to refer only to technological innovation. This is too narrow. Innovation is a broad and dynamic process that applies equally to the technologies, product development, production-process smoothing, management, marketing, organization and learning capability of a firm. So a technical breakthrough or technology fusion may well be based on one or a series of technical innovations, but it may not be identified or used effectively unless the firm itself can reorganize, or is already flexible enough to internalize the technology. This involves social innovation. Thus an innovative firm does not have to be in a high technology industry. It may use the technology for its internal purposes (word-processing pools or inventory control) or production purposes, in which case the technology becomes embodied in the business and products or services of the firm. Or it may begin, as its main business, to create, modify, or assemble the technology itself (as in the case of computers, numerically controlled machine tools, and so forth).

Technology

Technology is knowledge that is embodied in an artifact. It contributes to the creation, fabrication, and improvement of economically and socially useful products and services. Such knowledge relates not only to physical artifacts but also to forms of organization needed for their production, distribution, and use. We clearly depart here from the widely held assumption that technology is simply a form of 'information' that has the properties of being costly to produce, but virtually costless to transfer and to use. On the contrary, technological knowledge is mostly tacit (that is, it cannot be made fully explicit in the form of instructions), is embodied in individuals, and is mainly firm-specific. Technological knowledge is not largely generated by basic research activities, but is instead developed by firms to improve specific product lines or to solve specific problems. Depending on the type of technology, industry, or firm, such activities may be defined in terms of design, development, or production engineering.

Technological know-how and technology acquisition for firms is a cumulative and highly specific process. For example, two firms that make, say, light bulbs (as with GE and Sylvania) may do so based on very different core technologies, core competencies and corporate cultures. Given the firm-specific and highly specific nature of products, processes and related technological knowledge, the majority of firms tend not to engage in broadly based in-house research, but instead tend to closely watch technology and market areas that are germane to their existing activities. What firms try to do technologically in the future is strongly conditioned by what they have been able to do in the past.

Basic Research

In many instances, at the defining edge or frontier of much technical innovation is basic research. It is most often thought of as an international activity that is (mostly) publicly funded and carried out in universities. Its principal output is usually the publication of research results in scientific journals. As a result, the national benefits of basic research do not stop at national borders. Attempts to deliberately contain basic research by isolating it from international exchange are counterproductive not only to science, but to the rapid advance of scientific understanding and ultimately to the advance of the society funding it. This 'free-floating multinational' character of basic research does not imply that it has little economic value, nor does it suggest that basic research does not factor into the competitive advantage of firms and nations. In fact the opposite is true.

Basic science has strong economic ties (i) in its own right as a form of intellectual consumption, (ii) as a foundation to the technical training of future generations of researchers and technicians, (iii) as a source of fundamental knowledge needed to solve practical problems, and (iv) as a source of future generic or strategic technologies. It is for these reasons that a great many large firms are constantly involved not only in monitoring basic research results, but in contributing to and using them. It is also for these reasons, although in a decidedly more constrained and focused way, that many small, very high technology firms engage in basic research.

Having said this, it is important to recognize that there are two extreme, but still popular, models of the linkage between science, technology and innovation that are not valid. Unfortunately, they still seem to have currency – especially in policy circles – and must be discarded. The first can be described as the 'science push' or 'linear' model, where 'R leads predictably to D' and then to innovation (defined here as the first commercialization of a product or process), and diffusion. The second model can be described as 'demand pull.' It assumes that the rate and direction of technological change are by-products of other forms of economic activity: in particular, investment in plant and equipment is assumed to be the means through which innovations are commercialized. Both these popular models ignore the vital importance of interaction between research, corporate culture, and the market or users. They ignore the considerable variations among sectors, products and technologies. They ignore the institutional sources of knowledge and the growing importance of (and problems associated with) inter-institutional linkages (as in university-industry and inter-firm connections). They ignore the unpredictability or serendipity of all research. And they assume that 'science' feeds evenly into 'technology' at a consistent or dependable rate. In fact, while the relationship between science and technology is known to be extremely important, it is also very poorly understood.

As a result of the economic importance of basic research, it is important to underscore four critical reasons for its public support. First, if left to itself, a market will tend to invest less than is optimal in basic research because a profit-making firm can never capture all the benefits of the research that it sponsors. Second, basic research underpins the development of strategic technologies, which ties a firm into the international marketplace and which ties a country – via its researchers – into the world pool of new knowledge and new technologies. Third, facilities for basic research form an important part of a nation's infrastructure for future technological and productive activities. Fourth, basic research provides the critical training and research skills needed for the development of many future employees.

Strategic Technologies

Strategic technologies are so called because they have a firm footing in advanced research and an extremely wide applicability across industries and sectors. It is a characteristic of strategic technologies – such as microelectronics – that they transform entire industrial sectors while creating new ones. It is characteristic of strategic technologies that a large portion of their knowledge base lies in the public domain in the form of published papers and patents. In part this is due both to the novelty of the technologies themselves and to their rate of development. These features create an incentive for firms and researchers to keep informed about alternatives to those technologies that the firm is currently backing. In some sectors, it is essential for a firm seeking to be at the forefront to have an in-house knowledge base that enables it to monitor and absorb knowledge from public sector research institutions – most notably, universities. This is even (perhaps especially) important for smaller firms near the forefront, as it is (albeit in a different way) for firms following an adopt and adapt strategy. It is because of the knowledge-intensive, rapidly developing and public nature of these technologies that firms increasingly are moving into collaborative arrangements. These arrangements include research consortia (in which companies and university labs share recent results), contract research, joint ventures and strategic alliances.

Leading firms in strategic technologies tend to be drawn along a technological trajectory that improves their performance and leads them into new products with high growth in demand. Their technologies often spill over into adjacent sectors, creating in turn new technologies, new products, and at times new industries. Conversely, firms that are well behind the technological frontier – both as generators in some niche areas, and as users in broader areas – may find that their future performance is 'dynamically penalized' by their current industrial structure. In such a case, the national economies drift into lower value-added production and exports. One of the challenges to smaller interdependent nations is to shift their industrial mix into more, not less, value-added production and exports. This underlines the importance of strategic technologies and innovation.

By being active in strategic technology areas and by defining narrow niche areas in ways that build on indigenous strengths and market opportunities, a nation's industrial structure can be made more knowledge-intensive and more competitive. In Britain, France, Germany, Japan, Sweden and the United States, for example, carefully defined strategic-technology niche areas and niche policies have been set or sought. This is less so in countries like Scotland, Norway, Canada, Finland, Ireland, or Mexico. Those stronger countries believe that by focusing on certain specific capabilities, they will move their industrial structure into higher value added products and processes. Canada, by contrast, has not yet identified key niche sectors or technologies, nor has it adopted a more dynamic understanding of value added based on innovation, knowledge, learning and connection. This is true despite the fact that Canada has superb indigenous capabilities in such important technology areas as remote sensing, satellite technologies, advanced software, fuel cell technologies, and so on. Smaller nations need a clear, well-articulated, goal-oriented innovation strategy.

Despite the critical contribution that basic research makes to the competitiveness of a country, it is its role with regard to strategic technologies, or other disruptive technologies, that most often is of interest to policy makers. As has already been suggested, the general importance of strategic technologies stems from the fact that they set the performance standards for the next generations of technology and they are applicable in a wide variety of industries and products. They can be generated and developed by a large number of industries, and they can be 'stretched' or modified over time to underpin subsequent families of technology. However, to fund basic research on the expectation of developing strategic technologies is shortsighted and only follows the now-dead linear models. Indeed, it may seem unusual that disparate technologies – such as informatics, biotechnology, and new materials – are being clustered together by policy makers and afforded similar special treatment as strategic technologies. After all, there is much that they do not have in common. Some form the basis for enormous international industries while others, such as high-temperature superconductivity, are little more at the moment than promising laboratory phenomena. What they do have in common, however, is that they are knowledge intensive and they are likely to become pervasive. (It is these characteristics that have contributed to Japanese firms spending more on R&D than physical capital.)

SUCCESSFUL FIRM-LEVEL INNOVATION

Firm-level innovation must be seen as being more than just research and technology. More broadly, it has to include development and design activities, finance and marketing, market surveillance, firm organization and firm strategy. Competitive firms, regardless of size or industry, have to be innovative. But innovation is multifaceted. There are no simple, single-factor explanations. However, factors underlying successful innovations are fairly easily generalized.

1. *Successful innovation is people-centered.* It is based on competence and an ethos that encourages and rewards creativity and innovation wherever they may be found. Formal management techniques can enhance the performance of competent managers, but they are no substitute for management of high quality and ability. Just as research and technological innovation are the result of creativity and insight (people-centred characteristics), so too is successful innovation dependent on key individuals top management, technological gatekeepers, and product champions

2. *Successfully innovative firms forge extremely strong intermediate-and end-customer linkages.* Traditionally, the role of marketing is to scan the marketplace to identify new and evolving customer requirements as a basis for initiating new product developments or modifying existing ones. This is a passive, or at best reactive, attitude, regarding the user as simply responding to a marketeer's questionnaire. The marketeers then assess the answers for themselves and feed what they feel is appropriate into the product development or design function. The interaction ends there. In high value-added competitive firms, however, the user is seen as an integral part of the design and development process. Product improvement is based on a relentless focus on customers' needs and markets. Strong customer service, customer training, and follow-up are key.

3. *Truly innovative firms are internally integrated.* In firms where functions are separated – competing strategic business units, for example – products or product ideas are essentially 'thrown over the wall' to the next group that has to deal with it in order to get it to market. There must be integration of management, ownership of the new product or idea, corporate sense of direction, and feedback from the market to the engineers. Without these there will be no impulse to improve products, processes, or services. The firm will not be in a position to set the terms for competition and will be forced to accept the terms set by a rival.

4. *High value-added competitive firms see innovation as a corporate-wide task and set the conditions for innovation.* Top management must be seen to be receptive to risk, as well as committed to and supportive of

innovative ideas and practices. There should be a long-term commitment to major projects and there should be, to the extent possible, a willingness to seek finance internally.

5.   It should be said that business schools, in coordination with engineering schools, should tag up and create the next generation of people who will innovate.

Just like firm-level innovation, successful innovation at the level of the nation must be seen as involving much more than just research – although, again, a critical (and healthy) mass of research and development is essential for the development of a competitive nation. Innovation depends, for example, on the culture of the nation – on the willingness of its people to learn and to put their know-how and vision together in action.

It depends on the ability of the country to constantly enhance its technological capabilities. Successful innovation (and 'imitation,' which is the 'next best practice' upon which all countries including Canada depend for diffusion) requires high levels of technological activity to be performed and financed by firms. It requires publicly funded systems of basic research, which provide skills, instrumentation and delivery of know-how to practitioners through a multiplicity of channels. Over time, the mix between innovation and imitation (in both science and technology) will and should change, reflecting the fact that a nation is either moving towards or away from the world's best practice.

It should be realized that successful innovation and imitation does not come cheap or easy. The infrastructure for innovation in Canada must be continually built up and maintained at international best-practice levels. This necessarily requires strong and interlinked policies for research, training, finance, management, communications, and even transport. Imitating best practice German, Italian, or Japanese technology is difficult, not only because of the technical aspects but also because of distance and language. Many Canadian firms – though nowhere nearly enough – have recognized the importance of person embodied knowledge transfers and have pursued a variety of activities through which to enhance their technology and marketing capabilities. These have ranged from personnel exchanges with universities and R&D labs to foreign language courses and joint ventures.

CAN SMALLER NATIONS COMPETE?

Canada, Scotland, Sweden, Ireland, Finland, South Africa, Australia and others all have some superbly innovative firms and some extremely strong research and technology. Standards of living are high. Social security systems, and the commitment to social re-distribution and social democracy, are strong but under discussion. Small countries can have a surprisingly big economic global presence. For example, Canada has a very positive international reputation – geo-politically, environmentally and economically – and is consistently ranking by the United Nations as one of the top places in which to live.

However, Canada – other such countries have similar but specific issues – is vulnerable because it is still dependent on undifferentiated resource industries for a large part of its wealth creation. We are heavily dependent on trade with the United States, and our trade pattern is narrowing. We are technologically dependent and our industrial structure is narrow. Canada contributes roughly 4-5 percent of the world technology pool and of the world research results. Canada has a deficit in its technological trade balance. More than 80 percent of its exports go the United States, while less than 5 percent goes to Japan. Although we have tremendously talented individuals and firms, more than 65 percent of all our industrial R&D is done by only 100 firms. High technology exports are concentrated in four commodity groups: aircraft and associated equipment, telecommunications equipment, ADP machines, and non-electric engines and motors. The emphasis of most firms on the bottom-line, quarterly statement situation is squeezing our ability to save and re-invest in productive activities. Many argue that Canada probably has too many lawyers per capita – as compared with Germany, Japan and Sweden – and that we need more engineers, scientists, teachers, and entrepreneurs. Canada's population is rapidly growing and will be requiring the services of our health care system in increasing numbers. As it is now, we are not creating enough wealth to be able to pay for this surging demand on the health care system.

Surveys regularly point to the fact that Canadian managers do not understand research, technology, or innovation, and prefer to focus on short-term finance and sales. Other surveys show that our business and engineering schools offer ludicrously few courses in technology management, technology policy, or the economics of R&D. They are training for a marketplace that existed 20 to 30 years ago.

It is clear that we are not adjusting to the new competition fast enough. Between 1971 and 1990, Canada's high technology exports as a proportion of total exports increased from 11 to 14 percent and remained at that level in 2002. In the United States, the proportion of high technology exports rose from 27 percent in 1971 to 33 percent in 1990 but declined slightly to 32 percent in 2002. In Japan, the proportion rose from 12 to 24 percent during the 1971 to 1990 period and remained at that level in 2002. With respect to the newly industrialized countries of Asia, the proportion increased from 9 percent in 1970 to 24 percent in 1990. In 2002, the proportion ranges from 60 percent in Singapore to 17 percent in Hong Kong (we do not know what they are as a group in 2002). Contrary to the optimistic expectations of the 1960s and 1970s, the world economy is not the exclusive terrain of the industrialized countries. The world economy grew by only 1 percent in 1990 and was growing even more slowly in 1991. In 1990, the economies of Latin America shrank by 4 percent, Eastern Europe by 11 percent, and the then Soviet Union by 14 percent. There is nothing magical sustaining smaller economies or standards of living. Countries can lose out. If we are to compete, we have to work and we have to invest – in our people and in our firms. We have to innovate. And we all have to create a climate that stimulates competition on the basis of final customer needs, high value added, and a vision.

But where is the clear leadership from our politicians, entrepreneurs, employees and teachers? We need everyone pulling together. What we need from our leaders is a very clear agenda for action – even if it seems controversial. But most are too preoccupied with the trees to see the forest. Our leaders must be willing to take unpopular stands when necessary. And when such stands are necessary, they have an obligation to explain their positions to their constituents. They must solicit the support of their constituents and win not only their approval but their involvement. Canadians for example know that we must work to shed the 'woodshed of the OECD' image. The linkages between research, technology and innovation – coupled with a belief in people – give us the building blocks.

A first step in becoming more competitive is for our leaders to take responsibility for ensuring that every citizen realizes what being competitive really means and why it is important to every individual. In this way, the vision of our leaders can be translated into reality. To date, however, such leadership has not been forthcoming. There seems to be a preference in some business circles for opinion over vision and a reliance in academic circles on old practices, while some government circles seem to have opted for a process of excessive – or at least, unfocused – consultation. To be sure, in Canada's case, consultation is an important element in our parliamentary democracy. But it has practical limits. Unless clear questions are asked, and clear mechanisms exist through which to translate business and public concerns into action, there is a real danger smaller nations will see consultation processes as mere proxies for leadership – as indications of the absence of vision. And, after all, competitiveness – like research, technology, and innovation – is a visionary activity.

3. Some Economic Consequences of Knowledge

Let us talk more deeply about innovation, interdependence and strategy. The revolutions in information and communications technologies (ICTs) are driving fundamental changes in the world economies. In the wide sense, ICTs are in large part responsible for facilitating the processes of globalization and international integration. This means a fundamental challenge to be competitive, and in this context 'competitiveness' means something quite new.

Traditional notions of competition assumed that the world economy was based on the production and exchange of tangible goods. Key features of competition included a focus on prices, cost of labor, cost of capital and stable exchange rates. 'Value added' was thought of in terms of what we had.

Today, value added is based on what we know and do. Competition is increasingly based on intangible services. Low-cost labor is no longer an answer to high standards of living. In a knowledge economy, Canada needs skills and knowledge in the emerging areas of information, data, media and communications development, manipulation and acquisition. These will not be static skills. Instead, we need skills that are continually adaptive. They will be based on learning and on learning how to learn. In the early part of the century, Alfred North Whitehead (1920) said that 'the most important invention of the 19th century was the invention of the process of invention'. This was fitting for the industrial, mass production world that was emerging around mechanical technologies. Today, the most important innovation for a person, a firm, a community, a region or the nation will be the ability not to innovate once, but to innovate continuously. The place to learn these skills is in schools. Schools – which are not traditionally considered part of a nation's science system – provide the building blocks for the future of nations. A well prepared, skilled and literate youth will lead to considerable gains in economic growth and productivity as well as health. As the economies of countries like Scotland, Taiwan and Canada continue their rapid shift towards knowledge work, the governments should continue their commitments to innovation and developing innovation systems. By so doing, they will put in place a distributed system.

Thus, smaller nations are standing poised at the edge of a very challenging, one might say revolutionary, period. The challenge arises from two sources: 'hardware' and 'software'. The first arises from developing and distributing the technology: i.e.

- promoting advances in ICTs through leading edge R&D;
- facilitating the availability of information infrastructures through the Information Highway programs, and
- ensuring and extending access to communities, schools, and remote regions.

A second arises from:

- promoting indigenous content in all its forms, richness and diversity.

Together, these create real socio-economic opportunities which require strong public support, vision and commitment.

BACKGROUND PERSPECTIVES

Economic historians (Hobsbawm 1968; Jewkes, Sawers and Stillerman 1962; Landes 1969, 1983, 1998) are fond of noting that recent changes in the world economics are in fact not so much *revolutionary* as *evolutionary* in nature. Many point out that long before the advent of MBA degrees, accountants were well employed; that well before globalization, international trade was common; and human societies have long existed and have been notable for their use of language, information and communications. Therefore it seems that in an economic historical sense, a case can be made that there have been few major discontinuities. In the long haul, this is true.

But such sentiments mask the experience of contemporary students, citizens, workers, managers and policy makers who are now accustomed not only to such phrases as 'the new economy', the 'infobahn' and cyber-space, but to the *experience* of knowledge based economic change and adjustment. In short, while scholarly precisions may be important and interesting, they are not at times particularly helpful in the day-to-day navigation of the immediate waters that are so obviously fraught with transformation and apparent discontinuity.

More helpfully perhaps, industrial sociologists, economic sociologists and organizational strategists (Bell 1971; Drucker 1970; Schumpeter 1942; Swedberg 1991; Waters 1996) have improved the analytic lens in the public's mind – not only by breaking down historical epochs into pre-industrial, industrial and post-industrial phases (in which we are now engaged), but more importantly by highlighting the rise of the service sectors, the growing importance of the professional classes (Galbraith 1967; Reich 1991; Gershuny and Miles 1984), the primacy of theoretical (R&D based) knowledge and the driving importance of technological change. In short, they highlight that something 'new' was indeed going on in the economy and as a result, knowledge is now seen as being – along with capital and labor – a key factor in productivity, competitiveness, employment and economic growth.[1] (Nelson 1996)

THE ECONOMIC UNIQUENESS OF KNOWLEDGE

Knowledge is not a usual commodity (Hayek 1945). It is largely a public good. Unlike physical resources, it can be used and re-used without losing value and its intellectual property can be transferred without losing ownership. Uncertainty is high in its production (i.e. research), but this drops rapidly as it is diffused. There is considerable social leakage in the transmission of knowledge. There are also considerable spill-over effects which result in secondary benefits of proximity to the source of knowledge production, such as the development of high technology clusters, the attraction and retention of skilled workers, the attraction of investment, and the spinning out of new firms, jobs and industries. Markets – traditionally conceived – handle physical commodities well, but they do not handle 'non-commodities' (knowledge and information) well. Moreover, while the world of Alfred Marshall in the 1880s was one based on bulk production and diminishing returns on investment, today's world is one which features customization and niche production in which there are *increasing* returns.

These important characteristics are telling. But the economics of knowledge and information is an area in which there is still a serious dearth of language, conceptual schemes and empirical research (Winter 1987). Nonetheless, they appear in economic models in two forms. In microeconomics, the most fundamental assumption is based on the idea that individuals will make rational choices. Thus how much and what kind of knowledge and information economic agents have, and how powerful their ability is to process and act on this knowledge and information, are of great importance. The other major perspective is one in which knowledge and information are regarded as assets. Here knowledge may be in the form of a competence (an economic input) or an innovation (an output). But we must differentiate between knowledge and information in an economic sense.

Information is not knowledge. Knowledge is often defined as organized information, just as information is organized data. Knowledge is a human practice rather than a thing that resides in artifacts. Knowledge may be shared between people, but this involves a process of learning and experience about each other's knowledge. Sometimes, this knowledge sharing can be carried out in order to exchange information. But the goal here is to render information useful. It is for these reasons that (a) much work is being carried out currently at the OECD and elsewhere in order to improve our understanding of these processes of interaction, and (b) why we tend to differentiate between differing types of knowledge.

Thus codified knowledge and tacit knowledge differ importantly in that the former can be written down (in a patent, drawing, design, formula, ... and transmitted) whilst the latter is skill based, talent based, experiential and therefore is difficult to transfer except through demonstration (learning by doing) or appropriation (hiring the person who has a talent or the experience that you want). Additionally, knowledge can be seen as belonging to four classes. Know-what refers to knowledge of facts. Know-why refers to knowledge about principles and natural laws. Know-how refers to skills. And know-where refers to a kind of network knowledge, knowing who would have certain information or influence and how to access it.

Traditionally, the attention of government policies has focused on stimulating the production of new knowledge and information through the funding of research and development and through science and technology policies. (As we will discuss below, the emphasis has begun to focus more both on facilitating the provision of physical 'smart' infrastructure and the diffusion (connectivity) of knowledge and information.) But in a country such as Canada, however, we only produce an estimated 4 percent of the world science and technology, thus revealing our dependency on the rest of the world for new knowledge. Moreover, while only 0.4 percent of all firms in Canada carry out any R&D and while this is highly concentrated in six industries, more than 40 percent of manufacturing firms report carrying out knowledge-based innovative activities. Thus the production of new knowledge is only part, albeit an important part, of making a nation a knowledge-based economy. The ability to access, diffuse and apply new knowledge will be key to the future and continuing success. The effective use of knowledge and information is also a function of the new forms of competition.

Technology-led globalization has not only dramatically shifted competition towards high value added activities which are based on service, quality, customization and ideas, but it has also increased the importance of social capital (Putnam 1993; Fukuyama 1995; Woodcock 1998). Social capital – the 'glue' or culture of an organization, group or community – allows firms, institutions and even local regions to interact, exchange knowledge and conduct their transactions quite easily. Organizations which have a decaying social capital (one might think here of the 1980 comparisons of GM and Toyota, IBM and Apple – the iPod culture may be 'pay-back' time for Apple –, or even of Route 128 near Boston and Silicon Valley). Using a two dimension matrix (micro/macro, inward/outward), some analysts have suggested that the most supportive arrangement for social cohesion and economic development is where a locality (sub unit of a firm, municipality, etc.) is both closely *interconnected* and *open* to a wider world of opportunity. Describing the social milieu in this way emphasizes the importance of factors like trust and the capacity to build 'extra-family' collective loyalties. In situations where technology is characterized by rapid change, or where the knowledge base is not well documented (i.e. is tacit), then inter-personal and inter-group interaction is essential to solve problems (more on this shortly).

The nature and dynamics of social capital in highly localized technology intensive regions, such as Silicon Valley or the M4 Corridor, have long been recognized by industrial geographers (Florida 1998; Saxenian 1998, Wolfe and Gertler 1998). This has resulted in recent interest in municipalities to 'technopoles', clustering, proactive cities, including the growing importance of Ottawa, Tuscon, Raleigh-Durham, Shanghai. The widely asked question is 'how can we build a smart community?' This observation has also been an integral part of Canada's historical and economic legacy. For example, Canada has been a world leader in 'space binding' technologies (such as railroads and telecommunications) because of the vastness of our physical landscape. The key to understanding the clustering phenomenon through which knowledge, information and investment are energized into value creating activities is to recognize that the knowledge economy is really a network economy. In a location, economists often speak of 'externalities' and the 'spill-over effects' of knowledge-based activity. They often also speak of the important observation, empirically supported by the work of Edwin Mansfield and others, that the social rates of return for investments in knowledge production, while variable across industries, are typically significantly higher than the private rates of return.

At the level of community – a concept that is being questioned because of what is perceived in some camps as being the negative impacts of 'cyber culture' in which traditional values are somehow hollowed out – sociologists have begun to redefine the term away from a conception dependent on *place* towards one based on *space*. In so doing they are able to explain not only why knowledge production and clustering takes hold in some locations and not others. In addition they are also able to address the idea that computer networks that connect people can *positively* result in new forms of community and culture. In a sense, 'community' can be expanded to include networks of expertise as well as computer-mediated communication (CMC), computer-supported social networks (CSSN) and so on.

At the level of the firm or institution (including schools and libraries), this same idea has taken hold in the observation that no one can know it all, and no organization can 'do it all'. Thus, we find the logical explanation for what is happening all around: that is, that all forms of organization are forging alliances, linkages, partnerships, and consortia in an effort to become more flexible and adjustable in an environment typified by change and complexity (Axelrod 1984; Jervis 1997; Rycroft and Kash 1999). Thus people and organizations are learning to cooperate as a competitive and survival strategy and in so doing they are using new information and communications technologies to network and reformulate the nature of their activity and to solve problems.

Of course, problem solving has two aspects. On the one hand, it is adaptive or responsive. A team or firm responds to a challenge or competitive threat. On the other hand, it is creative. A team of researchers solves a scientific or technical problem through creativity. The various types of knowledge needed in each circumstance (from codified to tacit) is clear. But in questions of economic growth and sustainable social development, knowledge and information must be harnessed in the processes of innovation.

There are two reasons for regarding innovation as in important outcome of knowledge production and use. One is that innovation represents something new and therefore adds to existing knowledge. The second is that innovation is knowledge that is in demand. It is often defined in the OECD and European Union circles as an invention that has been introduced into the marketplace and thus represents knowledge that has proven its relevance for the market economy. Thus it is an idea that has been commercialized.

But on the other hand, it is important to note that innovation, as Schumpeter emphasized, is part of a process of 'creative destruction'. Innovation may therefore both open *and* closed markets, firms, and sectors, and may terminate as well as create jobs. This is of importance as an observation and leads directly to the emphasis, visible in many discussions of the knowledge economy, of the need for life-long learning, the learning firm, and so on.   Importantly for policy makers, these ups and downs are rarely felt evenly within the same sectors, regions or countries and almost certainly do not equally effect skill sets. As Schumpeter noted, innovation is not only a matter of technical change but importantly can be found in the opening of new markets, the discovery of new sources of material, as well as the social organization of work.

Smaller nations, regions and cities have been investing aggressively in innovation with the view that it provides a key to higher productivity and improved quality of life. Many believe that innovation is the major, if not the sole, sustainable source of economic growth and the major determinant of the wealth of a nation. Indeed, expanding our knowledge, and improving our ability to do new things, and old things in better ways, is central to Industry Canada's economic strategy. The innovative economy must embrace all industries and all Canadians need to strive to develop an innovation culture. However, the OECD has determined that Canada faces an innovation gap as compared with our G-7 competitors. Evidence of this gap includes having the second lowest business sector R&D spending rate among the G-7. The government and the private sector have recognized that Canada must increase its pool of highly qualified and skilled people, and we must extend and improve the usage of computers and the Internet. (This is a point to which we will return.) Indeed, despite a highly educated workforce and an extremely highly population literacy rate, Canada ranks low in the number of knowledge producers per 1000 labor force. Shifting the industrial structure of Canada, or any smaller nation, towards high value added shares of higher technology.   Indeed, as a recent study has highlighted, in Canada's knowledge-based economy, policy and government programs need to focus on developing social capital, distributing information into communities, and concentrate on social inclusion of distant or disenfranchised groups and communities, as well as help build the information and communications infrastructure and sectors.

KNOWLEDGE PRODUCTION, USE AND DISTRIBUTION

The context for these developments is beginning to be well known. Indeed, in a knowledge-based economy, knowledge, science and technology play principal roles in generating economic growth. This is new in the sense that the structure and composition of industry, worldwide, is shifting.

Briefly put, but essentially, the importance of knowledge production (S&T) distribution and use can be highlighted with reference to globalization, through which physical boundaries and the old economies of scale are collapsing. The revolution in information and communications technologies (ICT) – which has dramatically reduced the cost of micro-chip production, long distance telephone calls, data storage, and so on[2] – now permits instantaneous transmission of ideas and value. However, these assumptions of R&D equal and/or similar to economic growth must be reinforced as departments of Chemistry in the UK (by the way, chemistry is an essential science for the future of our well being in the full sense, from nutrition and health to engineering) are being closed.

So as not to let this point be missed, since the 1970s, the world flow of ideas and technologies – as captured in foreign direct investment and trade in intangible products such as software – has vastly outpaced trade in physical commodities in terms of value. Put another way, international growth in investment surpassed growth in trade and output in the 1980s. This has been augmented by a rapid expansion in international and inter-regional transportation which also serves to buttress the expanding global village through the flow of highly qualified people; as well as by a widespread reduction of barriers and impediments to trade, capital and technology flows between countries. All of these developments are portentous for workers and learners. This reflects the idea that the information and communications revolution, combined with flexible management structures, makes it easier for small businesses to compete with larger firms domestically and internationally. Very often, these small enterprises are the locus of smart, skilled, entrepreneurial people who fuel economic growth.

Consistent with the move towards an information and knowledge-based global economy, the occupational shifts over the past 20 years have led to an acceleration in the demand for highly skilled and qualified people – in the administrative, managerial, professional and technical areas. Further, there is a growing wage disparity between skilled and unskilled workers. The new economy is demanding higher skills. (This is reflected in the unemployment rate when correlated with years of education and schooling.) And these skills are highly associated both with new knowledge and with information and communications technologies.

Such broad observations are common in smaller nations, regions, cities and communities. Indeed, employment trends across the OECD show similar patterns in terms of reductions in manufacturing employment, increase in high technology exports and other knowledge-intensive outward flows, and so on. Moreover, and of great importance, there is occurring worldwide both a growth in the number of non-traditional performers of science and technology (such as Malaysia, Chile and Taiwan) which are beginning to have a marked effect on the flow of knowledge-bearing foreign direct investment and world production *and* there is an apparent world economic convergence when measured in terms of GDP per capita. It has been argued by Graham Vickery of the OECD that such developments are the result of the impact of technical change in countries like Argentina which are now experiencing knowledge-induced productivity gains as well as the early impacts of an emergent knowledge worker class in newly industrializing nations. Such patterns suggest strong challenges to other smaller nations in the next years and decades in terms of standard of living, competition for export markets, the attraction and retention of skilled workers, entrepreneurs, and other knowledge workers.

THE KNOWLEDGE WORKER

A knowledge worker is not only to adjust the traditional notion of 'worker' to the new economic context but is to highlight a number of new features. First, a class of knowledge work comes into existence when a body of related information must be collected, applied and built upon for subsequent action. Second, knowledge work is often created by the introduction of some new knowledge handling technology. Third, knowledge workers increase in number in environments where complexity of work expands at the same time that either the volume of work or the size of the organization in which it is done grows.

Human Capital

Machlup (1962) was the first to look at how information was created, distributed and used in the American economy. His was an 'occupational approach' to human capital in that he looked at how technology and market demand worked to change occupation structure instead of looking at trade, investment or production factors. By looking at white collar, manual and service jobs, he differentiated between knowledge producing and non-knowledge producing workers and noted resultant income shares, that were closely correlated to years of education, type of employment, and so on. This occupational approach has been carried forward in the work of Rubin and Huber (1986), Betcherman (1996) and the OECD (Miller 1996) and in the path breaking work by Keating, Hertzman *et. al.* (1999) in which the social and economic determinants of health are powerfully demonstrated.

Learning and Training

In general, the rates of return to graduate with bachelor and first professional degrees in Canada have been in the order of 12-15 percent. In assessing the rates of return for public policy purposes, however, it should be recalled that they omit most external benefits and therefore underestimate the true rate of return. Some estimates suggest that an under-investment in education results in higher unemployment and lower productivity and represents a net loss in output of more than $1 billion per annum.

With regards to the costs associated with learning, these can be differentiated in terms of fixed and variable costs. Fixed costs for new instructional media usually are much higher than for conventional technologies, because of the greater time and expense for installation of hardware and the preparation of courseware. But the variable costs are usually lower to the extent that there are fewer contact hours between instructors and students. Networking costs are mainly fixed costs, for transmission lines, routers that perform packet switching, and so on. When these fixed costs are spread over the several million users, these long-haul communication costs average a few dollars per user per year. The larger cost factor for users is in the access circuit that connects users to the backbone network and the on-going charge for the use of the circuit. Recent costs estimates however should *not* be projected into the future because new technologies will be cheaper than digital services over voice networks. We are seeing the emergence of convergent voice-data technologies

There are several benefits associated with learning and training that accrue to the economy as a whole, rather than directly to the individual, as a result of public investments. These benefits, while difficult to measure, are of considerable value. Some of the most important 'externalities' include:

- a greater number of trained persons increases the supply and transfer of specific skills to the labor market;

- for many professions, the combining of skills results in increased creativity, innovation and greater productivity;
- more educated people have a lower incidence and duration of unemployment;
- higher levels of education and training provide the basis for a faster acceptance and diffusion of innovation; and education increases the potential to undertake more education and training.

Training and Adult Education

Another element of the ICT revolution and the transformation of economies is the fact that the training market is growing. A significant portion of this may well be on their own time and initiative, even if it is job related, and this raises the need for access to distributed information services through public libraries, schools, and so on. Though the majority of training is still based on traditional technologies, this is expected to shift rapidly in the next five years. Although not as large as the K-12 post-secondary education market, the training/adult education market is seen as being the main driver for growth. In Canada, the 40-64 age group is growing from 8.7 million to 14.2 million by 2004. Moreover, the average age of BA earners is increasing as well. Other important influences include the shift in work patterns to higher levels and longer periods of unemployment Such shifts clearly raise implications for training, the upgrading of skills, the type and technology of delivery, the content requirements, etc.

Job-related training can be delivered using learning technologies at schools, libraries and home to the home-based self employed, another growing segment of the workforce. This is particularly important, not only for those in the metropolitan centers of Vancouver and Montreal, but also in more sparsely populated or remote locations. In addition, employers' increasing reliance on flexible work practices requires continuous learning of new job skills that in turn requires courses to be developed and delivered in short periods of time.

Telelearning is one way that individuals can have access to the training they need outside of the workplace setting. The challenge is in connecting individuals to the learning resources they need. In 1997, 36 percent of Canadian households reported having a computer but only 13 percent had a modem and used it to connect to the Internet. Location is a determining factor, and this statistic is positively correlated to income level. For example, 66 percent of 24-44 year-olds in urban areas have access, as opposed to 54 percent in rural areas. (This has grown massively.) And even though nearly all Canadian households have access to phone lines, many of those lines still require conversion to single party lines that support touch tone, and therefore can handle computers. Such compatibility is especially true in northern and remote communities. Gender and age also impact on user demographics for information and communications technologies. Still, almost 60 percent of all online services are men, and men account for 63 percent of total usage. Moreover, 84 percent of 15-19 year-olds report being able 'to do something' with computers compared with 10 percent over 65. Also, 67 percent of the employed use computers compared with 50 percent of unemployed, and 84 percent of PhD and MA holders can use a computer compared with less than 31 percent of individuals with less than high school qualifications. All this shows that as Canada's demographics continue to change in response to the information revolution, the need to connect communities and individuals will represent an imperative, a challenge, and a real growth potential. An example, pertinent to remote aged persons, is the advent of telemedicine.

POLICY ACTIVITIES AND CHANGES

Evidence of the shift can be seen in numerous countries, from the Netherlands to Sweden, Canada to Scotland. In Canadian documents such as *Building a More Innovative Economy* (Industry Canada 1994), Program Review I and II, the Science and Technology Strategy (1994-1996), the creation of an 'Industry Portfolio' have highlighted a number of important changes in how Canada would be guided into a knowledge economy, and the Innovation Strategy (2003). Moreover, the Liberal 'Red Book' (1993) adopted the language of the 'innovation system' as an organizing principle. This framework allowed the government to back leaders (instead of picking winners), to adopt the role of facilitator, and to become engaged in the whole innovation process (and not just selected portions of it, such as R&D which stands at the gateway of new knowledge). Part of this shift of action can be seen in the Networks of Centers of Excellence, in the matching grants policies, and in the management principles of transparency and horizontal coordination. And directly, part of this shift can be seen in the CA*Net3, the Information Highway activities, the Connectivity Agenda and in the SchoolNet program. But this has not been in isolation.

In terms of macroeconomic measures, the Canadian government carefully monitors and manages a number of metrics. Canada exceeds the OECD average in terms of its investment in knowledge as a percentage of GDP. In terms of R&D

intensity, Canada is below the OECD and slightly above the EU average and 15th in terms of business R&D. Canada is even with the US in terms of flows of graduates in science and engineering as a percentage of total employment and ahead in terms of flows of graduates in S&E as a percentage of total new degrees. However, Canada's share of services in business R&D exceeds the average of all OECD countries and is second among the G-8.

In terms of information and communications technology (ICT), Canada stands 10th as measured by the ITU's Digital Access Index. Personal computer penetration in Canada is 6th, following the US, Singapore, Sweden, Denmark and Norway in terms of PCs per 100 inhabitants. Canada ranks 14th in terms of Internet hosts per 10,000 inhabitants (which include smaller countries such as Iceland and Tonga). Worldwide, the growth of main telephone lines installed is growing rapidly, while the growth curve of cellular mobile subscribers worldwide is even steeper (World Telecommunication Development Report, 2003). Growth is also impressive in global cable TV and global satellite DTH (Direct to Home). Additionally, the number of Internet users is on the increase while the Internet use patterns is on the increase for managers, professionals, and students. Surveys (Neilsen Media Research, 2002) show that Internet users in the United States and Canada tend to use the technology for product information (>70 percent) as opposed to public information and collaboration. This observation supports the trend towards electronic commerce, vendor support, etc., but still reveals a minority use vis-*à*-vis education.

In terms of policy discourse and action, Canada is not alone in its attention to knowledge and information. The European Union (EU) has fully understood the nuances of the information society (even if the operationalization is more difficult). Nonetheless, the EU has not rushed into a narrow corporatist debate but has instead embraced the parameters outlined above. Its stated vision is to move from information to knowledge, from technological determinism to social embeddedness. It has focused on the changing role of the public sector, its governance, policies and programs. It has also embodied the changing nature of work, employment and quality of life, while embracing the growing need for flexible organizations and careers.

Similarly, the UK is actively focusing on smart cities, or what it calls the 'Information Age Town', the idea of 'Learning Direct' and 'Individual Learning Accounts', 'National Learning Grids and Targets', key skills, new library networks, etc. This idea of social capital is especially clear in Ireland, echoing locally the core rhetoric of 'New Labor's Third Way'. Indeed, in the UK, Prime Minister Tony Blair is challenging the country – with the help of the government

– to connect all schools to the superhighway free of charge by 2004. The main challenge in Britain has been identified as the need to train teachers and to create a market of high quality British educational software.

Australia too is fighting the 'tyranny of distance' in an effort to liberate and mobilize telelearning, telemedicine, etc. There, the focus is on electronic commerce, e-shopping, PC penetration, modem speeds, and so on. Thus the social inclusion element is not so visible as in Europe and parts of North America. But in Canada this is rising of necessity.

Across the APEC too, technology for learning has been declared a clear joint priority. By 2005, the region is driving towards

- distance education and learning;
- wired learning and pedagogy;
- the development of an Electronic Education Institution, and
- a focus on knowledge transfer.
- The December 2004 declaration of 12 Latin South American countries that they want to form a southern EU, following on an APEC suggestion of 1998 for Knowledge and Highly Qualified Personnel exchange in the region.

CONCLUSIONS

Clearly, smaller nations, regions and cities are all engaged in the transformation to a knowledge and information-based economy. But are they well positioned in terms of penetration of ICTs and in terms of being home to a number of ICT leaders? The speed and style of international competition make it imperative that countries like Canada be aggressive in promoting the growth of its ICT sectors, including (and perhaps especially) the emerging related sectors such as multi-media educational software. Moreover, the economic importance of promoting technical *and* social innovation, synergistically, will reveal and realize potential. Thus, we all must embrace the benefits of social inclusion, community access, digital collections, learning consortia, networking of schools and libraries, and regional development, as well as of technology development. To maximize the potential benefits of the cyber-economy, governments should continue to strive to facilitate competition, infrastructure development and innovation, and assist individuals and businesses to seize the opportunities associated with the information revolution.

NOTES

1. In economic growth theory and accounting, this reflects a move of knowledge and technology from being exogenous to endogenous. See the growth theories of Robert Solow (1957) as opposed to Paul Samuelson (1938).
2. The processing cost per instruction sent (1975=100) fell to 0.01 in 1994. The cost of a 3 minute phone call from New York to London fell from $250 (1990) in 1930 to $3 in 1995. The time to transfer a 1MB photograph using conventional phone lines versus integrated services digital networks has fallen from 82 minutes to 2.4 minutes; and from 7 minutes to 0.3 minutes for a 10 page fax. The sending cost for a 42 page document from New York to Tokyo varies from $US26.25 (24 hour overnight delivery) to $28.83 (31 minute fax) to $0.095 (2 minute Internet). The impact of technology on efficiency is also evident in the cost per retail banking transaction whether through the branch ($US1.2), the telephone ($0.65), the ATM ($0.25) or the Internet ($0.1) See *The Economist*, September 28 1996, the World Com 2002 Annual Report.

4. Technology, Trade and Investment in Interdependent Economies

No policy area is quite as domestic as international trade policy. Perhaps nowhere is this truer than in smaller economies, where the character of international trade policy and performance is tightly bound up with both the jurisdictional limits of its political system and with the expectations of policy to bring about the transformation of its industrial structure. Traditional wisdom regarding trade policy holds that countries such as Canada or Portugal with their longstanding reliance on natural resources must continue to colour their nation's industrial profile. It holds that this reliance should be encouraged politically, cherished culturally, and enhanced industrially. In making this claim it suggests that the country's current technological capacity is adequate for its 'resource future,' that its current contribution to the world technology pool is somehow fixed (having reached some sort of 'natural' limit), and is sufficient to allow smaller, interdependent nations to participate (and compete) fully in the emerging global economy. This traditional wisdom suggests that through the wealth generated by our natural resources and mature, dependable industries, Canada, or Finland, or South Africa can (and should) continue to buy their technologies off foreign technological shelves-that this pattern is cost-efficient (as the generation costs of new strategic technologies are very high) and implies no undesirable effects. This view, however, is being challenged. Increasingly, a revisionist view is emerging that holds that smaller nations, for example, must escape the 'woodshed of the OECD' (as is said in Canada, or 'get off the back of sheep' as is said in Australia) image and that the industrial structure of smaller nations must be transformed towards knowledge-intensive industries. Technology, along with strong education/research training programs and investment strategies can aggressively promote this transformation and that in order to achieve this, they must be viewed as major elements of trade policy.

BACKGROUND TO NATIONAL TECHNOLOGY DEBATES

That this revisionist view is beginning to gain centre ground politically attests not so much to the natural maturation and evolution of the Canadian economy as it does to a long series of minor victories that have been won on the political battlefields of the country. These various and disparate victories, which have been nonpartisan in nature, have only recently begun to focus on a national technology (innovation) policy debate. In so doing, the numerous stakeholders in the debate have realized that continued insularity and preoccupation with vested concerns is no longer in their best interests. They have recognized that the OECD nations are all approaching an important politico-economic crossroads, but that the competitiveness of each nation will depend on its own unique and individual responses. Well-designed technology, training and investment trade policies, it is now sensed in Canada, will play a key role in Canada's future economic viability. While this revisionist view has a distinctive history, it is also undoubtedly being fueled at present by:

- the opening of a continental market through the Canada-US Free Trade Agreement, and NAFTA as well as the proposed FTAA, which place premiums on trade in value-added goods and services;
- the growing technological sophistication of the European and Pacific Rim countries, which are showing an aggressive predilection towards strategic industrial and research alliances;
- the increased technological 'appetite' brought about by the twin challenges of Eastern European and Asian newly industrialized countries (NICs); and
- a shift in governments' views in Canada, namely, the parameters of their legitimate roles in stimulating technology generation and acquisition as well as industrial development through foreign trade policy efforts.

On balance, the first three conditions have been collectively perceived as presenting more threats than opportunities to Canada but the resultant tension regarding appropriate government roles is nonetheless being transferred into constructive debate and activity.

This chapter will review important elements in the history and scope of this revisionists' debate. It will highlight some of the mitigating factors that have worked against the development of a well-articulated, civilian technology-trade strategy. It will outline aspects of the new international environment in terms of its implications for Canada and national efforts to bring technology, investment and education/training into central public policy debates. And this chapter will outline how changes in Canada's corporate, academic, federal and provincial governments' approaches will affect Canada's plans to become a full partner in the new international economic structure through technology, trade, investment, and education.

Small, Open Economies

It has been said that the only thing that small countries have in common is that they are different. One thing that makes Canada different is that while it is a 'small country' technologically, it considers itself to be a 'big country' both geographically and geopolitically. Clearly, Canada falls within the ranks of the advanced industrialized countries, falling fourth (behind the United States, Switzerland and Norway) in terms of per capita Gross Domestic Product (GDP), fourth in terms of overall GDP, and ninth in terms of actual expenditures on R&D. But, there are several other factors besides overall economic performance that make size an important limiting factor in the technological competitiveness of countries. To begin with, small countries tend to have limited domestic markets. This means that firms in small countries must export to foreign markets in order to gain economies of scale. Increasingly, they also need to justify heavy expenditures on R&D, for as technology increases the sophistication of products and processes, so the scientific, technological and industrial resources and skills for development become more costly and complex.

Furthermore, small nations tend to have less money, proportionally, to spend on R&D; they tend to have fewer research personnel per capita, and there is a considerable tendency for researchers from small countries to emigrate. In addition, small countries tend to have problems in concentrating R&D resources. They need to fund across the spectrum of scientific research for educational purposes, but in so doing they fail to define their own technological niche areas — buying into, or falling behind, the research agendas of larger countries. As a result, and although it may be a dubious exercise to generalize about small nations, technologically 'successful' small countries seem to adopt an R&D specialization strategy. They *tend* to seek market niches in which larger firms (and even large countries' small firms) do not bother to compete, while the industries in which they tend to focus are those in which they already have strong multitechnology corporations. Thus, as one might infer from Kuznets the effective rate of growth in a small, open economy is mainly influenced by the existing level of economic development (which is high), technological development (which is low), the growth of innovative activity (which is low), and the factors influencing the innovative and knowledge process, as these have a decisive influence on the long-run performance of an economy. Contrary to popular belief neither growth of relative unit labor costs, nor differences in welfare state activity seem to have strong effects on the balance of payments constraint and growth, whereas the 'brain power' ability to identify, create, adapt and diffuse technology clearly do. This has implications for policy makers in that it underlines the importance of technology, investment and education/training policy for trade competitiveness.

Canada clearly 'fits' the general criteria for being a technological small country. Its domestic market is confined to 33 million consumers, versus 340 million in the United States, 500 million in the new Europe, and 123 million in Japan. Sixty-five percent of industrial R&D is performed by 100 firms in six industries, and half of this is performed by foreign multinationals. (Crown corporations represent a significant portion of industrial R&D as well.) Canada's Gross Expenditures on R&D (GERD) represent 1.85 percent of GDP compared with approximately 2.7 percent in the United States (1989). Its share of research scientists and engineers in the labor force is the lowest of the G7 summit nations. Government worries over the emigration of researchers from Canada have resulted in a registry of Canadians abroad, and debates over the appropriate concentration of R&D funds are evidenced by the not too distant discussions over forming Networks of Centres of Excellence and over the funding of such 'Big Science' projects as the Sudbury Neutrino Observatory (SNO) and the KAON Factory. Moreover, the importance of trade to Canada's economy is evidenced by the fact that trade constitutes 34 percent of its GDP. Technological dependency is suggested by its $7 billion high-tech trade deficit. Its contribution to world science is 4 percent (depending on the research field); its technology share of exports is about 3 percent; and its indigenous patents-to-labor-force ratio is one of the lowest of the industrialized nations (19 patents per 100,000 labor force). Given the anomalies that Canada's economically advanced but technologically immature state represent, it is not surprising that Canada is moving itself towards a more managed and technology-oriented trade profile. But the wish for this orientation is not new.

TECHNOLOGY AND POLICY FORESIGHT IN CANADA

In 1971, the noted political economist, Robert Gilpin, produced an assessment of Canada's science and technology system. In his paper entitled 'Science Policy for What?' Gilpin focused on how one could categorize nations in their approaches to technology strategies. Gilpin distinguished between:

1. strategies to develop science and technology across the broad front (e.g., USA);
2. specialization strategies (e.g., Sweden, Switzerland and the Netherlands); and
3. importation or imitation strategies (e.g., Japan and Canada).

Gilpin argued that Canada fitted the third category, but it did so in quite a different way from Japan. Like Japan, Canada has historically imported technology through direct purchases off foreign technological shelves. *Unlike* Japan, Canada has stimulated technology use and diffusion through foreign direct investment via its tariff policy. He went on to argue that in 1971 Canada was trying to move from the third category to the second category while holding clear first-category ambitions. In this observation, Gilpin not only encapsulated the techno-economic tension that is alive in Canada today, but he also previewed a deep-seated energy, However, in order to realize such transformative ambitions, Canada – like other small nations wishing to achieve and sustain advanced knowledge economic status – faced a number of challenges.

ELEMENTS OF CANADA'S NATIONAL TECHNOLOGY DEBATE

First, Canada did not have a high degree of entrepreneurship as did such countries such as Switzerland and the Netherlands. According to Gilpin, the high Canadian tariff had become a proxy for an indigenous entrepreneurial culture. Second, it did not have a significant number of either large, indigenous high technology corporations or technology-driven threshold firms upon which to develop a strong corporate technology base. Finally, Gilpin underlined the lack of an informal consensus system of decision-making (such as is found in numerous European nations), which enables quick-shifts to new paths of technological development. But, despite Gilpin's ability to identify these features, he nonetheless had difficulty in categorizing the Canadian model, leading him to conclude that 'in science policy, Canada is *sui generis.*' Gilpin's perceptive assessment of nearly forty years ago identified major structural features of the Canadian economic mosaic that have since become pressing issues of national concern. His sense, for example, that the increased integration of the Canadian and American economies when combined with tensions between national industrial development and regional (provincial) development would have significant implications for Canadian science and technology policy, was prescient. In tandem with this, many local and federal civil servants are focusing no longer on 'systems of innovation' (which they never understood) but on 'commercialization' which has been recognized as an issue for a half century but which has only been fodder for consultants and local bureaucrats, not entrepreneurs.

Of course, Gilpin did not foresee the debate over, and signing of, a major trade agreement between Canada and the United States. Nor did he predict that innovation policy would take on a higher profile as an instrument of economic development within Canada's regional economies. (Indeed, this has happened to such a degree that to some, political leadership has begun to pivot on the question of 'technology policy for what?' (to borrow from Gilpin's title). This is now a major source of consultation between national and regional authorities in many countries, as well as among Canada's stakeholders in the science and technology system. Nevertheless, Gilpin's assessment did flag *key* concerns in a debate that has evolved considerably in the past decade.

The Canadian technology policy debate that led into the new millennium spilled, of necessity, into the international trade arena. Recent commentaries on Canada's technological path reflect concerns about the crossroads we are approaching and recognition that precautions are in order to ensure well designed public policies. As in 1971, it is still difficult to categorize Canada's technology policy model (if indeed there is one) partly because of the dynamic nature of the debate. Whilst generalized assessments of technology, investment and competitiveness in small open economies have been put forth and have some obvious lessons for Canada, they cannot do justice to the high specificity of the debates, nor do they respond to the structural and jurisdictional issues that are unique to Canada. However, the urgency of attention that technology policy is now receiving demonstrates how the numerous stakeholders have moved science, technology and innovation from the periphery of decision-making circles in Canada to the center (the establishment of a new Cabinet in 2004 may have trashed this anticipation with the collapse of the Secretary of State for Science position and the appointment of an Industry Minister with a doctorate in

Economics who has stated that the department needs to move away from high-tech and towards resources like forestry).

As the cohesiveness of the debate in Canada has gelled domestically, more attention has been paid to international developments. Canada's approach to international science and technology has moved from a rather marginal activity focused on strengthening academic and scientific exchanges abroad, to a more strategic component of investment and trade strategy. Canada's federal and provincial agencies have, one by one, gradually moved from their sheltered 'womb with a view' mode to a more connected and aggressive recognition of the techno-global reality. As a result, they have undertaken a number of initiatives to help set their agenda for a knowledge-based economy. It is an agenda that features:

- strategic partnerships (in all forms) between firms;
- acquisition of appropriate technology from abroad;
- attention to and support for global requirements for unfettered diffusion of strategic technologies worldwide;
- continued active participation in multilateral and bilateral fora designed to strengthen the movement of goods, technology and services abroad; and
- on the national front, greater attention to improving the diffusion of science and technology throughout the economy.

The current debate about technology and Canada's participation in the new global economy is really part of a long standing domestic argument about national technological choice. To achieve an effective and coherent policy thrust, Canada is not taking the quiet-path scenario. Indeed, to reverse Robert Reich's phrase, Canada was until recently taking a 'loud path' to technological development and is mobilizing its sectoral stakeholders in an aggressive war to compete. These 'war' metaphors are probably as understandable to the Canadian psyche as the Japanese and Soviet 'threats' have been to Americans. To illustrate, recent reports on the Canadian technology situation refer to 'The Aggressive Economy,' 'Adjusting to Win,' and 'A Call to Action.' In a speech on global competition, former Ontario Premier David Peterson argued that the 'new weapons of power are not missiles and mortars, but scientific and technological leadership'.

Much of Canada's experience in gaining political autonomy and a sense of national identity and purpose came from participation in two overseas wars. The metaphor of a technology-driven global trade war is thus not incomprehensible to the Canadian political imagination.

The national science and technology infrastructure that Canada has inherited and created to meet the global challenges has its roots in a combination of borrowed traditions and novel experiments. Its academic institutions are a mix of European and American models. Its engineering tradition, for example, developed from specific technologies that were highly oriented towards Canada's vast geographic expanse and were thus heavily reliant on transportation, communications and energy. Many of Canada's earliest public sector research organizations, such as the Central Experimental Farms and the Geological Survey of Canada, were established to meet the direct, practical needs of a developing nation. The Canadian private sector's R&D capability evolved in large part from these public research organizations and, because of the structure of the economy, through technology transfers obtained via head office-subsidiary transactions. Business has now become the major performer and funder of R&D in the country.

Because they are still young countries economically, scientifically and technologically, the roots of Australia's, South Africa's and Canada's scientific and technical heritage have yet to be explored extensively. Historians of Canadian science and technology, for example, have gradually been filling in the gaps and in so doing have addressed myths about Canadian R&D, such as that Canada's industrial-academic research linkages are not well developed and are a recent phenomenon. The lack of appreciation for Canada's historical legacy (both domestically and internationally) has much to do with its deficient scientific culture and a negative self-image Canadians often have of their contributions to world science and technology. Recent surveys of the public view of S&T issues evidence this continued undervaluation of Canada's own scientific knowledge and heritage and have spilled over into debates on the importance of the science curriculum in Canadian schools.

CHANGES IN CORPORATE CANADA

The corporate sector has gradually moved from being on the defensive to being supporters and even path-setters. Whereas a decade ago the business enterprise sector was not willing to accept its share of responsibility for the weak national performance in innovation, today it has become more responsive to the issues. The Canadian Advanced Technology Alliance (CATA), the Canadian Chamber of Commerce, the Ottawa Centre for Research and Innovation, the Canadian

Research Management Association, and the Canadian Manufacturers' Association (CMA) represent just a few of the more active business associations that are tackling technology, trade and competitiveness The CMA, for example, along with the federal National Research Council, provided a centralized source of information and advice (CAN-MATE) to help Canadian manufacturers compete by adopting new technologies. The Chamber of Commerce and CATA sponsored several regional roundtables to stimulate technology in the major municipal communities across Canada, and as the discussion paper of that consultation stated: scientific and technologically based competitive strength is not found in countries, but within their communities. Given the nature of this 'new geography of competition' it may no longer be useful to think of Canada as being in competition with Japan, the US and other technology leaders. It is more constructive to think of Canadian cities being in competition with Japanese, American and other technology oriented communities.

Encouraging signs were also evident in the alliances formed by Canadian corporations with public-sector R&D institutions. The single most important source of technology for Canadian corporations is the university sector. In 2004, 65 percent of companies surveyed indicated they purchased R&D from universities. This has continued to increase.

ROLES OF PUBLIC POLICY

Corporate trends and assessments of S&T performance and capability put in question the 'proper' role of government at all levels in support of R&D and innovation. Traditionally, such support has centred on the advancement of knowledge, assisting in the training and supply of highly-qualified personnel, support for mission requirements and national objectives, and provision of fiscal and tax incentives for business. Increasingly, however, government S&T investment strategies have begun to shift from the input side to the output (diffusion) side of incentives. This has paralleled developments throughout the OECD as the rate of growth of R&D spending has slowed since the mid-1980s (reflecting the priority of managing national budgets) bringing science and technology spending into a 'steady state'; and as the share of government in financing the national R&D effort has declined (the US excepted). Indeed, the Canadian research councils have seen a set back in funding in 2005. This has been a function of conscious policy to transfer public R&D to the private sector — the engine of growth for any economy — and of increasing support for high technology sectors rather than for sunset industries. The role of governments in 'targeting' economic development in certain sectors or in 'backing winners' is the subject of much debate. The Nobel economist Wasily Leontief has compared the role of government to the game of curling. It is up to business to throw the rock down the ice toward the house. Government's role is to act as sweep, providing more or less broom activity, depending on the ice conditions. In tandem with this latter orientation, smaller OECD governments have, to varying degrees, become engaged in optimizing their participation in differing forms of international science and technology arrangements. This, of course, has clear implications for the design of domestic policies. Indeed, technology should be recognized as the true determinant of comparative advantage. This means that trade agreements not only need to allow for 'neutral' technology promotion policies, but must also accommodate reasonable use of technology programs to engineer constructed advantage.

There remains considerable debate over the most appropriate mix and focus of government R&D support. In the arguments between techno-globalists, mercantilists and general protectionists, Canadian policy-makers are struggling to resolve the 'bleeding edge' of nationalist economic rhetoric into the 'leading cdgc' of technological opportunity. (In some respects, this debate is but a larger version of the national debates over unfettered diffusion of scientific knowledge of the republic of science ideal and critical technological sovereignty which is prevalent in some nations.) However, to effect this change, it must be understood that, for a small country, protectionist policies towards technology and diffusion or any other kind of similarly distorting trade or tax practices are to be strenuously avoided.

As Sylvia Ostry has warned about the threat of high-tech mercantilism:

> the policy predisposition to contain the diffusion of technological knowledge within national boundaries runs counter to a powerful globalizing trend in R&D both by corporations and by research institutions and universities. The internationalization of research is also fed by emerging global markets for research personnel who can produce and apply it. Any attempt to 'nationalize' technology in the face of such powerful trends is unlikely to be successful but can be very deleterious by fostering duplication of effort and thus lowering the private rate of return to technological change, reducing the accessibility to scientific knowledge, and lowering the potential benefits to world growth. For this reason, what is required are not only policy proposals to deal with the current issue of access, but a more thorough review of policy options for mutually beneficial international cooperation appropriate to a new era of 'borderless technology'.

LOOKING OUTWARD

It is this attention to dealing with new ways of conducting international business that has led Canada to undertake innovative policy measures designed to lever Canada into the age of borderless technology.

In October 1989, Prime Minister Brian Mulroney announced a new three-pillar trade strategy. The strategy places a primacy on international science and technology partnerships, and can be viewed both as Canada's recognition of its obligations to the international S&T system as well as a demonstration of its commitment to maintaining and expanding a liberalized trading system.[57]

While there has been debate on how R&D and firms would fare under the NAFTA, the jury is still out, even in 2005. The issue was the subject of a conference held in September 1988 before the agreement was signed. The fact that the NAFTA did not treat R&D *per se* did not go unnoticed, although the agreement did address related issues of government procurement. A paper by Chris Hill, the then Director of the National Academy of Sciences' Manufacturing Forum, for example, made the following interesting observation, which can relate directly to Gilpin's earlier assessment that entrepreneurial drive had been stifled by the high tariffs:

> What is more difficult to quantify or otherwise project is the degree to which the NAFTA may give greater impetus to Canadian entrepreneurs and new entrants into the game of R&D and technology-based economic development, in part due to the psychological boost given to them by the promise of easier access to the large and lucrative market to the south. This may be especially true in view of the fact that most Canadian manufacturing and advanced technology enterprises are located near the US border.

Indeed, some of this may be borne out by a Conference Board of Canada survey on industrial R&D spending intentions. According to the survey, respondents viewed the technological implications of the NAFTA positively, although with caution. 17.7 percent thought that the NAFTA will increase their R&D over the next five years, while only 6 percent expected a decrease in R&D spending. The majority (51.7 percent) saw no imminent change in their spending plans because of the NAFTA. The survey noted, however: 'Many companies that did not expect any change in their R&D plans, or found the NAFTA not applicable to their situations, responded that they had already been trading in international markets. . . (or were) operating in a free-trade environment before the NAFTA was implemented. In point of fact, the number of companies performing R&D in Canada has decreased!'

In addition to strengthening the trade and technology opportunities for Canadian SMEs, Canada's 'Going Global' initiative also targeted the European Community and Pacific Rim regions as windows of science and technology opportunities. Science and technology funds for both regions were developed to encourage joint partnerships and collaborative R&D projects between Canadian organizations and their counterparts in Europe and Japan. Much of this built on the existing bilateral arrangements Canada has with these regions, and the funds are designed to complement this activity. For example, the Japan Science and Technology Fund responded to a Canada-Japan Complementarity Study that was commissioned by the Prime Ministers of Canada and Japan and reinforced the existing Canada-Japan Science and Technology Agreement.

Such an approach to providing a more strategic focus to Canada's international science and technology arrangements across a range of federal departments in the future will no doubt become more prevalent as stock is taken of the role of governments. There are over 250 formal bilateral science and technology arrangements managed by federal departments, agencies and provincial institutions. They cover a wide range of scientific disciplines and technology sectors.

LESSONS FROM CANADA

The Canadian climate for technology, trade and investment has matured considerably over the past several decades – recent changes to the national patent system and to Canada's active participation in world intellectual property organizations are examples. The nation looked like it was beginning to position itself to become a full innovation partner in the global economy. (We may be slipping under the Martin government which has abolished the Secretary of State for S&T.) Domestically, its S&T infrastructure has developed, and the role of provincial economies has become more active in viewing technology and innovation as central to growth. This is especially true in Quebec, Ontario and British Columbia, as well as in Canadian cities – many of which have embraced not the innovation systems notion but the idea of clustering. Canadian participation in international technology ventures is on the rise as both governments and the private sector recognize the necessity of this approach for survival. While Canada has borrowed much in its scientific and technological legacy, it can also provide some lessons for nations pursuing the 'technology niche' strategy of specialization. Its experience with a federalist structure, with its attendant federal-provincial dynamics, interprovincial liaisons and national consultative mechanisms, paradoxically leaves it well-placed to deal with global trends, which are moving to regionalization of formal trade arrangements.

Canada's role as an interdependent middle power has positioned it well to deal more effectively with a multipolar world order with all its implications in terms of shifting alliances, rapidly changing diplomatic strategies, and the increased need for commercial intelligence and anticipatory decision-making.

Canada's small expenditures in military technology has meant that it has focused much of its national energies on diffusion of civilian technology. As we have discussed, its approach has been and continues to be to maximize access to foreign technology, rather than simply minimize access to Canadian technology.

These trends have critical implications for overcoming myths or stereotypes of smaller nation technological dependency. As one observer has put it: 'The trouble we face is not offshore interest in our high technology, but the apparent short-sighted attitude toward it at home.'

Some of these stereotypes follow:

- That Canada, for example, has little perceived excellence in science and technology with which to participate in global programs has more to do with cultural attributes at home that have rarely placed a premium on S&T as a national resource than it has to do with the recognition of Canadian S&T abroad. Attempts to change this through the educational system, and through internationally peer-reviewed Networks of Centres of Excellence, are examples that will have a gradual positive effect.

- That the 'woodshed of the OECD countries' image has been propagated has more to do with the Canadian historical contribution of the natural resource sector than with the proper appreciation of the resource sector's increasing orientation to value-added production. Industry structure only accounts for part of the difference in Canada's lower industrial R&D effort. Again, here, attempts are being made jointly by the resource sector and governments to revitalize the technological sophistication of the industry in meeting global challenges.

- That the stereotype of government as industrial R&D surrogate has been promulgated is as much a function of the historical development of science and technology in a cold colony, as it is lack of appreciation for the rise of corporate R&D expenditures. The private sector is the major funder and performer of R&D in Canada and has assumed the role of champion not only for increased industrial R&D, but for other components of the innovation spectrum such as science education. As the Chamber of Commerce has put it, 'Canadian industry (must) regain control of the science and technology agenda.'

- That Canada has been a slow adopter of new technology is a perception that is gradually being challenged. Attention is now being given to a combination of acquisition of foreign technology, strengthening of provincial and community-based technology infrastructures, and diffusion of knowledge-based developments across the country.

- That Canada somehow missed a window of opportunity in setting the world lead in major technology development/commercialization programs following the Avro Arrow fiasco, for example, does not do full justice to Canada's other technological achievements such as the Candu nuclear reactor, remote sensing, the space program, consulting engineering, oil sands technology and cold regions/frontier engineering research, among other accomplishments. Indeed, several initiatives are underway to augment major national programs in environmental technologies, for example.

These myths are gradually being tackled by national major science and technology stakeholders. The success of this enterprise will be largely conditional on continued strong national leadership attention and unfettered access to foreign developments abroad and a strong and effective training and education system at home.

The challenge in engineering constructed advantage in the twenty-first century will be to ensure that infrastructure for science-based innovation – the currency of global trade – is strengthened and that public participation in this dialogue is fostered.

It is not an easy challenge to meet. In a small open society, stakeholders in the innovation or cluster system are limited in number with a consequent overlap of views and recommendations. Considerable lip service continues to be given to major societal issues such as public awareness, regulatory matters, management issues and development of human resources. A fiscal restraint agenda can make it an economic conundrum. Preoccupation with technology and trade questions tends to overlook the contribution of science and its development. This has significant implications for morale in the public sector research infrastructure and the ability of this sector to cope with increased expectations of change brought about by the competitiveness agenda. Labor has, up until recently, been marginalized from the debate.

Nevertheless, as this chapter has argued, the signals have been given; the debate is vigorous; and the agenda over the next decade will involve:

- Increasing awareness amongst decision-makers of the importance of science, technology, investment and education to international competitiveness.
- An understanding that R&D must be considered in the context of the entire innovation chain, and that in and of itself R&D *per se is* not a solution to the technology and trade question.
- A continued effort for a greater degree of concertation/networking across the country to meet the challenge of a global society.
- Greater effort in scanning for and increasing acquisition of foreign science and technology to strengthen domestic capability.
- Real measures to increase the level of debate on Canada's scientific and technological options, including a major effort to address deficiencies in scientific literacy and the scientific curriculum.
- Increased attention to the 'softer' areas of the innovation system, including management, marketing, financing (cost of capital) and regulatory issues impacting on the development of technology.
- Greater appreciation of the increased role of the community-based efforts to enhance the science and technology base of Canada's regions, including linkages with foreign subnational 'technological engines.'
- Finally, a major signal needs to come from the private sector to Canadian decision-makers that trade in today's global economy is inextricably linked to the new tools of technology and investment.

These constitute elements of the competitiveness agendas for numerous smaller, competitive nations in the twenty-first century.

5. Innovation, Institutions and International Development

Now, having discussed innovation strategies in the context of competition, knowledge, trade and investment – or what I have called the texture of the new economy – let us consider institutions and development. It is now something of a commonplace to chat about globalization, development and the world economy, about interdependencies and about the importance of technological change and innovation. We could easily add to the list: the expansion of free trade, for example – with the 'fast-track' move towards a hemispheric agreement involving 34 countries, and the current discussions concerning a Canada-US Customs Union (excluding Mexico) whilst operating within NAFTA and the South America proposal for their own 'EU'. We could add the security, border, immigration and identity card agendas that have emerged since 9/11and since the 'Eurozone'. We could easily add issues concerning the protection of, and access to, oil and natural gas – in the Middle East but also from Canada and Mexico into America, in some cases traversing environmentally sensitive national parks and animal reserves. And we could add concerns regarding the ownership and intellectual property of the environment, as in rain forests such as Brazil's. All of these issues beg important fundamental questions of innovation and development. But the agenda regarding innovation is shifting. So-called 'developing' areas of the world are now being economically differentiated. Official agencies from the OECD, the UN, UNESCO, the WTO, the WEF, the IMF and the World Bank now regularly refer not to the simple but still poignant phrase 'Third World', but to Dynamic Emerging Economies (DEE), Newly Industrializing Countries (NICs), and so on. At the heart of almost all successes and failures, beyond stable political contexts and an indigenous culture of economic entrepreneurship, is innovation.

This chapter is concerned with the political and economic thinking behind sustained development, using technological and innovation systems as its basis. As such, technological and innovation systems are by definition concerned with processes of catching up, falling behind, and – most importantly – leaping ahead.

It is about the institutionalization of creativity and the new production of knowledge. Anyone even casually aware of economic history knows that these issues are not new. Anyone even casually aware of China's rise and fall in technological prominence between the eighth century AD with I-Hsing's water leverage devices and the eleventh century Su Sung's astronomical clock tower (which stood a mighty 30 feet), with Britain's nineteenth century fall from empire, Argentina's lost ground as a regional, cultural and economic power early in the twentieth century, or the post-war rise of Singapore, Japan and South Korea would recognize the importance of this complex of innovative dynamics. These have all been extensively discussed throughout the writings of such scholars as Christopher Freeman, David Landes and Eric Hobsbawm. They might also recognize traditional approaches to understanding growth and development — such as Ricardian comparative advantage and trade theory. The Listian account suggests that a small national state can develop infant industries and services that are *not* based on abundant or cheap factors of production (now here he strays from myself and other neo-innovationalists) *providing* that it rejects free trade in favour of protection, state support (for which there is in my view a robust and diverse case to be made) and state guidance (which gets us back to the Polanyi/Bernal debate). Vernon's obsolescence bargain, or neo-Porterian notions of competitive advantage, do not posses sufficiently robust explanatory power.

With such developments in mind, this chapter will proceed as follows. First, it will briefly sketch political economic notions of development in a 'third world' sense. Second, it will briefly present an overview of the traditional views regarding obstacles to development. Third, it will discuss approaches that introduce 'innovation systems' as a conceptual framework through which economic performance across countries can be explained. The ability of having access to international networks and the difficulties of elaborating political and corporate strategies through which to achieve such access is the topic of the next section. A simple model is presented next while the last section attempts some modest conclusions from the perspective of innovation and its governance.

MOVING TOWARDS DYNAMIC EMERGING ECONOMIES

Paul Krugman, now of Princeton, has usefully reminded us that the term 'third world' was originally intended as a political badge of pride. Jawaharlal Nehru coined it to refer to those countries that maintained their independence, allying themselves neither with the West nor with the former Soviet Union. But soon enough the political intent of the phrase was overwhelmed by economic reality. "Third world" rapidly came to mean backward and poor. And the term came to carry a connotation, not of righteous demand but, of hopelessness, Krugman (1999, 16). Today however, the dynamic processes of globalization, complete with its science, technology, innovation and knowledge-based implications, can offer new opportunities for sustainable development paths.

The rapid advancement and distribution of information, communications and transportation technologies, the transfer of both technologies and capital from high wage to lower wage economies, the growing knowledge intensity of investment, the growing interdependence of nations, and the subsequent erosion of sovereignties have all rendered the socialist dream of isolation moot in light of the global quest for economic growth and development. It is also been rendered archaic given the widespread policy search for generating economic opportunities, capturing an increasing world share of higher value added activities, and distributing benefits across economies and down into the more marginalized elements of a society. Once protected elites became subjected to the tsunami of globalization, the challenge to science, technology and governance became unavoidable. By focusing on knowledge, education, skills, technologies and innovation, public policies – as being conceived and deployed in nations as diverse as South Korea, Taiwan and Singapore – are beginning to give rise to terms such as Newly Industrializing Countries (NICs) and/or Dynamic Asian Economies (DAE) thus suggesting that trend is not destiny, that countries may not be relegated to a slow or eroding development curve and instead that they may be able to move rapidly up the value added curve. Note though that the 'tap' cannot be turned on and off. India's excellent success in call centers and computing (and more and more in biopharmaceuticals – especially combinational chemistry) and South Korea's success in engineering are the result of decades of investment in mathematics and theoretical physics. Remember Ramajuan.

Note that, in the industrializing world, two different patterns can be distinguished. One is the DAE pattern, where the modes of governance of a large variety of exports-led incentives and institutional systems supported the process of upgrading technological capabilities. As it is depicted, for example, we can see the acquired competencies for the design of new products in high technological sectors. The second regards the largest Latin American economies. Around the mid-eighties the set of rules under which the Latin American economies operated changed dramatically, particularly in the cases of Argentina, Brazil, Chile and Mexico. The new set of rules included a different trade regime of incentives determined by the elimination of many of the barriers in effect during the previous decades; in addition, the government adopted a more limited role in the development process which implied a modification in the management of the nation's macroeconomic variables. This was an institutional change that created a whole new environment in which the firms and institutions operate, and there are important implications in their interactive interplay in developing technological capabilities. However, after all, the above-mentioned globalization process of Latin American economies has not yet further developed in a pattern based on dynamic comparative advantages and upgrades of technological capabilities. In general, the specialization pattern that dominates most of Latin American economies is based mainly on static comparative advantages, abundant natural resources and cheap labor forces.

BROAD TRADITIONAL OBSTACLES TO DEVELOPMENT

As Nehru's optimistic political framing lost currency, the transition reflected two broad meanings. At an early stage, a dominant approach to development and the economics of growth deferred to a neo-Marxian set of presumptions – typified by the classic contribution of Paul Baran (1956)[1] – regarding growth and accumulation and the disruptive effects of technological change. Ostensibly, two features are common to all traditional developing societies. One is low per-capita income. The second is the absence of growth.

Economically, the use of terms like 'third world' have tended to obscure the diversity of specific conditions that detracted from potentials being realized. In Asia, Latin America, Central America, South America and Africa the range of political and cultural experience is vast indeed. Some elements of economic 'backwardness' can be traced to colonialism and civil war.

Political obstacles to development traditionally include the lack of political stability and the presence of political independence. 'Bad' economic policies can also prevent economic growth from getting underway. And they can bring growth to a halt once it has started, so countries can fall behind just as they can progress.

On the basis of development economic theory, it is well-known that trade, free trade and the internationalization of production were not necessarily neutral in the different countries' growth paths (de la Mothe and Ducharme 1990; Dosi, Pavitt and Soete 1990). Thus, some countries have selected a road that is characterized by increasing gaps in growth. Trade liberalization and foreign investment flows are not the only elements that help to create a prosperous development path. The firm's and sectoral learning patterns as well as overall national capabilities are dynamically coupled via input-output flows, knowledge spillovers, backward and forward linkages, complementarities and context-specific externalities. Together, they contribute to shaping the organizational and technological context within which each economic activity takes place. In a sense, they set the opportunities and constraints that each individual production and innovation process faces — including the availability of complementary skills, information on intermediate inputs and capital goods, and demand stimuli to improve particular products. This has a direct link with the analyses that focuses on structural change and development (here, within a vast literature, contributions that come immediately to mind range from Hirschman to Rosenstein Rodan, Gerschenkron, Chenery and Sirquin, among others).

A traditional statement of that rationale is stated by Hirschman as follows:

'One suggestion along this line was that development is accelerated through investment in projects and industries with strong forward or backward linkage effects. I argued that entrepreneurial decision making in both the private and public sectors is not uniquely determined by the pull of incomes and demand, but is responsive to special push factors, such as the linkages, emanating from the product side. By now, the various linkages and their interaction have taken on a new character and importance. They appear to constitute a structure that is capable of generating an alternative path toward development or underdevelopment for the different staple exporters. In other words, some of the principal features of a country's development in the period of export-led growth can be described in terms of linkages deriving from its staple.' (Hirschman 1977, 70 and 80).

Taken together, these typical macro views on impediments to development and growth also embody the view that the development process invariably insists that economies pass through the historical experience of the advanced industrial economies. Thus the history of the consumption-intensive industrial revolution and of classical political economics became the focus and the template for many development economists (Hirschman 1971; Griffin and Gurley 1985).

International obstacles to development and growth can also be found in traditional views regarding gains from trade. For example, the theory of comparative advantage states that nations with differing endowments of capital, labor and natural resources will gain by specializing in those areas where their relative costs of production are low and importing in those areas where their relative costs are high. Furthermore, the greater the differences in endowments between countries — and the differences between rich and poor countries are indeed great — then the greater the gains from trade will likely be. However, in order to participate in a high value added sense and not be simply a source of low wage labor and production for advanced economic units, then a country must have a capacity to absorb and retain talent, to produce new knowledge, and so on.

TECHNOLOGY, TRADE AND DEVELOPMENT

The concept of 'take-off' is frequently cited in the development literature and is in many ways at the centre of Walt Rostow's analysis of the stages of economic growth. Since the 1960s, the central purpose of most contributions in the field of technology and trade has been to highlight the crucial importance of technological change and innovation in explaining the international trade pattern; for example Posner (1961), Freeman (1963), Hufbauer (1966) and Vernon (1966). This approach has stressed international *asymmetries in technology* as the main determinant of trade flows and specialisation patterns.

In Posner (1961), the pattern of trade is explained by the initial asymmetric access to technological knowledge in a world characterized by similarities in demand patterns. In this context, trade between countries will be maintained if the differences in national abilities to innovate and imitate persist. After a time lapse, most countries can imitate the new commodity and restore technological parity, also eliminating the basis for trade. Freeman (1963) and Hufbauer (1966) have stressed the differences in the factors which determine specialization before and after the imitation process takes place. Thus, during the innovation process the effects of patents, commercial secrecy, static and dynamic economies of scale prevail. However, once imitation occurs, specialization will be determined by the traditional process of adjustment in production cost and competitiveness.

In Vernon (1966), technologies are associated with distinct phases in the evolution of a technology and a specific international distribution of innovative capabilities in the production of new commodities. Innovative advantage is the main feature of the initial phase, explaining the production of new commodities in the advanced countries. Over time, technology evolves into a mature phase, characterized by the standardization of products and processes. In this latter phase, international competition is based on production cost advantages and technology can be transferred to less developed economies, whose comparative advantage lies in their lower real wages. In this respect, the pattern of trade is considered a process of technological divergence and convergence, for which the innovative process induces divergence while imitation and diffusion induce convergence between countries.

In doing so, many of these studies have undoubtedly scored points with policy makers who have increasingly come to recognize the significance of technology for international competitiveness. The basis for policy of these contributions remains, however, poor. This is in fact not surprising. The introduction of 'technology' in any kind of model, whether of the classical or neo-classical sort, raises many challenges. The complexity of the phenomenon of technological change on the one hand (with its dual impact on efficiency and new demand) and the essential dynamic 'change' perspective implicit in the concept of technological change on the other, are difficult to handle in their normative proposal in any normative economic model.

Recent formal approaches put increasing attention to uneven international technological change as an engine of growth.[2] These approaches have pinpointed the importance of the interplay between absolute and comparative advantages as determinants of the participation of each country in world trade, the dominance of technological gaps in the process of international specialization, and the bounds imposed by the dynamics of innovation and trade on the 'growth possibility sets' of each economy. On the determinants of absolute and comparative advantages, technological gaps – in terms of product and process innovation – and institutional asymmetries – in terms of the main form of organization of labor markets – contribute to determining the pattern of specialization and its evolution over time. On the demand side, on the other hand, asymmetries in national consumption patterns, regarding price and income elasticities, play a crucial role on the interplay between specialization and macroeconomic level of activity. Finally, trade balance conditions determine the growth rate differential of trading economies.

Under such an approach, it has demonstrated that the growth of relative trading partners depends not only on the demand structure of each economy constrained by the conditions of the balance of payments, but also, particularly, on differences in technology. Furthermore, the technological gap is introduced as one of the main variables explaining the pattern of growth possibilities through the effect of what we will refer to here as the technological gap multiplier which accounts for the initial distance between countries in terms of technological capabilities (Cimoli and Soete 1992).

Wide differences apply to the capabilities of developing new products and to different time lags in producing them after they have been introduced into the world economy. Indeed, the international distribution of technological capabilities regarding new products is at least as uneven as that regarding production processes. For example if one takes international patents or the number of discrete innovations as a proxy for innovativeness, the evidence suggests that the club of the innovators has been restricted over the whole past century to a dozen developed countries with only one major new entry, Japan. Second, the processes of development and industrialization are strictly linked to the inter- and infranational diffusion of 'superior' techniques. In a related fashion, as already mentioned, at any point in time, there is likely to be only one or, at most, very few 'best practice' techniques of production which correspond to the technological frontier. In the case of developing economies, the process of industrialization is thus closely linked to the borrowing, imitation and adaptation of established technologies from more advanced economies (Archibugi and Pianta 1992; Kim 1997). These processes of adoption and adaptation of technologies, in turn, are influenced by the specific capabilities of each economy.

NATIONAL INNOVATION SYSTEMS, CAPABILITIES AND ECONOMIC PERFORMANCES

A significant body of recent literature exists explaining the importance of institutions and their role in economic and industrial development. In particular, regarding the Pacific Rim NIEs, the work of many helps us to understand not only how institutional successes are achieved, but also institutional failures as well. Bardhan (1996) analyses such issues as one of coordination, which has to be seen in terms of the interaction of distributive conflicts with state capacity and governance structures. The author suggests that the success of institutions in some NIEs (namely South Korea and Taiwan) has to be understood in terms of the capacity of establishing and applying rules of performance criteria, so that, for example, credit allocation by the state was tightly bound up with export performance. In this way, international competition was used to foster internal learning. Most of these approaches point out that growth is not automatic. Growth needs a 'social capability' which can be viewed as a '... rubric that covers countries' levels of general education and technical competence, the commercial, industrial and financial institutions that bear on their ability to finance and operate modern, large-scale business, and the political and social characteristics that influence the risks, the incentives and the personal rewards of economic activity including those rewards in social esteem that go beyond money and wealth' (Abramovitz 1994).

All the above mentioned patterns provide examples of the functioning of what could be understood as a National Innovation System (NIS).[3] In a narrow way, we shall propose a concept and representation of NIS whereby its main feature will be related to empirically capture the main features that explain technological asymmetries and their interplay with growth performance. It now proposes the idea of a set of technological capabilities that essentially refers to a firm's, organization's and country's ability to solve both technical and organizational problems on the one side, and performance – as measured by such variables as competitiveness and growth – on the other. In between these two, and shaping their interaction (and therefore causing the magnitude of the span that exists between the two) lies the innovation system, acting at both the national and regional levels and therefore possessing an inherently local nature.[4]

At a national level, innovative capabilities are clearly difficult to quantify. Thus, a country's efforts to create these could be considered a proxy for the main capabilities available in each economy. Capabilities can be identified as those which pertain to the following groups:

1. Educational (literacy rate, secondary and tertiary level enrolment ratios, third level students in maths, science and engineering),
2. R&D efforts (scientists and engineers in R&D, R&D in GNP, ratio of private and public R&D),
3. Technology transfer efforts (FDI stock, imports of capital goods).

An essential aspect of capabilities regards their interplay with the catch-up argument. In particular, when a country that is behind the world innovation frontier is considered, most of the capabilities variables could be considered as a support for the scope for imitation. Thus, through the approaches introduced above, a catch-up process based on borrowing, imitation and adaptation of established technologies from more advanced countries is captured (Gomulka 1971; Abramovitz 1989).

Economic performance depends on how each country implements policies (to stabilize the macro-economic setting and to promote the industrial sectors) and organizes its institutional infrastructure and efforts. The relevant variables which can be considered as a proxy for the scope of catch-up are: GDP per capita, rate of growth of GDP, exports as a percentage of GDP, productivity growth, technological sectoral distribution for GDP and exports in terms of technological classification (for example: Pavitt's taxonomy), international market share of exports and imports and employment in manufacturing sectors.

In this framework, the possibility of institutional failures becomes incorporated into a broad structure which is able to account for the interactions among the main agents in the process of development. The essential feature of this system is constituted by the interface between competencies, efforts and performance and the role that the NIS plays in it as the wider representative of institutions (both public and private). Knowledge flows are embodied in individuals and their organizations, as already stated, and therefore it is obvious that the central part in the system is played by a collection of institutions. Most countries are characterized by different types of institutions which, however, could be distinguished according how these contribute to the development of technologies and the role that they play in the whole system. Thus, one can think at the following institutions as a sort of representative sample of those actually existing in different countries: higher education institutions (HEIs), research and technological development organizations (RTOs), industrial research laboratories (IRLs), government research institutes (GRIs), military research institutes (MRIs), agencies for education and training programs (AETs), certificated research and technology organizations (CRTOs), technological information centers (TICS), organizations supporting science parks (OSSPs), and technology transfer institutions (TTIs).

A few examples of how the system functions are provided by the historical case studies discussed in Dosi, Pavitt and Soete (1990), showing the mechanisms through which the NIS, by fostering R&D, has been enhancing the capabilities of firms and industries, ultimately inducing an improvement in performance. The same type of relationship is also confirmed by the case studies recently conducted by OECD, that revealed the extent and types of collaborations between enterprises and the public sector research base (formal collaborations – such as commissioned research, joint R&D projects, co-patenting and co-publications; informal transactions – informal contacts and use of published scientific knowledge; spin-offs from universities, and transfer of technology to enterprises – patents and product developments).

At a more specific level, and in particular by focusing on the educational policy, another example of the relationship running through the NIS to enhanced competence and better performance is provided by the analysis of the Taiwanese experience supplied by Nelson (1993) and Della Giusta (1996).

In Germany, Japan and Sweden it has been often observed that, at least in most of the post-war period, education and training systems have been particularly efficient in providing people with the requested standards in terms of knowledge and skills. University and government laboratories can therefore be considered as an important source for technological capabilities for the firms. In this respect, one can also mention the cases of Korea and Taiwan, emerging countries where it seems that education-led growth contributed to shift international specialization from standard products to much more sophisticated ones, gradually characterized by a higher content of technological complexity.

In other words, a specialization increasingly oriented towards innovative commodities and practices has been often supported and associated, particularly with the successful cases, by long-term planning initiatives and public investments in 'human capital'. While — as counterfactual examples in the cases of Argentina and Brazil — it seems that the weak links between the science and education systems and the industrial and R&D system contribute to an explanation of their weak competitive performances. Taking into account this institutional supportive environment reduces, at least in part, the serious analytical and empirical difficulties that the scholars have faced in explaining within an incrementalist perspective the incredibly fast technological learning trajectories experienced by some Far Eastern firms (Freeman 1987; Amsden 1989; Hobday 1995).

Moreover, taking this analysis to its logical extreme, one might say that the international performance can be obtained only according to the differences of NIS-capabilities displayed in each economy. Thus, international competition could be based on a 'protected piece of the NIS-capabilities', or on industries supported by government policies in terms of resources for science and technology development. Such has been the case for Korean *chaebols* as well as for the American computer, software and semiconductor industries, supported by research resources from the Department of Defense (Nelson 1993).

A more recent analysis referring specifically to the NIS approach in the NIEs can be found in the works by Kim (1997), Lall (1997) and Katz (2000). The argument here puts the emphasis on the 'message' that growth and catch-up potentiality are clearly related to country historical paths and development of a local NIS. Institutions, industrial and S&T policies — such as those that support science, human capital and learning capabilities — are the main variables introduced to explain differences between the NIS developed in Latin American and Asian NIEs.

An implication of this view is related to a broader set of approaches that look for a framework in which the mechanisms that support technical change and innovation could be understood, so that governments could form and implement policies in order to influence the processes of innovation. Moreover, by systematizing the difference between competence and performance, it could also become possible to create a concept of measurement of the 'goodness' or 'badness' of the NIS. Through the representation introduced above it is possible to explain why technological gaps among countries reproduce themselves over time due to the fact that individual behaviors (in response to the existing patterns of incentives and opportunities) produce sub-optimal collective outcomes. In other words, the existence of diverse institutions and organizations, and their modes of interaction, determines specific national systems of innovation which over time present certain invariant characteristics which account for their phases of relative 'technological success and failure'. When organized appropriately, an NIS is a powerful engine of progress. Poorly organized and connected an NIS may seriously inhibit the process of innovation (Metcalfe 1995).[5]

CAPABILITIES OF ACCESSING INTERNATIONAL NETWORKS

The purpose of the above sections was to discuss the empirical and analytical features that support an NIS analysis in order to understand their impacts on the sources of technological asymmetries and growth. However, most of these studies have implicitly stressed that growth benefits can be mainly obtained from local and domestic efforts. Today, policies oriented to increase local investment in technological variables and linkages – that essentially refer to the improvement of local functionality of the system – are not enough. In fact, with the growing internationalization of technology and production, the improvement of capabilities has to be related to the ability of accessing international networks where knowledge and technology are produced.

Since the world economy is becoming more interdependent, this phenomenon is adding a new dimension into the analysis of the technological asymmetries. The growing interdependence between all the economies and regions, through raising commercial and financial flows, along, with domestic institutional constraints, are affecting the traditional trail of knowledge elaboration and technology.

In fact, today, firms and countries have large opportunities for accessing knowledge and technology at the international level. The globalization of industrial research – traditionally a headquarters function – also increased in the 1990s and this will continue into the twenty-first century. The factors driving this are becoming more complicated and diverse as firms join university-based and private-public research consortia, cross-industry strategic alliances and so on. Traditionally, the industrial propensity to invest in research abroad was highly correlated with the internationalization of the firm's functions, such as production and marketing. In an economic sense, *market access* is still an important factor in the globalization of research, particularly in those sectors that have high levels of foreign manufacturing. As product cycles shorten and technology becomes increasingly complex and specific, more R&D facilities are created near foreign plants but also, shared R&D activities are developed to reduce the time of transfer of knowledge. In recent years, *personnel access* and *knowledge access* have become the more significant factors in the globalization of research. Research has shown, for example, that personal contacts and proximity are a *sine qua non* to network realization and research productivity. Cyber-networks without loyalty, trust and interpersonal relations, are not sustainable.

A New International Scenario: Policy, Globalization and Complexity

Top achieve international access in an economic environment in which firm-level profitability and state-level competition is no longer grounded in tangible goods and natural resources (which themselves feature quantity-based pricing), economic agents now have to trade with intangibles, which are much more difficult to monitor, price and produce. This results in an environment of economic competition which is not only more fierce and more open to competitors, but is also open to greater risk. This is true for two reasons. Globalization means that firms must compete at great distances from their home. Production abroad becomes costly; being represented and distributed in far-off markets is costly. And servicing clients in foreign countries in a timely fashion is costly. Together these mean that firms must stretch their resources considerably.

Technology is a co-aspect of globalization which drives up risk in so far as the most advanced technologies emerge from R&D. R&D is based on creativity and discovery. Thus, R&D can be considered inherently risky as it cannot be guaranteed to generate commercially viable or useful results every time. Nor can the next breakthrough in any given research field be guaranteed to emerge from labs in this-or-that location. As has been noted, in order to overcome the twin dilemmas of both global presence and technological advance, organizations in regional clusters and networks increasingly operate through cooperative strategies. In short, they are cooperating in a complex environment in order to capture value from ideas, innovation and people.

The new complexity has created an environment of uncertainty because of the velocity and specific intensity of technical innovation (Figure 5.1). Complexity in such a context can be expressed in terms of the systematic overlap of economics and technological factors. Some of them can be now briefly summarised: firms face increased costs because of the globalization of production and markets, as well as due to the costs of carrying out R&D. The increased risks associated at the firm level by sunk costs of in-house R&D activities, by decreasing product life cycles and, at the more national level, by both the increased pace of competition and the increased emergence of international interdependencies, restrict, to some degree, the flexibility and autonomy that governments may feel when dealing with such matters as financial markets and market access. The increased pace of competition, fueled in part by the availability of worldwide telecommunication networks and information systems, and coupled with the concomitant reduction of reaction times when faced with market signals, emergency response, or environmental emergencies, are good examples of the nature of the current world complexity.

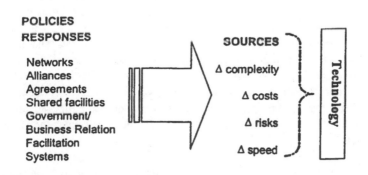

Figure 5.1 Summarizing Complexity

A Need for Coordinated Governance

Let us refer to the case of the modes of governance technology and development in Latin American countries. In an extreme synthesis, from the above points, it is clear that access to international networks is important because they are the expression of cooperative exchanges between economic agents, and generate effects at the micro, meso and macroeconomic levels. The importance of networks does not rely only on the support of information inflows, but on the specialization of knowledge as well. While production activities become more complex and economic agents more interdependent, complementary actions among firms and organizations are necessary in order to improve the global market position of the former. However, equal distribution of benefits cannot be generalized when interdependencies and networks are developed across countries. The benefits of networking activities are not necessarily equally distributed. In an interdependent world, who captures the benefit of the above networks and externalities is an important element which should be more frequently evaluated. For example, the modernized Latin American firms are becoming increasingly globalized in terms of the orientation of its production and its capacity to acquire foreign technology. More important, the liberalization process provides incentives to develop networks with firms and institutions located abroad (Cimoli 2000).

What is the main consideration related to the effects of innovation in the experiences of some Latin American countries? We know that the building of national innovation systems is a social process that involves knowledge and learning, not only about the way to do things, but also essentially on how to produce cooperative environments in which the economic performance can be intensified. Consequently, the modes of governance of local institutional frameworks, educational and training systems, R&D incentives and industrial relations affect the innovation system itself and the kind of knowledge networks which support the innovation system. Our conjecture here is that Latin America presents a rich case where the modes of governance have been exclusively 'delegated' to the market driven by the process of trade liberalization and globalization of these economies. Consider as an illustration the following stylized facts.

1. Most of the Latin American production structure has gone through important changes from the import substitution period through the new scenario characterized by macroeconomic stabilization policies. The largest economies, after trade reforms, have increased their participation in the world arena in terms of exports and imports. Most of the surviving and efficient

firms (MNCs and large domestic firms) have increased their export of final commodities and automobile components, chemicals, plastic products, glass, beer, electronics, steel, cement, etc. On the other hand, their imports of intermediates, machinery and equipment also have grown. Thus, the image that we have is that countries such as Mexico and the Central American nations have greatly globalized their production activities, and a new pattern of specialization in the global production chain is emerging.

2. In recent years, a new pattern of sectoral and production chain has appeared, while at the same time economic activities are coordinated and integrated across geographic borders. In fact, production activities now are widely recognized to be the centre of gravity for the newly industrialized economies' increased participation in the new 'world specialisation'. This new globalized scenario has increasingly modified the nations' competitiveness, as well as their integration in terms of production capacities across firms, industries and nations. Industries and firms now are integrated in an international network according to different types of linkages designed as networks of contractors, or they have formed more coordinated, integrated and organized production chains in different sites around the world. Many other factors give specific shape to these networks; one such factor involves the rules of action for NMEs as they decide whether to invest locally or export, based on the trade-off concerning proximity of trade for local investment compared to the gains in concentration or scale that come with exporting.

With a difference in timing, it is possible to infer that an 'optimal cycle' of globalization, which relates growing production capacities to dynamic and higher technological efforts, will prevail in the long term. At the beginning of this process, foreign firms start their production activities in a domestic location, adapting organization equipment around their main headquarters-based business. Manufacturing activities are located mainly on the basis of labor costs and local markets that have specific regulatory frameworks (think of NAFTA as introducing a new regulatory framework). For some authors, local technological competencies become an early ingredient in persuading multinational enterprises (MNEs) to establish subsidiaries in a large range of industries. However, in general, in the following stages, local firms are expected to develop their own technological competencies by adapting the production organization/processes and product designs. In the last stage, R&D is expected to move ahead, establishing research centers and linkages with local centers that specialize in the production of applied research and the formation of human capital.

This last phase, associated with the new phenomenon in the globalization of industrial research activities, generally has occurred throughout the most industrialized economies in the OECD area, as more of the multinationals' investment is directed toward research abroad and the acquisition of laboratories. Nevertheless, recent evidence on the large multinational firms' contribution to the world's technology shows that, in spite of increasing talk about the globalization of large firms, technological activities, they remained remarkably oriented toward domestic activities. MNEs prefer to keep technological activities at home, in contrast to their attitude toward production activities. For foreign firms, the overall evidence seems to point to the contrary of the expected convergence. Technical literature cites international evidence about large MNEs keeping most of their technological activity at home (Pavitt and Patel 1995). In fact, analysis carried out through empirical studies at the meso and micro industry level in countries such as Argentina, Brazil and Mexico has shown that this hypothetical phase remains a 'dream' for most of these countries.

Under these circumstances, foreign direct investment (FDI) refers to the activities and decisions that MNEs make. These activities and decisions, developed considering international production, exert a strong influence on the direction of trade flows, scale and content as well as on trade specialization, competitiveness and the host and home countries' foreign trade balances. This is the case of a host countries in Latin America. In fact, to a significant degree, their patterns of trade specialization and performance (for example, international competitiveness) can then be analysed as the outcome of the processes that are a result of the MNEs' decisions concerning the location and quality of direct foreign investment. In this context, regional integration through NAFTA has played a crucial role as an institutional regime or framework that has supported incentives for the MNEs. Today, technological development occurs mainly in the MNEs' home bases, and only a small portion is transferred to host countries. This process determines, on the one hand, that Latin America countries do actively participate in the globalization of production and, on the other hand, that their participation in the globalization of scientific and technological activities is very poor. As companies transfer only some of their R&D activities, we can expect that the present concentration of corporate R&D will by and large lead to an even stronger international divergence of technological development. The internationalization of R&D is carried out within developed economies and regions with already-proven technological advantages. Technological cooperation between firms seems, in practice, to exclude firms that do not already have an established reputation within the developed economies. This view supports the results obtained by empirical research on the organization of research activities in multinational firms; here, it is clear that even multinational companies perform most of their innovative activities in their home country (Patel and Pavitt 1995) and with some specificities (Cimoli 2000).

3. Most production activities in Latin American countries have increased their demand for the knowledge and technology that foreign sources provide. Our evidence indicates that most countries have modernized their plants that are specialized in exports, which suggests that industrial adjustment has occurred preferentially through process innovation such as the improvement of production organization, improvement of skills and adaptation of machinery and equipment – not the renewing of fixed capital – which would permit the MNEs and large domestic groups to achieve a better competitive performance. Moreover, there are three main reasons why the dynamics of inter-industry flows simply are not functioning to improve R&D efforts and linkages with the local institutional framework. For example, in Mexico and Central America, Maquiladora operations dominate the production of science-based components, thus allowing for very limited links and flows to other domestic suppliers of intermediate goods. Specifically, when analysis is developed for the most recent years, it seems to confirm that the Maquila industry is one of the leading actors in the industrial modernization. The diffusion of this type of industry introduces only very weak connections with the domestic productive firms and institutions. The 'maquila innovation system' mainly supports and stimulates networking activities in the firms and institutions located abroad, thus reinforcing the knowledge and technological advantages in the developed economies.

4. The imported equipment used throughout the industrial system replaces the learning capability that could accumulate in specialized domestic suppliers of equipment in a well integrated industrial system. The main changes could be observed in the modes of how sectors and the type of firms (considering Foreign Firms and Non-Foreign Firms) are interlinked with foreign production networks and sources of technology. Specifically, the pattern related to R&D efforts and other modes of technology transfer has

been replaced mainly by greater integration with imported inputs, stronger linkages with foreign engineering services and institutions (such as universities and other research institutes) for the most successful export sectors. Their direct contribution to R&D and technology transfer is not substantial. The evidence on R&D activities and technical collaboration (technology transfers) shows that the efforts and local interactions for this kind of activities are scarce and scattered (Cimoli 2000; Katz 2000)

5. The personnel employed in activities such as R&D, quality control and local adaptation of design mainly interact within the multinational firms where they work and, furthermore, those firms are characterized by reduced linkages with the domestic higher education institutions; local research centers and laboratories. In this context, for example, universities show increasing efforts to improve and create linkages with the production system. However, those efforts are inhibited by two principal factors: first, the bureaucratic organization in most public universities, and second, the more modernized industrial sector and the science-based sector's demand for knowledge from institutions and research centers abroad.

The above-mentioned factors have inhibited local networking activities. Moreover, local networking activities did not have sufficient support, in terms of linkages between the different agents in most of the innovation systems in the Latin American countries. In others words, the production system has modernized a small part of the economy, due to the effects derived from the opening-up of the economy; however, this process has not been accompanied by an increased effort to stimulate the creation of local networks, such as non-market system of linkages, a business culture and institutions that enable firms to interact with each other.

Most policy makers have held that the liberalization process is a sufficient condition and that they only need to support the acquisition of foreign technology and to locally capture and absorb the benefits from the internationalization of trade, investment and technology flows. In fact, policy makers point out that the openness of the economy has expanded the nation's technological opportunities, thus improving its technological efforts. Up to now, the modes of governance that are likely to be specific to local institutions, local regulatory frameworks and 'authorities' for privatization rules have only played a passive role. Furthermore, efforts to promote more integrated systems, which would allow firms to rapidly address technological and organizational problems, have been not carried out.

In general, our conjecture is that the outcomes of this process at the microeconomic level are that the technological trajectories of each economy can be completely divergent. The instrumentation of networks generates conditions for gaps in the creation and absorption of knowledge and of technical change. In this sense, the macro convergence of economies does not mean equality of the members, yet implies different capabilities in capturing the benefits of networking activities. The microeconomic divergences observed in the technical paths of different countries at the regional level is explained by the differences in the institutional framework of each economy, that is, the functioning of networks does not imply uniformity of the technical procedures.

In this context, it is possible to infer that the technological performance of the economies is mainly determined by the *composition, size, flexibility* and *international accessibility* of the National Innovation System. On one side, it is possible to find economies that are successful in developing local abilities through strength of linkages between different parts of the NIS, while on the other side, it is possible to find prosperous economies with intensive connections with the international technological knowledge system. Fundamentally, there exists an irrefutable fact — the economic success of a society relies upon the abilities they develop to generate and incorporate knowledge and techniques produced in other economies.

FORGING AHEAD, CATCHING UP AND FALLING BEHIND: A SIMPLE MODEL (with Mario Cimoli)

By referring to the trade and growth analysis summarized above, it is possible to draw an interpretation and representation of the main interplay between the NIS, capabilities and growth performances.

Within the learning economics, the mechanisms of adoption and learning substantially modify — and add new interpretations to — the cost functions faced by the sectoral country's productivity. The description of the process proposed here explains how unit costs decrease in accordance with a technologically determined learning curve, with capabilities clearly possessing a cumulative character. This process has been adapted from the evolutionary-structuralist models which introduced some sort of Verdoorn-Kaldor law for the explanation of the interplay between learning, dynamics of productivity and trade specialization. The introduction of endogenous dynamics increasing return is displayed by a mechanism which explains gains in specialization in terms of an increase in exports and higher international market shares.

In the following figure, we have a representation of the interplay that exists between labor productivity (p) and exports (z),[6] whereas each schedule p minus z shows that changes in productivity are led by exports increasing. Thus, under the assumptions that a change in productivity affect the whole range of commodities produced,[7] an increase in the country's exports — higher participation in the world economy and market shares for the commodities already exported — will lead to higher productivity via learning mechanisms, organizational change and quality improvements.[8]

By referring to these relationships, different schedules of specialization and productivity can be obtained. Looking at Figure 5.2, one can discern an increase in domestic capabilities (literacy rate, secondary and tertiary level enrolment ratios, third level students in maths, science and engineering, scientists and engineers in R&D, R&D in GDP (private and public R&D), accessing international knowledge networks, direct FDI stocks, imports of capital goods, etc.) moves the function on the right side and will increase the number and type of commodities exported. In the high NIS-capabilities area, the number of commodities produced and exported will be increased (new international markets could be gained for 'new' commodities that has been already imported or produced only for the local market). Two simple and schematic processes are described here. First, a country can gain in terms of dynamic comparative advantages when a path of productivity growth is taking place. General support could be found, among others, in the learning mechanisms, organization of production and product quality improvements. Second, a country's efforts to increase its participation with 'new' commodities in the world market are mainly embodied in the changes of NIS-capabilities addressed to support innovation, its diffusion and access to international knowledge networks. In sum, we describe here the two patterns with respect to the Latin American economies. The pattern in Latin American can be described by the movement along a single schedule, thus these economies improve their productivity on the basis of a modernization process held in the larger exporter firms and their comparative static advantages. The pattern on the other side seems to be characterized by an increase in their productivity, along a single schedule, and the movement of the schedule on the right side. In other words, these are economies that not only gain in terms of a continuous process of modernization but they also have created new capabilities and competencies for the design of new products and process.

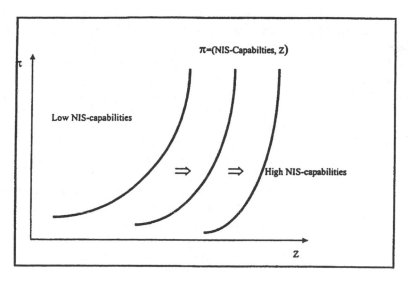

Figure 5.2 NIS-Capabilities and Specialization

In Figure 5.3, the interplay between NIS-capabilities and catching up processes is graphically represented. Looking at the left side, think of a 'NIS-capabilities frontier' which could be identified as the actual created asset that each economy has shown to built-up in order to support innovation and its diffusion. Each p minus y schedule is build-up on given NIS-capabilities. The figure tells us that an increase of domestic productivity will lead to a higher domestic income (with respect the world economy). In other words, an export led growth approach is assumed here.

On the right side of the figure, the growth trajectories are displayed (where y approximates the GDP as a proxy for the scope for catch-up). The export leading growth process is taking place on a single schedule relating y changes over time. Thus, if our country is behind the international frontier, a process of catch-up is taking place when its productivity increases and learning mechanisms (associated to organizational changes, improved adaptation of imported capital goods and quality improvements etc.) in the production activities are obtained.[9] Two limits are represented when the catching-up path takes place $(Y)_1$ and $(Y)_2$ which could be considered as the physiological bottom-up of relative growth possibilities; in particular, y_1 represents the 'international frontier' capturing the performance attained by the developed economies.

Again, on the left side, an successful effort to increase this NIS-capabilities asset would shift upward the schedule *p minus y*. The same could be obtained when the set of institutions, which jointly and individually contribute to the development and diffusion of new technologies, improves the transfer and absorption capacity of knowledge flow and, consequently, the diffusion of the innovation process and the access to international knowledge networks. Thus, an effort to increase NIS-capabilities and improve its functionality would produce a jump of the schedule *y minus t* reducing the gap from the international frontier.

In other words, a stronger effort to obtain a functional (well organized) NIS and higher capabilities of accessing into international knowledge networks will lead to an upward shift of the schedules *p* minus *y* and *y* (the income increase from y_a to y_c). Thus, a higher participation and higher income with respect to the world economy could be reached; and a process of catch-up is taking place reducing the growth gap from the international frontier.

Most of the effects described before can be neutralized by a higher effort to increase the NIS-capabilities and improve its organization in the advanced countries. In this case, a jump of the international frontier (y_1) and an increasing gap from the others' growth trajectories could be obtained. A scenario of a stable gap in the growth trajectories in terms of the international frontier could be viewed as the result of similar efforts in NSI capabilities.

The catch-up process introduced here put its emphasis on differences in the scope for export led growth and a country's potential to support innovation systems and international access.[10] In this sense, there are two mechanisms introduced and described in Figure 5.3. First, a country could exploit growing productivity on the basis of improved competitiveness and increased exports. This process is building up on a given NIS-capabilities framework. Thus, learning mechanisms, organizational changes and quality improvements in the production activities are the main sources of catch-up. Second, it can be put that since the catch-up process is shaped by the actual NIS-capabilities, an effort to increase this asset and improve its functionality would jump the country's growth trajectory nearer to the international frontier.

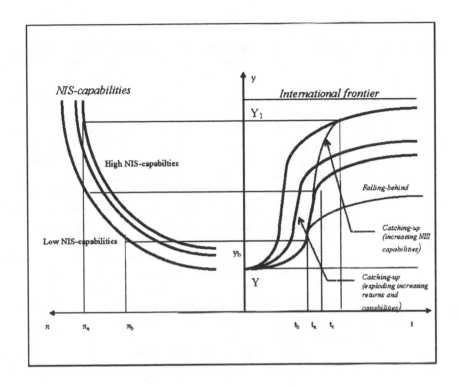

Figure 5.3 NIS-Capabilities and Trade Growth Performances

The model sketched above accounts in a relatively straightforward manner for the following general property that all efforts addressed to improve the functionality of the NIS-capabilities — related to both institutions and resources — by a country could be viewed as a necessary condition to improve its economic performance. In the same sense one can see that a catch-up (or forging-ahead) growth trajectory is taking place. Conversely, a falling-behind trajectory is associated with NIS-capabilities that are poorly organized, do not have access to international networks and make less efforts to increase these assets.

CONCLUSION

From international research on innovation and the governance of technology, we know that there is an increasing amount of empirical evidence supporting the phenomenon that the rate of introduction and transfer of innovations among firms and between sectors seem to be increasingly influenced by the ability and capacity to co-operate with other firms and organizations. Networking activities are, without doubt, key in understanding policy implementations. Therefore it can be drawn from all these new international contexts that one of the determining factors driving the internationalization of R&D is the capacity of firms to efficiently manage decentralized complex systems on a world level. Also, other types of networks – for example, between universities and research centers – need an increasing capacity to manage complex linkages with and between government and international organizations. It is likely that the lack of such a capacity is a main obstacle to the internationalization of research and networks. These observations thus provide a framework for analysis in which the traditional neo-classical and political economic trajectories for growth and development are deemed largely moot. Questions of technological choice, appropriate technology and transfer, low wage-low skill employment, and so on – all based on dependency theory and hegemony – become de-emphasized in light of innovative practices, knowledge and learning.

The globalization of economic production and knowledge activities might even increase the divergence across nations and regions if local knowledge externalities are not captured by the developing nations. As the number of non-traditional nations becoming active in the performance of science and technology increases, and as regional cooperation pacts and networks are forged by countries across regions in an effort to pool education, labor, innovation and technological resources (as is happening across APEC and the CARICOM), the ability to catch up and forge ahead becomes real. As mentioned earlier, our general conjecture is that national (and regional) innovation systems deeply shape the development pattern of each economy. However, the new opportunity and needs for an increasing accessibility to markets, personnel and knowledge have to be captured too. In this context, the potential conflict derived from the modes of governance of the national system and its international accessibility go together with a specific and new set of incentive structures which should promote the local distribution and diffusion of knowledge. These are the times when the discretionality of modes of governance is the highest, and orthodox approaches may produce a development path characterized by a continuous loss of technological and knowledge opportunities.

NOTES

1. Many of these deal with accumulation and can be traced back to Marx's *Das Kapital*, the first volume of which was published in 1867. More specifically, one of the centerpieces of Marx's theory of capitalist development held the view that the rate of profits (and hence of accumulation) inevitably declines as growth takes place. These profits were produced by labor from surplus labor. Competition in the face of this declining rate of profit leads to stronger owners of capital swallowing up the weaker who are then driven into the pool of workers (proletariat). Gerhard Mencsh has also explicated such lines in his *Stalemate in Technology* (1982).
2. See: Metcalfe (1989), Metcalfe and Soete (1984), Amable (1992), Soete and Verspagen (1992), Verspagen (1990), (1991), Dosi and Freeman (1992), Dosi, Pavitt and Soete (1990), Cimoli and Soete (1992).
3. The Abramovitz notion of differentiated 'social capabilities' is quite consistent with this view (Abramovitz, 1989).
4. Anther definition of National Technological capabilities which capture the main features of learning and institutional setting is associated with '...complex of skills, experience and conscious effort that enables a country's enterprises to efficiently buy, use, adapt and improve and create technologies. The individual enterprise is the fundamental unit of technological activity, but national capability is larger than the sum of individual firm capability. It comprises the non-market system of linkages, business culture and institutions that enable firms to interact with each other, exchanging the information needed to co-ordinate their activities and to undertake what effectively amounts to collective learning' (Lall 1997).
5. There also exists an international dimension given by MNEs strategies that provokes the slipover effects of technology policies of one nation on those of the others. The increasing mobility of firms' resources (FDI, strategic alliances etc.) and the globalizing of the world economy can modify the main elements that explain the origin and the orientation of the NIS competence, in terms of whether it is biased in favour of the MNEs strategy or mainly determined by the country's scientific and technology policy. On the other hand, the national unit is too large to understand the effects of the innovative process in a particular area: it therefore becomes important to focus on the appropriate unit of analysis, and therefore on geographically and institutionally localized distinct systems.
6. In this respect, p is considered as the average labor productivity in the industrial sectors. However, this analysis could be extended to a reconsideration of capital inputs; see Dosi, Pavitt and Soete (1990).
7. In this case that a similar consumption pattern prevails and production costs are given and fixed in both economies.
8. This figure is obtained from a model with a continuum of goods whereas the dynamics increasing returns are introduced; see Cimoli, Dosi and Soete (1986).
9. In this context, the introduction of dynamics increasing returns is assumed to explain the interplay between productivity and income.
10. Most of the works on catch-up put the emphasis on the scope for imitation (Gomulka 1971; Abramovitz 1994). The scope for imitation here is considered as a feature of both competitiveness - organizational and quality improvements - and NIS-capabilities efforts.

6.   The Institutional Governance of Innovation

Let us continue. We are all connected in this global world. Interdependence is the name of the game. But how do we construct advantage? Through ideas and institutions.

I have introduced this already but will develop it more now. David Ricardo, in the nineteenth century, suggested that the comparative advantage of nations was based on what they had. Portugal, because of its excellent climate, produced and exported wines. Canada, because of its abundance of natural resources, extracted and exported timber, minerals, and so on, and later because of its waterways it exported both water to California and hydro electric power to the north east United States. This basic idea proved robust in our understanding of the economic notion 'value added' and tended to explain well the trade patterns and investment flows between nations, that is until the 1970s. At that time, much analytic confusion ascended in the minds of market traders and policy makers. With the seemingly simultaneous rise of the oil crises of 1971 and 1973, the formation of OPEC, and the undoing of the gold standard, many analysts failed to assess the long term fundamentals. Neo-Ricardian economics, which had been so helpful for so long with regard to how institutions interacted internationally, had not failed but had met a new reality. (We could easily extend this to the US$ 50 per barrel of oil in 2004-2005.)

Wassily Leontief (Nobel 1973) and Robert Solow (Nobel 1987) noted, separately, some paradoxes. Leontief stated, in his final speech as President of the American Economics Association, that the vast majority of articles in the *American Economic Review* dealt with imaginary data sets and econometrics instead of the real economies in which technological change was so central. He also noted that whilst neo-Ricardian theory suggested that nations – through their institutions – would only import items in which they were less advantageous and export those in which they were more so (acting as rational actors), and that nations would trade in areas in which they had advantage in factors of production (labor and capital), why would the United States – which was technologically intensive and had scale and scope-export labor -intensive products to Europe and Japan. This should have been expected of China or Mexico. Leontief noted that the US was exporting and importing power tools to and from Germany. The difference was in the Do-it-Your-Selfers (DIY) Black and Decker vs. the construction quality tools – that is, professional performance specs vs. DIY, that is technological performance.

Solow, for his part, noted that the dance between investment, productivity and trade – which Ricardo postulated should follow each other – had separated with investment sky-rocketing to 1200 percent between 1970 and 1990, leaving trade and production far behind. This signaled a critical shift in the nature of the world economy. This shift was thought by many to be about oil and currency. But in fact it was about technological change with the incredible rise of services, newly defined beyond restaurants, entertainment and tourism. Solow fathomed this, understanding that technological change, especially in services (including software, business and financial service) endogenized technological change in growth theory – importantly revising neo-classical economics away from the rational actor, perfect information, in which technology is evenly distributed across time and space (T bar). The now famous 'Solow Paradox', coined by Luc Soete at the University of Limburg, was that 'computers are everywhere in the economy except in the productivity statistics'. Hence, on two macro observations, the role of technology in the economy and in the society was noted and highlighted. Institutions are trying to facilitate these fundamental observations.

These avenues of thought were further extended by Michael Porter when he spoke about not comparative advantage but *competitive* advantage[1] in which the scale and scope of an economy which features large domestic markets is key. This introduced a broad 1980s discourse on 'the Triad', sometimes defined as the US, Japan and Germany, or after the 1992 Maastricht Accord, the EU. For countries that abut on hegemons, like Canada or the Nordics, and which do not have the large domestic markets that Porter suggested were required for indigenous technological development and high value added exports and employment, others, such as Alan Rugman and Joseph d'Cruz at the University of Toronto (working on behalf of Kodak), countered with the idea that Porter's conditions could be met by discussing not a Diamond, to use Porter's phrase, but a double diamond in which Canada, for example (which is the American's leading trading partner), could conceive of its domestic market to include the United States and now Mexico. This logic has resulted in the Free Trade Agreement, the North American

Free Trade Agreement, and the proposed Free Trade Area of the Americas, which will include 34 countries. Interestingly enough, this continental opening of markets, criticized by anti-globalizationalists and opponents of the World Economic Forum, the IMF and the World Bank[2], did not replace Ricardo but complemented him – expanding his bilateral trade and investment world to a rule-based (institutional) multilateral world in which technology-intensive goods and services add to the quality of life. (How this will unfold with China acquiring IBM's PC business in December 2004 and many other such deals on the horizons is most interesting analytically and important geopolitically.)

But this has led to another series of questions. In our multi-lateral, rule-based, world, how do we explain the impressive rise of small economies in some cases relatively resource-light, with low populations yet high value added, technology-intensive, knowledge-based employment with global market access and success? Examples abound, but using Porter and Ricardo, how can we describe the dynamic techno-economies of Taiwan, Singapore, Hong Kong, South Africa, South Korea or Finland. The answer may be in 'constructed advantage'. In this emerging concept, we can begin to look at cities – home to more than 85 percent of jobs and national growth. The most successful cities can be as small as Cornwall Ontario Canada or Toledo Ohio USA, neither of which is a burgeoning Metropolis like 'Gotham' but each of which is sustainable based on lifestyle. The combination for dynamic and sustainability includes local leadership, physical and smart infrastructure, talent (both technical and entrepreneurial) and capital. All these flow through institutions.

Institutions – local, national and international – are far more than agencies. Institutions are complex social systems. Relationships and networks matter, particularly in our global world community. In abject solitude, little of meaning occurs. [3] Innovation too is the complex combination of research, technology and managerial acumen within the context of social demand and individual creativity. It is the main driver of economic growth and sustainable social development. Institutions, or social structures, are the facilitators of innovation. Institutions vary in form and diversity. Ideas cannot be separated from institutions. Successful institutions are learning organizations, able to adapt to knowledge – to network. They form alliances and partnerships that result in robust supply chains, be they political, economic, environmental or social. Yet the patterns of innovation and the paths to innovation are uneven across sectors and nations.

Some Asian countries, such as Japan and Korea, tend to be mission oriented in their science and technology policies. Some, like the members of the European Union, like to approach innovation from a regulatory and social distribution point of view. Others, like the United States – because of its scale and scope and because of its culture of individualism and entrepreneurship – tend to be mixed but focused, while others, like Canada, Finland, Australia and Denmark, tend to focus on the 'D' side of the R&D spectrum with few companies – like Nokia and Nortel Networks – in the top 150 rankings of global high tech firms. Yet they sustain high tech economies, tremendously sophisticated science, highly skilled labor forces, and excellent access to major markets.

PRECIS 1: INSTITUTIONS

With the emergence of the so-called 'new' knowledge economy,[4] our international cultural, political and economic discussions have moved increasingly towards relationships, social contracts and institutional analysis around innovation, around the technology-society relationship. Many are displeased with the notion of 'globalization', yet it delivers benefits and it has long been so. Many regions or sovereign areas differ in their reaction to genetically modified foods, global positioning systems, energy grids, HIV AIDS, military preparedness, coastal erosion, climate change, border security and other technologically intensive social issues.

Institutional Economics

Highly esteemed researchers like Stiglitz (Nobel 2001) who worked on markets with asymmetrical information, Simon (Nobel 1978) who worked on economic organization, North (Nobel 1993) who worked on institutional change, along with Olson, Williamson and Furubotn[5] have together worked to explain the ways in which institutions and institutional change (adaptation) affect the performance of innovative economies. Their work is powerful and influential.

Evolutionary Economics

Nelson and Winter, formerly of Yale, operating from a different evolutionary economic perspective, have argued for the centrality of institutions.[6] Institutions exist, they argue, because of the uncertainties – not certainties – in human interaction. Institutions and relationships vary widely. They can include marriages, contracts, firms, universities, strategic alliances, government agreements, informal networks and treaties. This work has been supported by the 'Italian School', such as the 'badlly behaved dynamics' of Giovanni Dosi and his colleagues at the Santa Anna School in Pisa, and by the 'Manchester School', particularly the work led by J. Stanley Metcalfe.

Cultural and Social Economics

Cultural anthropologists, such as Mary Douglas[7] and Ernest Gellner[8] concur, raising a renewed focus on relationships in civil and progressive societies. Scholars such as Putnam at Harvard, Florida at George Mason, and Francis Fukuyama of John's Hopkins' have labeled this interest in institutions and relationships in terms of 'social capital', the result of creative classes, or community trust. This makes our focus on innovation (science, technology and innovation) local in an international setting.

System Theories and Effects

Scholars such as Robert Jervis, Gordon Pask, Stafford Beer and Brian Arthur[9] have highlighted the indirect and unintentional effects of actions. As Jervis said, 'in a system, the chains of consequences extend over time and many areas: The effects of action are always multiple'. (p. 10). Drawing on Charles Darwin he goes on to say that 'when chains of interconnections are long and intricate, the results are more likely to be surprising' (p. 21). We must then look at international institutions in a new way.

PRECIS 2: INNOVATION POLICY

But in so thinking, we must recall that innovation policy is concerned with stimulating, guiding and monitoring knowledge-based activities within a political jurisdiction, typically a nation or a region.

The goals of innovation policy are economic, although they are also stated in broad welfare terms (for example the advancement of knowledge, sustainable development, or social benefit). But this is changing towards health, development, environment and inclusion.[10] There is a new social contract for innovation emerging. The instruments for innovation policy are programmes and institutions, as well as ideas. However, as a policy area, not only is it deeply knowledge- and information-intensive but its subject is itself knowledge. Hence, given the variance of knowledge between the spectrum of explicit and tacit knowledge, knowledge management in innovation policy is by definition a domain that is fraught with ambiguity, uncertainty, judgement, creativity and spontaneity.

Meeting the challenges of innovation policy in a dynamic knowledge economy requires substantial advances in our understanding of how research, technological, innovation and policy systems or institutions interact. These systems include knowledge producers (such as laboratories), knowledge users and appliers (such as firms), knowledge regulators (such as food and drug inspection agencies, intellectual property agencies), knowledge diffusers (including information highways), and knowledge funders. This is why we, in this article, will briefly focus on debates, systems of institutions: cities and communities, smaller nations and international institutions.

Innovation policy is a complex process.[11] It is not a single product. It is a result of a set of programs and policies, all involving institutions. Yet traditionally, the individual policy-maker has been seen as a rational actor who has needed more and better information to make 'better' decisions. The decision-maker was portrayed as a thoughtful individual who could be convinced by evidence and who could make sound judgements based on 'state-of-the-art' knowledge. Knowledge, therefore, directly affected decisions, and decisions were policy. Yet, during the early modern work on innovation policy, there was little attention paid to understanding policy-learning processes, or the manner in which policy institutions produced, assimilated, used or transferred information. Adjustment, combinations and creativity are all central. We must look at innovation, institutionally, in a fresh way. This leads us to governance.

PRECIS 3: GOVERNANCE

Governance is the challenge of steering and positioning complex organizations. These can be committees, research groups, firms, networks, communities, regions and international agencies. Ultimately, it is a matter of leadership, of responsibility and of vision when it comes – as it does daily – with technology and society. A requirement is for policy groups to become highly adaptive organizations. It requires becoming effective signal processors, organizations that incorporate learning, in their strategy.[12] Their 'signals' come from the knowledge, which, as a factor of production, has different characteristics of traditional neo-classical factors, these being the supply-demand isoquants between capital and labor $[Q = f(K,L)]$[13] which assume that technological change is evenly distributed across actors and available over time and space, which of course it is not.

Successful institutional governance requires an understanding of the management of knowledge, but first it must the institutional context and value of knowledge.

PRECIS 4: SOME ECONOMIC CONSEQUENCES OF KNOWLEDGE

The reason that governance, institutions and innovation have become conjoined in our mutual shared economy is that knowledge is not a usual commodity. It is largely a public good. Unlike physical resources, it can be used and re-used without losing value. Its intellectual property can be transferred without losing ownership. Uncertainty is high in its production (i.e. research), but this drops rapidly as it is diffused. There is considerable social leakage in the transmission of knowledge. There are also considerable spill-over effects which result in secondary benefits of proximity to the source of knowledge production, such as the development of high technology clusters, the attraction and retention of skilled workers, the attraction of investment, and the spinning out of new firms, jobs and industries. Markets – traditionally conceived – handle physical commodities well, but they do not handle 'non-commodities' (knowledge and information) well. Today's world features customization and niche production in which there are *increasing* returns, unlike in the traditional industrial societies. Institutions are important facilitators to realize these returns. Today, institutions regard knowledge and information as assets which are to be managed.

Information is not knowledge. Knowledge is often defined as organized information, just as information is organized data. Knowledge is a human practice rather than a thing that resides in artifacts. Knowledge may be shared between people, but this involves a process of learning and experience about each other's knowledge. Sometimes, this knowledge sharing can be carried out in order to exchange information. But the goal here is to render information useful. It is for these reasons that (a) much work is being carried out currently at the OECD and elsewhere in order to improve our understanding of these processes of interaction, and (b) why we tend to differentiate between differing types of knowledge.

Thus codified knowledge and tacit knowledge differ importantly in that the former can be written down (in a patent, drawing, design, formula and transmitted), whilst the latter is skill based, talent based, experiential and therefore is difficult to transfer except through demonstration (learning by doing) or appropriation (hiring the person who has a talent or the experience that you want). Additionally, knowledge can be seen as belonging to four classes. Know-what refers to knowledge of facts. Know-why refers to knowledge about principles and natural laws. Know-how refers to skills. And know-where refers to a kind of network knowledge, knowing who would have certain information or influence and how to access it. In short, the knowledge economy is really a network economy, and innovative networks work through institutions. But debates have shaped our institutions and they continue to do so. I choose five historic debates to discuss.

Debates and Blueprints

Scientist-philosophers

Bernal[14]

In 1931, the Soviets sent a major delegation to London headed by Bukharin during which the physicist Boris Hessen presented a paper on 'The Economic and Social Roots of Newton's *Principia*'. Leading British scientists, such as J.B.S. Haldane, Lancelot Hogben and Maurice Dobb were sympathetic and impressed. In 1939, John Desmond Bernal (otherwise known as 'Sage') – a red-headed, Irish, friend of Picasso, Marxist crystallographer at Birkbeck College, London and who was a confidant of Winston Churchill, published a volume that was in many ways the beginnings of modern science, technology and innovation policy. Until then, the field and practice was a rather *ad hoc* affair, both conceptually and institutionally. His volume, *The Social Function of Science*,[15] argued that the scientific enterprise needed to be focally oriented towards the benefit of mankind, focusing on areas of global concern such as nutrition, energy, health and agriculture, as well as epistemological exploration.[16] Bernal was early in our recognition of the role of individual craft and institutional learning in human advance historically. He has been followed since in looking at the role of technology in society. His views, which included discussions of strategies for scientific advance, the financing of scientific advance, the re-organization of research, etc. were adopted and advocated by a number of prominent British scientists.[17] But, through a series of BBC Radio debates, it was made clear that Bernal had his opponents, arguing that his institutional proposals – putting science in the service of society and government – was too collectivist or socialist, thus undermining the individual creative spirit of the researcher. Yet Bernal's ideas bear directly on policy makers today.

Polanyi

What Bernal proposed, and how he typified the institutional practice of science, the Hungarian born chemist Polányi Mihály (Michael Polanyi) – who moved through Germany and then with the help of William Bragg, landed at the University of Manchester – opposed.[18] Starting with his 'Collectivist Planning'[19] in 1940 which was to be followed by the kernels of 'The Republic of Science' in 1942 on BBC Radio and later in the premier issue of *Minerva* in 1961 funded in part by the CIA (Congress for Cultural Freedom) and edited or influenced by the Chicago sociologist Edward Shils and the New York (now Washington) neo-conservative Irving Kristol.

Polanyi argued on behalf of the essential nature of discovery conducted by a 'Society of Explorers' (scientists and technologists) who should not be guided by government policies in their research goals or practices but who should be left alone, in their communities, to allow their creativity to help advance internationally reliable knowledge which could *then* be identified, diffused and applied in various contexts over time and in different spaces. Polanyi's most noted contribution has been his observations on tacit knowledge ('we know more than we can say'), but his work on the theory of money, the nature of intellectual property rights and patents, and on the role of governments laid the ground work for an institutional approach to research which was led by universities and industry rather than by governments which, given his experience with the National Socialist Party before he left Germany for England, he distrusted.

Yet, despite the academic view that there is a 'Bernal-Polanyi Debate',[20] there is not. Polanyi and Bernal actually saw more eye to eye than is generally admitted. Both were institutionalists. But Bernal worked science into his conceptions of governing institutions – as a government advisor – including funding mechanisms in exchange for research priorities while Polanyi worked more on the nature of knowledge and creativity *around* governing institutions, focusing on the process of creativity and the nature of knowledge.

Scientist-Pragmatists

Bush

In contrast to these early style debates, to which I have given only short shrift to their richness, there were 'designers' of the modern institutional architecture. Perhaps the most prominent was Vannevar Bush whose July 1945 report to President Roosevelt on *Science: The Endless Frontier – A Report to the President on a Program for Postwar Scientific Research* is still seen as seminal.[21]

Many read the report as a blueprint, with institutions like the National Science Foundation coming out of it. Some read it more shrewdly, like George Mason's David Hart (formerly of Harvard) who sees it more as a tactic rather than a strategy.[22] Nonetheless, taking a very Bernalian approach, Bush was backed by the President's supportive 'post-war language'.[23]

Bush outlined a program based on the role of science in the war on disease, the public welfare (including employment), the nurturing of scientific talent and skills and the institutional need for co-ordination. His final forays were into the new responsibilities of government, a new National Research Organization (complete with discussion of purposes, functions, and budgets). On the bases laid out by Bush, institutions and principles have been defined well beyond the borders of the United States.

Brooks
Early scholarly work on science and technology policy had been begun, at the new University of Sussex (including Geoffrey Oldham, Asa Briggs, Roy McLeod and Christopher Freeman), at what is now the Harvard Balfour Center on Science and International Affairs and at the OECD (with Alison Young, Yvan Fabian and Keith Pavitt). By March of 1971, the OECD's Secretary General's *Ad Hoc* Group on New Concepts of Science submitted its report. This was entitled *Science, Growth and Society: A New Perspective*, Chaired by Harvard's Harvey Brooks and including Umberto Colombo, Carl Kaysen, Alexander King and Jean-Jacques Salomon. The important conclusion of the committee was that 'the new orientation of our societies towards the qualitative aspects of growth and towards broader concepts of welfare will require a much closer integration of science policy with the totality of economic and social policy'.[24] In this report, again blending the epistemological goals of Michael Polanyi and the institutional goals of J.D. Bernal, Brooks and his colleagues began to break open the 'black box' of technological change starting with the assumptions concerning science, technology and society (especially economic growth), international competition and co-operation, underdevelopment, the formulation of technology-intensive problems, and the management of technological progress.

Rothschild
In March of 1979, Cmnd. 7499 was presented to Parliament in the United Kingdom. This was after the public and technologically intensive challenges of Sputnik, the Cuban missile crisis and the US space program. Popularly known as the Rothschild Report, named after its Chair, Lord Rothschild, this report was a

Review of the Framework for Government Research and Development (Cmnd. 5046)[25] and it had a revolutionary impact on the design of science, technology and innovation policy. It highlighted that no government has a single science policy. It has a range of policies that need to be coordinated and paid for. It argued that the role of government science must not conflict with private sector R&D. Instead, it professed the extension of the customer/contractor principle (advanced in 1976 in Cmnd. 5046), the strengthening of governmental scientific capabilities, the creation of an Advisory Board for the Research Councils to advise the Secretary of State for Education, to advise on the Science Budget and to promote liaison between bodies. This new logic was predicated on the Thatcherite notion of 'value for money' which transformed British government institutions including research departments, universities and polytechnics during the 1980s.[26] In Canada, for example, this Report laid the institutional groundwork for leveraging private sector monies, matching grants, community/university partnerships, industry/university partnerships, internet connectivity for all schools across the country, and a range of research networks between universities and private sector/industry associations.

INTERREGNUM

In the foregoing brief sections, I have sketched some themes which have import for any consideration of international institutions as well as some historical statements which are rarely linked. These are all about technologies in society, Together they inform how institutions are formed, perform and adapt – as through knowledge, innovation and governance. They are *social* formations which have economic impact. They involve the cultures of practice around creativity.[27] Remember that humankind or civilization is a function of *homo faber* and *homo economicus* (in other words, technology and society).

The Variety of Institutions

Cities

No better institutional example of the *homo faber/homo economicus* nexus can be found than in the city. Over half of the world's population now lives in cities and over 85 percent of the advanced industrial economies drive their growth through cities. Cities are complexes – value-added networks – of knowledge-based and skills-based institutions, made up of physical infrastructure, smart infrastructure, access to funds and investment, and leadership. The modern metropolis has been one of the crucial sites of the modern technological scene since Walter Benjamin wrote about creativity in the age of mechanical – and now electronic – reproduction in the early 1930s. Metropolises such as London, New York, Vienna, Berlin and Paris have been well documented. One can also think of Tuscon, Raleigh/Durham and Ottawa. What all feature is a complex of leadership, creative destruction, access to infrastructure (both smart and physical – airports, interstates, city services), access to capital, and access to talent. In many instances, this involves the spill-over effects of colleges, universities and volunteer organizations. It features the spill-over effects of knowledge and culture, of technology and society. One could easily extend this to smaller regions and their innovation strategies.

Smaller Nations

Smaller economic nations, such as Australia, Canada, Denmark, Finland, Ireland, Scotland and Sweden, have differing approaches to innovation, technology and society. In Ireland, for example, responsibilities for science, technology and innovation are very centralized at the national level yet deployed regionally. In Sweden there is strong coordination with regional and national innovation strategies. In Scotland, there is a strong culture of individualism, precluding a cultural of multilateral coordination. In Finland, R&D is heavily concentrated in a few areas (Helsinki, Tampere and Olou) and STI responsibilities are very centralized. But one critical observation for any future discussions of technology in society, including strategy – culture – and policy, is the striking difference between North America and Europe. North America is driven by the individual and the entrepreneur. Europe is guided more by the social distribution of services and drives growth through regulation. This will intensify as the EU expands and will be mitigated with the expansion of the civilian roles of NATO.[28] All involve ideas-based, and rule-based, institutions.

International Agencies

There is another level of institutions, that of the international institutions. We know them well. The WTO, the WHO, the UN and its numerous affiliates, and so on. As the current anti-terror experience is showing us, there is tremendous inter-connection between organizations. A speeding ticket in Vermont reveals to the police officer one's employment in Canada. Checking in through the 'Fast-Track' passport check at Heathrow can result in questions about visits to North Carolina. Institutions are quietly interconnected. Institutions can be voluntary in terms of membership. Institutions can carry the weight of legal compliance. They can be withdrawn from, as with nuclear treatises. Other treaties can be voluntary. They can use the powers of moral suasion. (These have failed the US at the UN in the case of Iraq.) Easy examples include the OECD which carry no 'weight of law' but yet can provide comparative analysis and suasion to the benefit of its members. NATO is more difficult, since it does 'carry strategic military weight' but is expanding its mandate beyond the North Atlantic through, for example, including highly successful programs on best practices between 'East-West' in technology and innovation management through its Science and Technology Policy and Organization Committee. The NAFTA is negotiated down to a very specific level of product code for trade. And so on.

CONCLUSION

Technology and innovation are social processes. They rely on institutions and ideas. They provide our collective economic growth, social development and environmental sustainability. Our ideas have come a long way, through science, engineering, management, medicine, environment and philosophy (all humanities and social sciences included). Technology in society will take us into greater contact with each other, it will certainly challenge us, and – in our increasingly networked societies – the critical roles and shapes of institutions will play a critical role in our future innovations. Today and tomorrow, to refer back to John Milton, there is no solitude. In solitude, what happiness? There are only social relationships. Institutions – from promises, marriage and contracts to the UN and NATO – enable us to live by rules, agreements and understandings. How we choose to shape our interactions, including our technological choices, will determine the future of our civil societies.

NOTES

1. This is interesting because, as the Club of Lisbon has reminded us in *The Limits of Competition*, MIT Press, Cambridge MA, 1998 p.1, the term 'competition' means 'to seek together'. It is also interesting that the new knowledge economy has shifted neo-Ricardian economics away from prices, cost of capital, ownership and property,

and access to natural resources to knowledge, talent and skills (creativity), access to smart infrastructure (such as internet access) and assets to entrepreneurial financial services.

2. See for example the recent work of Joseph Stiglitz (Nobel 2001) and his work on markets with asymmetrical information.

3. Sir Isaac Newton, a life-long bachelor who followed his uncle to become Fellow at Trinity College, Cambridge (1661) and became Lucasian Chair (1669-1687), who occupied rooms that would in time house Charles Darwin and C.P. Snow and who is buried at the Fellows' Pond, Christ's College Cambridge, next to C.P. Snow, author of *The Two Cultures and the Scientific Revolution*, might have disagreed. G.H. Hardy, also a life-long bachelor at Cambridge and close friend of Snow probably would have too. Cf. John de la Mothe, *C.P. Snow and the Struggle of Modernity*, University of Texas Press, Austin, 1992.

4. Roger Alcaly, *The New Economy: What It Is, How It Happened, and Why It Is Likely to Last*, Farrar, Strauss and Goroux, New York, 2003.

5. See his *Institutions, Institutional Change and Economic Performance, Structure and Change in Economic History*, Mancur Olson's *The Firm, the Market and the Law*, and *The Logic of Collective Action: Public Goods and the Theory of Groups*, Oliver E. Williamson's *The Economic Institutions of Capitalism*, and Eirik G. Furubotn's *Institutions and Economic Theory*.

6. Richard Nelson and Sidney Winter, *An Evolutionary Theory of Economic Change*, Belknap Press of Harvard University Press, Cambridge MA, 1982.

7. Mary Douglas, *How Institutions Thinks*, Penguin, London, 1986.

8. Ernest Gellner, *Anthropology and Politics*, Cambridge University Press, Cambridge, 1995.

9. Robert Jervis, *System Effects: Complexity in Political and Social Life*, Princeton University Press, Princeton, 1997; Gordon Pask was an extraordinary individual who worked on Conversation Theory, Characterization, Cybernetics, Evolutionary Models, and Adaptive Machines. His major books were *The Cybernetics of Human Learning and Learning and Performance* (1975) and *Conversation, Cognition and Learning* (1975). He was, along with Stafford Beer, my teacher in 1980. Stafford Beer might best be recalled for his *Cybernetics and Management* (1959) as well as *Designing Freedom* (1975), *The Heart of the Enterprise* (1979) and the *Brain of the Firm* (1981). For Brian Arthur, see *The Economy as an Evolving Complex System II*, Addison Wesley, Reading, 1997, and *Increasing Returns and Path Dependence in the Economy*, University of Michigan Press, Ann Arbor, 1994.

10. UNESCO, *World Conference on Science: Science for the 21st Century – A New Commitment*, Paris, 2000.

11. Robert Rycroft and Don Kash, *The Complexity Challenge*, Pinter, London, 1999.

12. Cf. John de la Mothe (ed.), *Science, Technology and Governance*, Continuum, London, 2001.

13. This is the simplified version of the Cobb-Douglas Production Function. See the work on technical change and growth by Paul Samuelson, Robert Solow, Zvi Griliches and Gregrory N. Mankiw.

14. Brenda Swann and Francis Aprahamian (eds), *J.D. Bernal: A Life in Science and Politics*, Verso, London, 1999.

15. J.D. Bernal, *The Social Function of Science*, George Routledge and Sons Ltd., London, 1939.

16. This also included detailed examples of clothing, primary needs, housing, work, play, production, mining, engineering and chemicals, transport, distribution, communication, administration and control.

17. Cf. Gary Werskey, *The Visible College: A Collective Biography of British Scientists and Socialists in the 1930s*, Allen Lane, London, 1978.
18. In 1948 Polanyi exchanged his Chair in Physical Chemistry for a Chair in Social Philosophy. He later became a general member of the Mont Pélerin Society, along with John Jewkes, Lionnel Robbins, Fritz Maclup, Frederick von Hayek and Karl Popper (a burgeoning group of social economists), and of The Moot, a more theologically based group including T.S. Eliot.
19. Michael Polanyi, in *The Contempt of Freedom*, Watts, London, 1940, pp. 27-60.
20. Cf. Karl Popper, *Conjectures and Refutations*, Allan Lane, London, 1963; Thomas Kuhn, *The Structure of Scientific Revolutions*, University of Chicago Press, Chicago, 1962; Michael Polanyi, *Personal Knowledge*, University of Chicago Press, Chicago, 1959; Imre Lakotos and Alan Musgrave, *Criticism and the Growth of Knowledge*, Cambridge University Press, Cambridge, 1970.
21. Bush, who is no relation to the Bush Administration, insisted that his name be pronounced 'Vann-E-var' (thanks to Eugene B. Skolnikoff of MIT for this little known fact) and who was NOT asked by the President to write this report but who asked the President to ask him, as Director of the Office of Scientific Research and Development, to prepare the report.
22. David Hart, *Forged Consensus: Science, Technology and Economic Policy in the US, 1921-1953,* Princeton University Press, Princeton, 1998.
23. President Roosevelt prefaced the report with the following epigraph: 'New frontiers of the mind are before us, and if they are pioneered with the same vision, boldness, and drive with which we have waged this war we can create a fuller and more fruitful employment and a fuller and fruitful life.' In so doing he linked the military mission with a civilian purpose, predicated on the demonstrated impacts of R&D performed during the war.
24. Letter from Harvey Brooks, dated Paris, 28 March 1971, addressed to Emile van Lennep, Secreatary-General of the OECD.
25. This was a 'White Paper'. I am grateful to Professor Ben Martin of the Science and Technology Policy Research Unit (SPRU) at the University of Sussex for this.
26. Actually, the Hayekian roots of the Thatcher 'revolution' are wonderfully described in Richard Cockett, *Thinking the Unthinkable: Think-Tanks and the Economic Counter-Culture, 1931-1983*, Fontana, London, 1995.
27. Anthony Storr, *The Dynamics of Creation* (1972), *Churchill's Black Dog* (1989), and *Solitude* (1997).
28. See Wolfgang Munchau, 'Bullying by Large Countries Could Split Europe', *The Financial Times*, Monday, November 24 2003, p. 13.

7.   Capacities and Priorities in Innovation

Of course, smaller interdependent economies must be concerned with questions regarding scientific and technological capacity. Questions of priority setting are therefore implicit in all discussions of innovation policy. For analysts, policy makers and politicians alike, they are both difficult and inescapable.

National debates over knowledge-based growth and prosperity are typically grounded in the capacity of a people to produce, use and diffuse scientific knowledge. Policy debates over GERD/GDP ratios, critical technology lists, or the proper role of government in the performance of science and technology reveal this clearly. And in operational debates, the issues over capacity and priority setting are directly linked to how science, research and technological capabilities are viewed as being best organized and managed to contribute to economic growth and social well being.

The scale of a nation's input of resources provides an indicator of this, as does the scope of its activity. Moreover, while debates across countries may seem to be thematically similar, their details in fact reflect the specificity of each national setting. For example, few countries can afford to spend and be active in so broad an array of research areas as the G-5. Smaller countries (that is, 'smaller' in terms of home market size, skilled population base, breadth of private sector R&D performers, and so on), need to continually balance policy between supporting breadth and selecting niches. Canada and Australia both fit into this context. And since so much of the discussion around developing a knowledge-based economy requires not only the production of new knowledge but the capacity to identify, attract, apply and distribute new knowledge, then questions of capacity and priority setting are key.

Indeed, within the context of the recent re-orientations of public policy in Canada vis-à-vis. 'innovation' and the changing roles and mandates of federal or national laboratories, capacity and priority setting have come to the center stage. How did this happen, what does it mean and what are its prospects?

107

THE RE-ORIENTATION OF PUBLIC POLICY

By way of background, it is important to appreciate the context for current Canadian policy. Similarities and differences will be evident to international readers. In its 1993 electoral blueprint document, popularly known as 'the Red Book', the Liberal Party highlighted science and technology issues as being critical to its planned economic agenda. It did so through the language of 'national systems of innovation'.

To economists of innovation and science policy scholars, of course, this conceptual framework was well known. The work of B.Ä. Lundvall, Christopher Freeman and Richard Nelson had already infiltrated the corridors of the OECD Committee on Scientific and Technological Policy (CSTP). But by 1993 this framework was new to policy makers and politicians in Canada.

The path through which this conceptualization found its way into the minds of central agencies was through a network of Toronto-based Liberal 'insiders'. More particularly, this included the Executive Director of the International Federation of Institutes for Advanced Study (IFIAS) – an organization which had funded research into the NIS concept, a Member of Parliament who was a contributing author to the Red Book, and a senior policy advisor to the Prime Minister's Office (PMO).

In February 1994, with the Liberal's first budget speech as government, the Finance Minister enthused – as part of what would become, polemically at least, Canada's move towards being a 'knowledge-based economy' and 'the most connected nation in the world' – that a Science and Technology Review would be undertaken immediately under the leadership of the Industry Minister. By the Spring, a series of cross-country consultations for the Secretary of State (Science, Research and Development) had been planned and two volumes of discussion papers had been released, including one on national systems of innovation.

In the same budget speech, it was also announced that a Program Review would be undertaken in order to ensure that government department spending was being done in an efficient manner and that duplication of services between departments was identified and reduced. To long time students of science policy, of course, it is perhaps not surprising that by the time the S&T Review was completed and released in 17 volumes two years later in March 1996, the dominant principles that had come to drive the government were the principles of the Program Review, not the S&T Review. In part, this was because

- the need for a Science and Technology Review was no longer being driven by central agencies;
- coordination for the Review was being led by a junior Minister from Industry Canada with no science budget while other Ministers for Environment, Health, Natural Resources, and Fisheries and Oceans were senior cabinet members with sizeable science budgets;
- Industry Canada (IC) had what could be described as cautious relations with the federal laboratories and science-based departments and agencies (SBDAs) predicated on the perception that IC's agenda was to control the SBDAs;
- the Office of the Auditor General released its 1996 Report criticizing the government for not setting priorities in its science and technology expenditures; and
- the, by now, dominant governance principles of the Program Review calling for transparency, horizontal coordination, and better management, coupled with the government's commitment to smaller government and deficit reduction, meant that science spending for both research granting councils and federal labs would not be protected or excluded from the political and policy goals of the day.

One clear message from this exercise, if one hadn't learnt it already from the 25 federal science reviews that Canada had undertaken in 35 years, was that science policy cannot be treated as standing outside of the body and the practice of public policy making. In and of itself, it does not hold a special place in government circles (unlike scientific knowledge which can still claim to be a privileged type of human knowledge)[1] *unless* it is directly tied to the national interest. Even, or especially, at a time when the production of knowledge itself is being transformed, to miss this point is to risk arriving at a distorted assessment of the science-government relationship.[2]

CONCEPTUAL AND PRACTICAL IMPLICATIONS

What does this shift in language connote? Conceptually, a rationalist's case could be made for the argument that the adoption of a 'system of innovation' language represents a major shift in the government's thinking about science. It could be argued that it represents a deliberate abandonment of linear models of innovation in which 'science push' variants (in which government has a prominent role) and 'technology pull' variants (in which government plays an important role but with more indirect instruments such as R&D tax incentives) prevail. In so doing it could mean a subsequent abandonment of the implicit centrality of research as the engine of economic growth, and therefore of the centrality of government research funding and its performance of S&T.

In its place, the new approach of government – featuring the core concepts of NIS approach – could be said to feature networks, linkages, learning organizations, and a wide band of knowledge types beyond research (such as tacit knowledge, network knowledge, skills, and know how). It could be said that the new prevalent image features the recognized interaction and importance of all socio-economic actors (not just the government),[3] the importance of partnerships and alliances between actors (and therefore, especially in the case of a small open economy, of the creation of synergies), and of the importance of clusters or 'smart cities'. Each re-jigging of the conceptual framework implies a differing role for government, reducing the centrality of government-led activity (e.g. picking winners) and instead imbedding government into a network of actors ('backing leaders'). Thus governments, in a neo-Keynesian way, can begin to think about providing 'smart' infrastructure (CA*Net3, SchoolNet, Canadian Foundation of Innovation, the Community-University Research Alliances, etc.) which links communities of practice, and designing federal programs which provide incentives for research (e.g. Innovation System Research Network).

Together, this shift in language can be cast as being seemingly in step with both the latest thinking about the research-economy connection *and* a 'devolving state hypothesis' in which, in an interdependent globalized world economy, the sovereignty of nations is in question. Government can thus portray itself as being both 'hip' and responsible. However, such an interpretation may provide something of a *post hoc* rationalization rather than a smooth, government-wide match between what central agency intends and departments understand.

In practice, the adoption of a 'system of innovation' language in government documents reveals less of a break with the proceeding administration's approach to science and technology than might be expected, and it has neglected, to some extent, the lost of capacity in the federal laboratory system which began in the mid-1980. Thus both the *rationalist's* analytic approach fails, as does the *ideologist's* reaction that there is a *de facto* break between Conservative and Liberal approaches (this only leads us to the complex *realist* pressures of governance). In point of fact, there are considerable continuities between administrations in Canadian federal politics (i.e. there is no 'third way' yet in Canada).[4]

The continuity between the two administrations could be seen in the ongoing commitment to increasing business enterprise R&D through matching grants, the creation of consortia and centers of excellence. It could also be seen in the move to reduce both government spending on R&D and government performance of R&D. However, as Sir Robert May has effectively shown, this is in no way unique to Canada. While GERD/GDP ratios have generally risen in advanced nations between 1981 and 1999, trends in government funded GERD *generally* have fallen significantly.[5] So, in fact, apparent continuities in trends belie less a tacit similarity between conservative and liberal governments in Canada than a broad shift in fundamentals, including the agreement to regain control over public expenditures and reduce deficits coupled with all the vagaries implied by an interdependent, globalized international political economy.[6]

GOVERNMENT S&T CAPACITY IN QUESTION: THE HISTORY

Within the broad context of the call for 'less government' that was popularized by Gaebler and Osbourne in their *Breaking Through Bureaucracy* and operationalized by the governments of Margaret Thatcher and Brian Mulroney, it is evident that recent years have been quietly typified by a questioning of what the 'proper' role of government *is*. In science and technology this is certainly true, but the question runs deeper than recent history would superficially suggest. First, while deep cuts have been made, no re-orienting mandate statements have been issued by the government and departments have been left to 'manage' the decreases. In most cases this has been reactionary in mode rather than strategic (understandably since no one knew where next year's budgets would go).

In terms of science capacity, this has come strikingly to the public eye in a variety of crises. Examples include such issues as 'tainted blood', Hepatitis C, the management of the fisheries, carbon emissions, risk from Radio Frequency Fields, and so on. The underlying public issue (of course, one of many) is whether the federal government can provide fast, high quality science in response to challenges to public risk. (The general concern is that the private sector and the university sectors are incapable of responding or not mandated to respond.)

Going back to the 1970s, in Britain such questions resulted in a (not entirely uncontroversial) set of principles such as 'value for money', project management, user or client re-orientation of labs, etc. that some reticent 'Republicans of

Science' still view as being anathema to science.[7] Nonetheless in Canada, similar developments have emerged.

In terms of concern over capacity and priority setting, the Glassco Commission report was able to highlight in January 1963 that 'there is no universally accepted pattern for arriving at these vital S&T spending decisions'. By 1984 the issue had not gone away and the National Advisory Board for Science and Technology noted that 'S&T [were] a clear priority for the government, but [they] were not managed as strategic assets.' By 1990, the Lortie Commission complained that 'outdated and seriously deficient operating and administrative policies' were making it difficult for federal labs to meet expected quality and productivity standards. It noted the emerging low morale in the federal lab system and the need to freshen and clarify lab mandates. (Many of the federal laboratories still operate with mandates written in the 1950s and before.)[8]

On the question of the management of federal labs, proposals have ranged over time from the need for a single federal departmental S&T institute with a CEO and a Board of Directors to a single political 'Science Czar'. Given the mood for decentralization in government, neither of these proposals has ever been seriously entertained.

Both the Lamontagne (1969-1972) and Wright (1985) Reports argued that reviews should be performed to see which aspects of R&D could be contracted out. As Doug Wright said, 'in our view R&D should only be done in-house when there is a need for secrecy or neutrality.' He went on say that there is a need to maintain scientific competence and to maintain contacts with the international scientific communities. 'In all other cases, we believe, the government should attempt to gradually shift the bulk of its research requirements to outside contractors.'

GOVERNMENT S&T CAPACITY IN QUESTION: 'THE THREAT'

Principles aside for the moment, the result of government action has delivered a government lab system that is under severe stress. This can be seen both in its capacity to deliver, in its ability to set priorities across departments, and the focus of mandate in a rapidly shifting environment. This can be seen from an array of indicators. Since 1993, total federal government spending on S&T has fallen. In terms of R&D this has dropped from $2.8 billion to roughly $2.5 billion while related scientific activity has slid to nearly $1.5 billion. This has been an erosion in both current and constant dollars. Moreover, total highly qualified personnel in the major SBDAs has dropped from over 35,000 to nearly 28,000. This erosion has been felt more deeply in some departments than others.[9] The loss of capacity is felt to be a result of these cuts coupled with a rising existing work load per person year (PY) and per dollar as well as of a rising demand by the public in such areas as public health and risk and in such private areas as federal drug approval.

On the more qualitative side, anecdotal evidence from interviews with Natural Resources Canada, Health Canada and the National Research Council[10] shows that some researchers are complaining that they are no longer conducting research, that the research is not being peer reviewed, that they are being told to change research areas by managers because of lost PYs, that they have become contract mangers, that they are being pressured by private sector interests to approve unchecked or un-validated research results, that research careers in government are no longer competitive or viable (so that the demographic curve goes up while uptake into research jobs falls to a trickle), and so on.

Augmenting these suggestions are the facts that government labs continue to have a public responsibility: the public interest (however defined). Despite misplaced arguments about 'market failure', recent work has shown that government labs (a) have been adaptive to changing contexts and environments over time (and therefore there is every reason to believe that they will continue to be so in the future), and (b) have a series of core tasks that cannot be taken over by university labs or industry. These include:

- provide technical assistance to small and medium-sized Canadian businesses which are working in a technology-intensive area and which do not have the needed in-house expertise or equipment. This is an important role for government which has enabled thousands of firms to grow, compete, and in turn create new value-added jobs. No firm or university could easily provide this service.
- pursue new technology development in areas such as data encryption where there is both a security issue (in privacy for example) that will involve government regulatory functions and an economic issue where the future technology can be stimulated in concert with universities and consortia and in which no one firm could afford to develop.
- establish and negotiate standards in order to harmonize Canadian and international regimes to protect Canadians and provide a favorable business climate. Again, state-to-state negotiations cannot be done by firms and

government science in the public interest is needed to ensure level playing fields and to avoid conflicts of interest.

- undertake testing and approval in areas related to drugs, bio-medical devices, vaccines, blood products, and the like which clearly require government involvement as well as a research capability in order to evaluate and verify outside results for the protection of Canadians.

- undertake environmental monitoring for the protection of Canada's eco-system and commons (in support of existing environmental standards and in anticipation of the identification of new environmental threats). The capacity of the government to carry out such work is critical as ecological threats emerge and as the government commits to meeting negotiated international treaty levels which would be difficult to contract out. Moreover, the capacity to conduct survey work and stock assessments in order to understand changes in the ecological systems of Canada (including the fisheries), geological transitions, and so on are key and are germane to government – not industry – goals and mandates.

- support emergency preparedness in areas like earthquakes, floods, and the like. Again, firms operating for profit would be hard pressed to undertake earthquake modeling and monitoring over the long haul and Canadians would rightly wonder if emergency preparedness, operated by the private sector, would provide the responsiveness, warning and universality that Canadians require.

- support policy in the science-based departments and agencies as well as in industry, heritage, foreign affairs, international trade, defense and transportation. To farm all these responsibilities out to academic or private sector concerns would not only create a government contract monitoring and management nightmare but could also lead to breaches of security, a de-coupling of government science from government policy, and a lost assurance that government and the public interest were matched.

- continue regulatory monitoring and compliance activities such as monitoring and regulatory control of food, drugs, consumer product safety, transportation safety, and the like.

- conduct basic research, not because government researchers should be expected to contribute to the international open literature, but because basic research will support government researchers to be involved in the latest developments, findings and techniques, and will keep vibrant an external research network which can be called upon in support of government science. Active research will serve to promote an attractive career path for researchers in which valuable scientific and technical work can be carried out, thus ensuring the revitalization of government science.

This taxonomy of mandated tasks for government science is complex and daunting to manage, but it does lend itself to a differentiation of sectors and incontrovertible government responsibilities in an 'innovation system world'.

GOVERNMENT S&T CAPACITY IN QUESTION: A SCENARIO APPROACH

In response to some of the developments noted above, the need for capacity and priority setting work has come to the attention of senior management in Canadian federal labs. This has in large part been driven by the work of the ad hoc Science Assistant Depute Minister's (ADM) Committee which represent 13 major departments and agencies.

One concern of the analysts who carried out the study for this committee revolved around the tacit view of some of the SBDAs' managers that the current context of 'lost resources' simply means (a) that a principle task is to retrieve these resources from the public purse, and (b) to put them back into those same activities which were cut. Instead it was the view of the analysts that following such a route would reinforce the longstanding territoriality that exists between departments and that has in part been responsible for the current situation. Rather, SBDAs should (c) take the opportunity to seriously evaluate and re-orient themselves, strategically plan and position themselves vis-à-vis. their core mandates, core clients *and* the central agencies, and proactively re-tool themselves managerially. In the analysts' view, 're-tooling' and 're-orienting' might well involve horizontal planning and management across the SBDAs (i.e. the creation of a Science Portfolio within government), striking alliances, and building networks and linkages both across government and between government-business-university.[11]

In order to assist managers move in this direction, 'capacity' in this study was broken into a series of 'drivers':

- scenario description drivers (Table 7.1);
- outcome drivers (Table 7.2); and
- implications for capacity planning (Table 7.3).

In the absence of any Canadian Foresight study of the breadth and scope found in Australia and Britain, this analysis was not intended to replace science capacity planning at the operational level. Instead, it was meant to help managers and policy staff test the robustness of their own capacity plans within a broader planning framework. To achieve this, the study postulated four different scenarios:

- what if the future context of the SBDA is largely as it is today?
- what if there is a gradual decline in the resources available for S&T performance across government?
- what if there is an increase in S&T resources?
- what if the future unfolds in a way that is very different from what we are planning for?

Although each scenario was grounded in the contemporary policy environment – in particular the federal government's S&T strategy and its government-wide planning exercise – they were not meant to define or measure capacity but were meant to be somewhat provocative in order for managers to test their own current thinking.

In Phase 1 of the study dealing with the scenario description drivers, environmental, economic, industrial, social, fiscal, policy and S&T elements were reviewed. In Phase 2, research, policy advice and staffing considerations were reviewed, along with infrastructure and partnerships. Finally, implications were sketched for SBDA roles, resources, personnel, facilities and equipment, science-policy linkages, and business arrangements. As a result, a number of themes thought to be worthy of consideration were revealed.

Linkages, Networks and Alliances are Key

In the emerging Canadian context, external lab linkages, networks and alliances will be critical for the SBDAs to meet their public responsibilities. In some cases, external connections are needed to make up for gaps in in-house capacities. In some, they are prerequisite to demonstrating the needed support to request further federal funds in order to build additional facilities. In some cases, linkages are needed to ensure a flow of young research talent into the SBDAs. In other cases, they are important for cross-departmental planning and resource sharing. In the case of priority setting, each SBDA should seek to fill sectoral gaps (e.g., in the case of Natural Resources Canada, remote sensing, mining and geology are obvious targets for assessment).

Money is Not the Solution

The 'reinvestment scenario', in which the federal government would make a significant amount of money available to renew SBDA research facilities and equipment, at first blush seems like a heaven-sent opportunity. But as already noted, and on closer inspection, it is unlikely that the government will have enough money to meet all the reinvestment needs of the SBDAs. Particularly in a time of surplus budgets, federal science is not the only mouth to feed as numerous programs and communities (many with political constituencies) feel that they have a higher level immediate claim on newly available resources. These conditions prompt the observations that each department will need to improve its science policy capacity in parallel with its research capacity.

Skills Planning Needs to be Future Oriented

It is essential that the federal labs ensure a flow of research talent into the future if capacity is to be improved. Given the pressures outlined above, it is clear that demographics (aging) and poor career prospects will make it difficult to attract high caliber researchers. This pressure is augmented by the fact that science and science-based public problems are both moving rapidly thus requiring that the SBDAs develop a human resource approach that is flexible and adaptive. One element of this response might not only mean building linkages with university departments, but also creating specialized (departmentally dedicated) 'farm teams'.

Technologies are Moving Too Fast

Research technology is moving too fast for organizations to afford to stay at the leading edge or to recoup their investment prior to technological obsolescence. For example, in the natural resource sectors, opportunities are growing quickly for applications of information and decision-making technologies as well as systems in remote sensing and GPS. This calls for developing creative partnerships with hardware, software and equipment suppliers as well as with external research groups so that edge technologies can be accessed without appropriating the full costs involved.

Cross-Department Cooperation is Increasing

As was noted in the December 1998 report of the Office of Auditor General, [12] cross-SBDA cooperation is beginning to yield positive benefits. This trend is being driven by both the need to address horizontal policy issues such as climate change and productivity as well as by common resource constraints. This latter condition will continue to hinder the ability of single departments to finance solutions themselves, thus suggesting that joint ownership and operation of facilities and equipment might be worth study. However in 2003 the Innovation Strategy could not pull off a joint paper on innovation and learning between Industry Canada and Human Resources and Development Canada, thus suggesting that corporate memory of science, technology and innovation plans in the past, non-territorial bureaucracies and continued political will at the Ministerial levels are essential.

Research or Science Assessment?

It is obvious that no government department can hope to perform more than a small fraction of all the research that is relevant to a particular issue. This simple observation is amplified when it is noted that Canada only produces about 4 percent of the world science and technology. The only Canadian firm in MIT's top 100 R&D spenders is Nortel. The vast majority of R&D performers is concentrated in six industry areas, dominated by Crown Corps and foreign-owned subsidiaries. Thus the vast majority of relevant research will be undertaken outside federal labs – in universities, industry, at home and abroad, and published in a vast multidisciplinary world literature. Moreover, this will often be transferred through personal networks or embodied in new technology.

Support for science policy often involves providing timely information to government decision makers about what to do on a particular issue. Given that information is often incomplete and results uncertain, scientists are often reticent to offer advice in this regard. This points to a gap in capacity that needs to be narrowed by government scientists in understanding their role *qua government scientists*, not 'scientists'.

CONCLUSION

Canadian policy has in recent years spoken of innovation systems, has reviewed its science systems, and has enunciated management principles. It has reacted to a variety of science-based crises and there is a worldwide anticipation that science-based issues will only increase in frequency and importance. (BSE, Hantavirus and GM foods are but three recent examples.) Yet Canada continues to have no effective system of science priority setting or management in government. International experience suggests that establishing S&T priorities in the public interest will be increasingly essential. But to get there government needs a framework and indicators to effectively monitor its performance. This framework needs to be linked to the strategic management of its SBDAs. Without such equipment, parliamentarians and government managers will continue to have no basis for assessing government expenditures on science, monitoring the capacity of its lab system (and adjusting to needs accordingly) or setting clear priorities. This chapter has outlined some pressures and possible principles for SBDAs to approach these issues. Beyond this, the SBDAs might well begin to act as a unified Science Portfolio, and not just as an adjunct of the Industry Portfolio which serves different purposes and interests. Moreover, focusing on science capacity and priority-setting issues (instead of reacting against decreasing resource envelopes) may well help the SBDAs within government and position the Canadian government to better identify, anticipate and respond to public interest issues and responsibilities.

NOTES

1. Cf. Imre Lakatos and Alan Musgrave (eds), *Criticism and the Growth of Knowledge*, Cambridge, Cambridge University Press, 1970.
2. Michael Gibbons *et al.*, *The New Production of Knowledge*, Beverly Hills, Sage, 1994; Michael Gibbons, 'Governments and the New Production of Knowledge', in John de la Mothe (ed.), *Science, Technology and Governance*, London, Cassell, 1999.
3. Susan Strange, *The Retreat of the State*, Cambridge, Cambridge University Press, 1996.
4. Anthony Giddens, *The Third Way: The Renewal of Social Democracy*, Cambridge, Polity, 1998.
5. Robert M. May, 'The Scientific Investments of Nations', *Science*, 281, 3 July 1998.
6.
7. Cf. Paul Cunningham (ed.), *Science and Technology in the United Kingdom*, London, Cartermill, 1999; and Philip Gummett, Deborah Cox, Rebecca Boden and Kate Barker, 'The Changing Central Government of Science and Technology', Draft Paper, NATO ARW, Manchester, England, June 1999.
8. For example, because the mandate for Therapeutic Products Division of Health

Canada was written in 1953, xenotransplantation must be treated under the category of biomedical devices.

9.   Please note that the abbreviations RSA= 'related scientific activities' (i.e. R&D+RSA=Total S&T); NRES=Natural Resources Canada; ENV=Environment Canada; AGR=Agriculture Canada; F&O= Department of Fisheries and Oceans; and NDEF=National Defence.

10.

11.   For a detailed discussion of the development of the federal lab system in Canada, see Paul Dufour and John de la Mothe (eds), *Science and Technology in Canada*, London, Longman, 1993. For a sketch of how this new governance structure might have looked like, see John de la Mothe and Gilles Paquet, 'Circumstantial Evidence: A Note on Science Policy in Canada', *Science and Public Policy, 21*, 4, August 1994, pp. 261-268.

12.   *The Federal Science and Technology Strategy: A Review of Progress*, Chapter 22, 1996.

Table 7.1

Scenario Description Drivers	
1. Environment	These are the environmental factors that are driving science policy within the federal government. They include such factors as climate change, global warming and greenhouse gas production.
2. Economic	These are the macroeconomic factors that influence the wealth creation status of the nation. These factors influence the economy at large, and thus the total resources available to the economy.
3. Industrial	This set of factors describes changes that are or could take place in the government's policies toward industry. These are discussed both in a domestic and an international context.
4. Social	These are the social factors that are influencing natural resources policy and S&T within government, or that are being influenced in turn by other factors, such as the economy. Social factors are those which will affect the 'social union'.
5. Fiscal	Fiscal drivers describe the government's ability to finance its operations, including its S&T activities. Improving fiscal circumstances may increase the scope for government funding of S&T while a deteriorating fiscal situation will have the opposite effect.

Scenario Description Drivers	
6. Policy	These are an amalgam of factors that are driving (or would drive) policy development in the federal government, emphasizing those factors that are influencing science policy: the government's ability to finance and perform S&T.
7. S&T	This set of factors relates to the nature and level of the federal government's future requirement for science and technology, and how those requirements might be met; for instance through in-house versus external R&D.

Source: John de la Mothe and Ron Freedman (The Impact Group, Toronto).

Table 7.2

Outcome Drivers	
1. Research	These describe the implications of each scenario for the SBDA's research activities.
2. Policy Advice	These factors explore the changing demands and resources for science policy advice in each scenario.
3. Staff	Staff drivers explicitly examine the implications for the different scenarios on retention, rejuvenation and recruitment of scientific, technical and policy staff.
4. Infrastructure	Each scenario will demand a different type and level of R&D infrastructure. These are explored here.
5. Partnerships	The value and necessity for forming external S&T partnerships changes in each scenario. Partnership considerations are described here.
6. Other	This group includes a set of miscellaneous outcomes that have a bearing on science capacity.

Source: John de la Mothe and Ron Freedman (The Impact Group, Toronto).

Table 7.3

Capacity Planning Implications	
1. Role	These examine the role that the SBDA's S&T play in achieving the federal government's S&T objectives (wealth creation, quality of life, advancement of knowledge) as well as SBDA's broader role in Canada's national system of innovation.
2. Resources	Here, the analysis examines different strategies for securing and deploying the resources needed to carry out an SBDA's mandate in each scenario.
3. Personnel.	Each scenario implies different personnel and skill set requirements. This analysis examines the type of skills needed and how they can be obtained.
4. Facilities & Equipment	Under each scenario the SBDA will have a different capability to operate and acquire the facilities and equipment it needs to fulfil its mandate. This category examines different strategies for matching requirements to available facilities and equipment.
5. Science-Policy Linkage	SBDA's capacity to provide science support to policy development changes in each scenario. Here we explore the nature and extent of those changes.
6. Business Arrangements	The ways in which an SBDA lab relates to stakeholders inside and outside of government are likely to vary under each scenario. This analysis examines different implications for business arrangements with external stakeholders and other SBDAs.

PART TWO

Constructing Advantage in the New Economy

8. Interdependence and National Systems of Innovation

We have now discussed a number of related themes. Let me now try to make some connections around 'constructed advantage'. Smaller nations are by definition interdependent. In the innovation system literature, the term 'national' often owes a debt to the Westphalian world system. This refers to a peace treaty between the Holy Roman Emperor and the King of France, as well as her respective allies, signed on October 24th in 1648.[1] Smaller nation states of course – such as, at the time, Bohemia, Burgundy, Carinthia, Carniola and Morovia – typically defined by population size and domestic market size – are by definition interdependent. They are interdependent in terms of trade, geo-politics and cultural histories. They share borders and rely on the world for their marketplace. They rely on the world for their exports and for their attraction of foreign direct investment (FDI). In today's terms, one can think of energy, environment and security policies in North America. And smaller nations rely on knowledge to build creative communities and high standards of living. It is most interesting that scholars such as Alberto Alesina and Enrico Spolaore have focused on exactly these issues, pushing beyond tradition, regional economics and industrial dynamics. This involves learning institutions, physical and smart infrastructure, access to the full range of capital – including risk-accepting funds and leadership. To these ends, the term 'National System of Innovation' is frequently used to describe a part of the national economy that puts science and technology (S&T) to productive use. Schumpeter argued that there are essentially five types of innovation as we have echoed throughout this volume.

- the introduction of a new good or service
- the introduction of a new method of production (process)
- the opening of a new market
- the acquisition of a new source of supply of raw materials (or the

replacement of material with a higher performance material – as in steel with composite steels in cars)
- re-organization of an industrial unit.

S&T operates principally on the first two types of innovation: new products and new processes. In the modern context, these would include government products and programs such as social programs and health care programs. The Organisation for Economic Co-operation and Development (OECD 1991) in its *Oslo Manual* sets out a theoretical and practical approach to understanding and measuring innovation resulting from scientific and technological activities. This work has been expanded after the completion of its Technology and the Economy Program (OECD 1992) to current systems analysis studies on complete national systems of innovation.

The purpose of this chapter is to describe the complex networks that are collectively described as 'national systems of innovation' and to link them to the situation of smaller nations, regions and cities.

THE ECONOMIC ENVIRONMENT

Citizens of modern smaller nations generally accept the idea that their economies – their ways of maintaining high standards of living, of creating wealth, and of distributing that wealth – are undergoing a major transition has become widespread and accepted. In acknowledging this shift, we have rather routinely said that the key to our future lies in science and technology, research and development, and innovation. We have said that the new economy is somehow different, that it is knowledge-based or information-based. We have said that the economies of the OECD nations have 'gone global.' But for a long time, we have had only vague ideas about what all this meant or what we could do about it.

Our framework for understanding economic growth and trade has worked well for the better part of a century. Yet in this older view, the new intellectual resources upon which we now rely never really played a big part. Moreover, the elements needed for growth were all thought to be contained within the borders of the nation state. Thus, it was not surprising that smaller nations such as Canada exported minerals and timber, Brazil exported rubber and bananas, Portugal exported wine, and the United States exported steel. Every nation – and the firms within each nation – was thought to have a natural comparative advantage, and competitiveness was defined by such factors as price, costs, exchange rates and productivity.

But times have changed. Growth can no longer be generated by simply taking resources from the environment and selling them. More than ever before, performance specifications, quality and design have become more important than price competition. Value-added has become increasingly a matter of what we do rather than what we have, and mass production (with its volumes of uniform, undifferentiated, products) is rapidly giving way to lean production which is fast, flexible and capable of delivering customized products and service.

As for the global aspects of the new economy, there is no doubt that international trade has been one of the main engines of growth since World War II. With the continuous liberalization of trade, which has reduced the average tariff barrier across the OECD nations from 46 percent to less than 5 percent, world trade flows in commodities (or merchandise) have increased between 1950 and 1975 by more than 500 percent, compared with an increase in world output of only 200 percent.[2] But international investment and technology flows have overtaken product-based trade (note that international services typically show up as investment – as in franchises – not trade). This is a subtle but important shift and suggests a number of changes. For example, traditional trade is largely based on tangible goods. Investment and technology flows, on the other hand, are highly intangible; that is, they are not embodied as a widget or a machine, but are encoded as information. One is material-intensive the other is knowledge-intensive.

Wealth creation and economic growth are often used interchangeably. Economic growth is a function of income, which itself is a measure of the flow of some resource of value (usually money, but it could include natural resources, intellectual property or human capital). On the other hand, wealth is a measure of the existing inventory or stock of a valued resource. The stock of wealth is therefore a factor in producing income. Wealth in this sense is in effect a 'cause' of income, rather than the other way around. Surplus income may be used to support higher levels of consumption or may be used to increase investment, which in turn adds to the stock of wealth.

A society can enhance its productive capacity in two ways:

- through investment, which adds to the stock of wealth, including physical and human capital; and
- through innovation, which improves the productivity of physical and human capital.

Innovation is central to many of the shifts resulting from the globalization of the major economies. Or more precisely, it is the innovative capacity of firms that is the major driving force behind economic growth and a country's ability to derive the benefits from international trade. Understanding the ways in which firms access and use external sources of knowledge is important for science, technology and innovation policy. And the availability of intelligent infrastructure, ranging from information highways and high-technology networks to universities, provides the environment within which innovation can thrive.

These important facts have led firms and public policy circles to pay increased attention to the ways in which they can strengthen their innovative capacity and hence smaller nation's competitive positions. But in order to discuss these ideas, we need a new framework to help us grasp how the system really works and how it does not. What follows is a brief sketch of this framework.

LINEAR MODEL OF INNOVATION

The linear model of innovation has been used to explain the links between research and development (R&D) and economic performance. It is so highly abstract that it does not really explain the complexities of innovation in a real world. Yet it still informs many policy discussions. This fact alone has led economic historian Nathan Rosenberg (1991) to say it 'is dead, but it won't lie down.'

The linear model has three principal variants referred to as science-push, technology-pull and market-pull. In the science-push variation, product development and commercialization are the result of broad-based, undirected basic research. Basic science discovers new principles or mechanisms about the natural world that – once a practical use is thought of – get taken up in more focused or applied R&D, which in turn leads to experimental development, design, prototyping and ultimately market launch. In this model, knowledge is discovered in universities, passed on to firms through publications, patents and other forms of scientific correspondence, and on to final customers in the form of a product or service.

The technology-pull model is essentially the same except that it shifts the emphasis away from scientists and onto engineers. Here, engineers working within firms come upon a technical problem dealing either with the production process or with new product realization. They pass the problem down the chain for the scientists to fix – through basic research – and then the solution is passed up through to market launch.

And in the market-pull version, the stimulus for basic research and new technology comes not from a knowledge-based problem, but directly from the market.

Of course, there are numerous flaws with all of the variants of the linear model. They are all highly stylized and thus do not accurately reflect the way real labs or businesses operate. They rely almost exclusively on the R&D process, thus excluding most of the social, organizational and financial factors upon which most innovation and economic growth are based. They artificially separate the process of knowledge creation into a series of hermetically sealed activities – basic and applied research, experimental development, design, etc. – that few in research or business would recognize. They have also, at least implicitly, separated scientists, engineers, accountants and marketers and, in so doing, have assumed that each possesses a clear set of discrete, non-transferable and inflexible skills.

INNOVATION AS A NEURAL NETWORK

In an attempt to move beyond this simplified view, and recognizing both the high information content of innovation and the unpredictability that underpins much creative research, some researchers have developed so-called neural network models of innovation. In these, ideas, techniques and commodities are all interconnected, attesting to the serendipity of innovation. The advantage of this kind of approach is that it places the cognitive nature of innovation and the flows of knowledge between actors at center stage. However, it does little to help in either the analysis of innovation and its links to economic performance or in the management of the process.

Chain-linked Model of Innovation

A more satisfying model is the chain-linked model of innovation which puts its emphasis more systematically on the inter-relatedness of the different phases of the innovation process and on the feedback mechanisms that are involved. In this conceptualization, knowledge and research are not dissected as they are in the linear models, and artificial distinctions – such as that between competitive and pre-competitive research – become rather obsolete.

National System of Innovation

The benefits of this chain-linked model are captured and extended in a framework that has been growing in intellectual coherence and policy relevance throughout the OECD countries in recent years. This framework is widely known as the 'national system of innovation.' The idea of a national system goes back more than 150 years to the writings of German economist Freidrich List in 1841 in his *National Systems of Political Economy*. But more practically, the idea – as applied to innovation – has grown in currency through the analytic and empirical efforts of B.A. Lundvall, Christopher Freeman and their colleagues.

The benefits of this approach are myriad. For example, there is a widespread conviction that in the new global economy, firms increasingly use external sources of technical knowledge to stay competitive. They may do so for a number of reasons. They may need to keep up with the increasing pace of technical change in their industry. They may need to share the increasing costs or risk of doing research. They may need to cope with the growing multidisciplinary scientific knowledge upon which much innovation is based. Or they may need to gain access to new markets by cooperating with other, knowledge-intensive firms.

The policy relevance of this approach also stems from a number of sources. First, policies aimed at improving the innovative capacity of an economy – and of the business sector in particular – need to be grounded in a sound understanding of the way that firms in a country access information and know-how. Second, governments are playing an important role in the development of intelligent infrastructure and technological networks. And third, governments are increasingly working with firms in an effort to negotiate access for them into new markets such as is found in the new European Union or Mexico.

Moreover, for a long time, the principal emphasis or preoccupation in science, technology and innovation policy has been on fostering the generation of knowledge, rather than on its distribution, improving access to knowledge and applying knowledge. Surely, for a country like Canada, which contributes only about 4 percent of the world pool of S&T knowledge and which ranks sixth among the Group of Seven (G7) most developed nations in terms of gross expenditure on R&D as a percentage of gross domestic product,[3] this kind of orientation needs to be carefully rethought.

The essential rationale for a national systems approach was outlined by Chris Freeman (1988):

the rate of technical change in any country and the effectiveness of companies in world competition in international trade in goods and services, does not depend simply on the scale of their research and development ... It depends upon the way in which the available resources are managed and organized, both at the enterprise and the national level. The national system of innovation may enable a country with limited resources ... to make very rapid progress through appropriate combinations of imported technology and local adaptation and development.

Clearly, this demarcation has important implications for a country like Canada where the S&T policy debate has long focused principally on the level of spending on R&D and on the scarcity and scattered distribution of resources for innovation due to the geographic and demographic realities of the smaller countries.

A number of broad characteristics become prominent with the adoption of a systems approach. First, it emphasizes that firms are the principal sites for the creation of wealth and cannot be viewed in isolation, but as part of a network of public and private sector institutions whose activities and interactions initiate, import, modify and diffuse new technologies. It emphasizes the linkages (both formal and informal) between institutions.

Second, it emphasizes the importance of location, the role of mayors and community and industry associations, etc. The core of growth is people, leadership, infrastructure and access to capital.

Third, it emphasizes the flows of intellectual resources between institutions. Fourth, it emphasizes learning as a key economic resource. And fifth – albeit counter-intuitively, given our global economy – it asserts that geography and location still matter. In a sense, the synergies of a national systems approach rely on local systems of innovation.

Essentially, then, the idea of a system of innovation asserts that a country's economy is more than the simple sum of its firms' activities, but is rather the result of synergies that arise from the interactions between economic actors in a country. In addition, a system of innovation can be considered important because of its distributive power; that is, the system's ability to distribute existing knowledge for recombination.

One of the originators of the modern concept of national systems, as already noted, B.A. Lundvall (1992), argues that an important advantage of this framework is that it allows analysts to examine the differences in the ways that countries, or even individual industries in various countries, organize their knowledge-creating or knowledge-using activities. Such variance can often be traced to differences in geography, language and culture. He distinguishes five areas where differences between national systems might occur. These are in the internal organization of firms, in inter-firm relationships, in the role and expectations of the public sector, in the institutional setup of the financial sector, and in the intensity and organization of R&D.

In dealing with innovation, it is useful to reinforce what is meant by the term. Some have said simply that innovation is anything a firm does to stay competitive. But this is not rigorous. Indeed, recall the last category suggested by Schumpeter. This involves changes to the organization of a firm, an industry or the way in which industries act within a society, both inside, outside and between institutions. Strategic alliances and joint ventures, which are often designed to gain access to new technologies or new capital, can be thought of as innovations in that they can allow small firms, for example, to act big and be present in numerous locations or markets at once. Clearly, then, R&D is not the only way a firm or a nation can innovate and generate jobs and wealth.

Of course, firms do not wish to innovate only once: they need to institutionalize the innovation process so that it becomes part of their corporate culture and makes them capable of innovating continuously. In a sense, they need to learn – and remember – how they innovated in the first place. Firms such as IBM and Nortel Networks are famous for having done just this. But as the experience of IBM in the late 1980s shows, it is entirely possible for a once-innovative firm to forget.

A number of large firms such as IBM have deliberately flattened their hierarchies into what they call a federation of firms. In effect, they are trying to enjoy the benefits of being both big and small. By so doing, they can get closer to their customers, closer to their suppliers and closer to the communities in which they operate. They can act faster, be more flexible or responsive to both new pressures from competitors and new opportunities from customers, and pay more attention to quality. These are all earmarks of innovative firms in today's global economy.

KNOWLEDGE

Knowledge is a term used to refer to a lot of different but economically important activities and processes. It is particularly important – indeed, it is critical – to any understanding of the new economy and the changing nature of growth. The advantage of knowledge is that it is a durable and public good. That is, it doesn't wear out or get used up and, when codified in the form of a patent application, a published article, etc., it is available to everyone. Multiple or joint use does not diminish the value of knowledge.

An important element of thinking about research and innovation in terms of knowledge is made clear by Michael Polanyi who reminds us that there is explicit knowledge and tacit knowledge. He describes the latter by saying simply but powerfully that 'we know far more than we can say.' Upon reflection, this seems obvious, but it captures the intangibility of the innovation process.

Beyond this, Arrow (1957) differentiated between various types of knowledge. These they describe as follows:

- *Know-how* usually refers to some form of knowledge that enables someone to complete an observable task, without necessarily being aware explicitly of how the task was done. Manual skills are typically referred to as know-how, but it may also be used with reference to the organizational abilities of individuals or social groups. Tacit knowledge is largely know-how.
- *Knowing what* refers principally to factual propositions like tax codes, regulatory or legislative details, commercial documents like balance sheets, as well as the kinds of knowledge that are needed for the identification and labeling of phenomena in the natural world.
- *Knowing why* refers to knowledge as understanding. Traditional conceptions of scientific knowledge tend to fit largely within this category.
- *Knowing who* refers to one's understanding the identities, reputations and the relations between the various actors within organizations. The greater part of an individual's knowledge about other human beings is gained through social interaction and is privately held. As a result, it is not something that can be confirmed. Its validity is tested through judgment. Social know-who thus parallels organizational know-how, except that it is, in direct terms, practically useless economically.

A further distinction should be made between information and data. Data refer to non-ambiguous and elementary bits of information. Information, then, can be thought of as structured or formatted data that are ready for transmission. From this perspective, knowledge can be considered as the conceptual and factual contexts that enable individuals or organizations to interpret or give meaning to messages. Of course, thinking about knowledge and information in an economic sense (that is, as a commodity) allows us to begin thinking about their transfer into use.

Not surprisingly, when we think of innovation, we often view scientists, engineers and technicians as different and perhaps special kinds of knowledge workers. Relying on this sort of view, or restricting our view of the system to the very highly trained and talented individual researchers, should be avoided. Instead, the critical interpretation ought to be one that is based on the social organization of knowledge, the distribution of knowledge and production.

Today, what fundamentally distinguishes scientific workers from others is not their methods, the nature of the knowledge they generate, nor the system through which they obtain financial support. Instead, research throughout the OECD strongly suggests it is the reward structures that exist for knowledge workers as well as the social and political arrangements put in place to organize this work, such as laboratories, institutes and universities.

The crucial distinction from the system point of view has to do with the ideas of an open community of scholars and the proprietary research community. For the open community, research and the research community are organized around the mission of adding to the public stock of knowledge. This is largely paid for from the public purse (that is, tax dollars) and is made generally and openly available across borders through journals, published articles, scientific correspondence, lectures and so on. For the proprietary research community, the economic value of research is appropriated by the organizations (largely firms) that sponsor or undertake it. This can be contained in the form of intellectual property rights, patents, licenses and so on.

The transfer of knowledge is perhaps the most important flow within a national system. But before this can happen, a first step is necessary in the process of making research commercial; namely, the transformation of knowledge into information, usually referred to as codification. Whether knowledge is in a codified form – patent, article, etc. – determines in part the cost of acquiring knowledge.

Within a national system of innovation, there are numerous ways to transfer knowledge. The most important of these are contractual tools, social networks and information systems or coordinating mechanisms. Examples of contractual tools are strategic alliances, joint ventures, licensing and distribution arrangements. Social networks are particularly important, not only because it is ultimately individuals who transform, use, modify and diffuse knowledge, but also because the primary form of technology transfer is through human movement or interaction.

The individual plays a critical role in technology transfer as well as in the creation and modification of knowledge. This is especially true for the researcher. Each researcher is bound to some degree by the state of the art in his or her specific field or specialization. This can shape the innovation process, particularly because much innovation in the private sector does not take place at the research frontier but rather happens along the border of different fields. For example, the Human Genome Project, a massive multinational research program in the life sciences, is made possible only by the existence of very fast supercomputers, a technology that came out of a different field of informatics.

NETWORKS

In the literature about national systems of innovation, the idea of networks has become pervasive. The OECD (1992) has tried to look at networks as being agreements that exist somewhere between the marketplace and the hierarchy.

As David Teece (1990) has noted, the main reasons for participating in networks are the complementarities to be gained by pooling resources. By joining a network, firms and other organizations in a sense cease to exist independently, instead, they exist in relation to each other. The motivation for collaborating in these ways varies from firm to firm, since each has unique profiles and capabilities. Some firms seek to share risk, some seek increased scale, others look to diversify their technology base or transfer technology, while still others collaborate in order to access new markets.

The core benefits of firm collaboration and networking include:

- elimination of duplication
- ability to pursue a broader research program
- ability to take advantage of both scale and scope
- improvement of research management
- reduction of innovation time.

But perhaps the greatest benefits of the network idea are to be found at the local level. It is generally accepted that technology and investment not only are critical to both economic growth and job creation, but also are footloose; that is, unlike natural resources, they are not tied by geography but are able to locate wherever there is an attractive environment. This helps us to understand the mechanisms that have made regional examples of success possible. One need only think of the Silicon Valley in California, or Route 128 near Boston, in the United States.

Canada too has clusters of technology-intensive firms and institutions, for example, around Montreal, Ottawa, the Niagara peninsula, Edmonton and Vancouver. What these examples have in common is a success resulting from government-business collaboration (involving governments at every level), the presence of infrastructure, the availability of knowledge centers (such as universities and colleges), good skill sets in its local people, and patience coupled with vision.

Of course, not every local system of innovation specializes in the same areas. Some have strengths in biopharmaceuticals or microelectronics, while others might focus on transportation technologies. This is another important characteristic of this networked reality – what some call the clustering or swarming effect. Once local centers have chosen to compete in a small range of industries, technologies are bought (technological trajectories) and firms, both competitors and suppliers, gather because of the availability of skills, etc., financial institutions learn to work with the peculiarities of the particular industries involved and competitive reputation builds. This combination of factors creates an attractive environment for other firms, more investment, upgraded and extended infrastructure (funded both locally and from government sources), and so on. In other words, mechanisms and synergies develop.

CONCLUSION

The preceding discussion was conceptual, but it has considerable importance or potential for reframing discussions about science, technology and innovation policy in smaller nations, regions and cities. Canada has a small, open economy. It has a limited market, limited resources available for research and development, a highly distributed population, and an industrial profile that still reflects both its national resource heritage and a heavy presence of foreign multinationals. Therefore, developing a critical mass in investment, technology and industry has long been problematic.

But we have an excellent string of universities across the country, a talented research base, a sophisticated consumer base, access and proximity to a large and highly developed market to the south, and recognized prowess in areas like telecommunications, remote sensing, multimedia technologies, transportation technologies and biomedical research. In other words, we have everything we need to compete internationally on the basis of our national system of innovation.

The keys to unleashing this potential will be found in our capacity to reframe the S&T debate. As important as they might be, we must not restrict our view of the new knowledge economy to the performance and funding of R&D with the vain hope that, if told to, our universities and government labs will do the kind of research that our firms need, and will pass on this new knowledge in a market-usable form. Innovation does not start in the labs and then spread evenly across the economy. Innovation and economic growth are systemic and depend equally on entrepreneurs, teachers, financiers, technicians and managers as well as researchers. We need to see innovation as a learning process in which we are all partners. This involves a major shift in the way in which the Government of Canada sees science, technology and innovation. But it also shares the responsibility (and opportunity) for local and regional growth with researchers, politicians and entrepreneurs in each locale. The OECD countries are waking up to the potential of national and local systems. We must not allow ourselves to fall behind. If we think that innovation and knowledge are too expensive, just think how expensive the consequences of ignorance and lethargy will be.

NOTES

1. For a thorough synopsis on this treaty and its importance for the notion of the nation state, see The Avalon Project at the Yale Law School.
2. Based on statistics from OECD and United Nations Statistics Office.
3. Based on statistics from OECD and United Nations Statistics Office.

9. Transitional Systems of Innovation

To thrive, innovation systems or clusters must be fed by universities, government funding and entrepreneurial cultures. Political stability is also a *sine qua non* (but note the recent poisoning of the new President in the Ukraine, or political killings in Afghanistan, Palestine, Iran and Iraq, all of which stymie foreign direct investment and the flow of workers, experts and other talent). This makes transition towards innovation and interdependence extremely difficult. In the case of the countries of Central and Eastern Europe (CEE), they share a long tradition of scientific, research and technological excellence. Within this tradition, the evaluation and management of their science systems focused on the highest quality research, on peer review, and on the custodial abilities of their national Academies of Science. However, as these regions continue the rapid shift away from centrally planned political economies towards more open, internationally integrated, and market-oriented ones, a series of major challenge to policy makers emerges from the need to revitalize, reconnect and dramatically reorient their research systems away from the republican view of science for national prestege[1] and towards their regional and national socio-economic objectives.[2] This is a general challenge, not specific to the CEE nations, that is being faced widely by small and medium sized-economies.

In order to meet this challenge, a first policy step must be to adopt an appropriate mental map. It must discard either antiquated assumptions about the nature and function of scientific innovation that no longer apply, or eschew frameworks that were devised for other contexts or countries with other capabilities. For many small and medium-sized economies, however, this has proven difficult to do. Not only do most smaller economies have longstanding politico-economic connections with a hegemon (be it the Triad or the former Soviet Union), but they also tend to have fewer resources to spend on S&T (and therefore cannot afford to support the full range of research activities, thus enjoying neither scale nor scope), they tend to have fewer researchers per capita, and so on. This lack of critical mass also can have a dampening effect on technology-intensive inward FDI. Seen from the perspective of economic policy,

138

despite macro-economic suggestions that there is an international convergence taking place amongst industrial and industrializing countries (an attractive observation that might cast powerful influence in some policy circles), disaggregated sectoral data shows that there is in fact a more complex global process of niche development, economic and market specificity, and so on, which requires specific policy responses that match the regional capabilities and contexts.[3] And yet, there is an understandable urge to 'catch up', to stave off the 'falling behind'.[4] The differences in observations belies the implicit debate that is buried in much of the literature on science, technology and development economics.[5]   Moreover, by adopting such mental frames, there is a presupposition, or rather an acceptance of, another country's preeminence or hegemony.

Such observations are particularly poignant for the Central and Eastern European regions. In the Czech Republic, for example, and at a time when science-based innovation and technology transfer is seen as something of a *sine qua non* of economic growth, total R&D personnel fell from 138,000 in 1989 to under 50,000 in 1996. R&D expenditures fell over the same period from 21,400 (millions CZK) to 16,250. Moreover, gross expenditures of R&D across the region as a percentage of gross domestic product were and are still low, with Hungary posting a 0.67 percent ratio for 1996 and Poland showing 0.76 percent (as compared with Canada, the lowest of the G7, at 1.65 percent – now at 1.9 percent).[6] Such apparently weak and even retrograde performance in science and technology requires immediate attention. As Provazník *et. al.*, and others point out, 'R&D spending has become an important issue', but lack of private funds, lack of local business interest in the long run, and government's concern with balancing interests has led to a policy view that the business enterprise sectors of the region (which does not have the capability as yet) must drive the transformation.[7] The framing of the issues in such a way may be problematic and points to some generalizable concerns to other regions for, as regions throughout the world are discovering, knowledge-based economic growth and sustainability are best realized through partnerships, collaboration, and linkages.[8]

With this background in mind, the purpose of this brief chapter is to 'clear the brush' somewhat in terms of frameworks that do not have a high utility of function with regard to transitional regions, and to propose some steps that might facilitate the re-engagement of the region. In so doing, this chapter will briefly critique the popular emphasis on research as a driving force in the linear model of innovation and suggest instead a variation of the national innovation system model – the regional system of innovation – as a more appropriate and adaptable model for transitional economies.

DEMANDING CONTEXTS AND POLICY CHANGES

The goal of many smaller, interdependent countries and regions today is to develop an innovative capacity. However, the pace of change and the contexts for competition have come to be very demanding. The rapid and widespread political-economic transformations that have overtaken full regions of the OECD, the APEC and the CEE in recent times are challenging policy makers and economic institutions to adjust to new circumstances. Moreover, they reveal a number of fundamental shifts toward what many casually refer to as 'the new economy'. Since the 1970s, this emergent set of circumstances can be cryptically sketched as follows. Trade in tangible goods (which long characterized the international division of labor between nations, and which was grounded in geographically determined comparative advantages) has been dramatically surpassed in value and in volume by trade in both intangible services and knowledge- or technology-intensive goods like software. Similarly, international investment traditionally 'landed' in physical plant and equipment (P&E) whereas today, with more than $1.2 trillion being traded on the currency markets daily, such investment is flowing to the capture and repatriation of intellectual property rights, research results, copyrights and so on *without* necessarily involving any new tangible P&E. As we have already said, traditional notions of 'value added' were defined according to what natural resources were at hand (i.e. minerals, forests, water, etc.) whereas it is increasingly defined by 'brain power' (i.e. increasing functionality, performance, quality, service, attractive designs, and so on which are derived from creativity and knowledge). The large multinational enterprise (MNE), long recognized as the core vehicle for international business, has been dramatically diversified in form by strategic alliances, joint ventures, the devolution of monolithic management structures, and so on to the point where the nationality and scale of an MNE no longer matters in the way that it once did.[9] In addition, in many advanced industrial economies, the majority of new jobs (as much as 70 percent in Canada and the United States) are coming from the tertiary sectors (services) while the majority of jobs in traditional sectors are becoming more knowledge-intensive and are 'moving up' the skill curve. Of course, the effect of these economic developments are only magnified in some ways for transitional economies because of the political events following 1989 which, among other things, brought the importance of government monetary and fiscal policy (as regards science, technology and industry, for example) into highlight.

This complex and turbulent context has had various opaque monikers attached to it, from notions of 'techno-globalism' and 'the end of geography' to 'turbo-capitalism' and 'head-to-head competition'.[10] Other favored descriptions have featured 'globalization' (of production, markets, cultures, etc.) as a dominant world logic in which technological advances (and advances in telecommunications and transportation in particular) are key and through which deep integration and national interdependence are realized (channeled through either negotiated common markets and free trade zones like the EU or NAFTA, or through common rules of engagement through the ISO, the WTO, and so on).

As appealing as such meta-frameworks might seem as useful as they might be for understanding certain important networks of rules that have been ascendant since the days of Ricardo; and as appropriate as such high level generalizations might be for certain economies; such horizons are not particularly helpful when looking at the transitional economies of Central and Eastern Europe. This is due to the fact that the frameworks typically offered up reveal faulty or inappropriate logics.

While the motivations behind such 'black box' analytic schema are highly variant, they have in common two types of distortions. First, they tend to mask (rather than reveal) the emerging dynamics that are at play in what Karl Polanyi called 'the real economy'. In other words, despite their stated recognition of conditions of change, adjustment and transition, what they tend to retain is a romantic attachment to either static explanatory forces (such as prices, markets and rational actors) or a hopeful sense of triumphalism in which future change and tensions are somehow mollified and the 'proper' order of nations is established (as with the 'end of history' thesis of Francis Fukuyama). Put another way, there is a sense in many of these images that the economic changes are taking place 'up there' whereas growth and industry in the 'real economy' takes place 'on the ground'. The challenge, as Richard Florida and B.Ä. Lundvall have aptly suggested, is to become a 'learning region' and a 'learning economy'.

How this can be done will be outlined below. Second, these meta-frameworks tend to implicitly presume a level playing field between actors or an equal access to opportunities. This is quite simply not the case. The 'meta-game' and the contours of the new topography are still being greatly influenced by the hegemons. In any case, the faulty or inappropriate logics fall from the fact that, from the point of view of contextually specific transitional economies, the units of analysis are typically ill-chosen, are deployed at too high a level of abstraction, or the dynamics of change are not properly diagnosed. This means that such frameworks are only marginally helpful to analysts or policy makers in transitional economies, and yet the policy challenges in such contexts are serious.

When considering the role of science in the new economic context, it is important to note that the optimal unit of analysis in terms of factors of production is knowledge, not research. While in terms of broad economic performance it is probably at the regional, not the national, level that this will yield the most meaningful results. These points can be explained in three steps of transition.

SCIENCE SYSTEMS IN TRANSITION (STEP 1)

There is little question that one of the important elements of political-economic development (and thus of policy focus) is to be found in the science, research and technology system of a nation. The preeminent position, historically, of the CEE economies in this regard has already been noted. Science and technology, of course, have long been recognized as being critical factors in determining the fortunes of nations[11] and as being important change agents. This is certainly true in the broad tableau of the 'real economy', even though the exact mechanisms through which science relates to the economy or the evolving relationships that science has with politics and policy are not very reliably documented across regions. But four broad features which have changed the topography of the policy challenges facing smaller and transitional nations are worthy of mention:

One is that the nature of *the science enterprise and research itself is changing*. Traditional images of discipline-based research which is focused on the breakthrough and the individual have been supplanted, as has the siloed view of institutions (universities, academies, firms, and so on).

A second shift is that a broad number of non-traditional national players are becoming actively involved in the performance of science and technology. In other words, *the world science base is expanding*, and given that science and economic performance are linked this means that the base for competition is also expanding. Indeed, smaller nations from Spain to South Korea and Singapore are now showing growth curves in their S&T activities that promise to match the relative level of activity as in Australia or Canada.[12]

A third and related point is that as the number of small independent states continues to grow, the S&T dynamism of regions which do not themselves have the capacity to be fully functional in all aspects of the science system, but which can enjoy the synergies of regional linkages in research, education, industry and government, can make these areas important innovation centers. *The case for inter-regional cooperation is taking on new importance.*

A fourth and final point is that in the new emerging context, *the number of transboundary issues that involve a science, research or technical component is on the rise.* These can be found on a variety of fronts, from the environmental and ecological fronts (0_3, bio-diversity) to issues of international rules (intellectual property rights, standards, technology export controls), security and conflict resolution. [13]

And yet outside the large economies of the Triad (the USA, Japan, and Germany), the exact roles of science, research and development in transitional regions or smaller economies have not been fully explored. In part, this is because the place of research-led growth in development economics is marginal. In part this is also because the dominant mental maps that have been developed to understand the socio-economic functions of science have been based on sets of expectations grounded in 'scale and scope effects'; in an 'endless frontier', breakthrough, notion of advancing knowledge, and in a 'first among equals' strategy that is well suited to the Triad but which is less well suited to less resourced economies.

SCIENCE SYSTEMS IN TRANSITION (STEP 2)

A long time cultural view of the relationship between science and economic performance privileged the role of research and can in some ways be seen as exemplifying a trickle down theory of science. Indeed, into the early part of this century, research (and the researcher) were culturally seen as being key. The tradition was one of a lone investigator (often a gentleman amateur) advancing a particular area of science and communicating with peers the fruits of research verifying the results. The sponsor of the research was typically a wealthy patron. The principle motivator was curiosity and the search for new knowledge while the principle community was the republic of science. The link between science and the industrial arts was *not* front and centre.

As science and economic performance became more clearly linked, and as the role of research became linked with security, research labs became more formally organized in firms, research became more professionalized with degree-granting institutions standardizing their curricula, and the principle sponsor for science became the government. To a large extent, the implicit 'trickle down' model of science benefits remained, even though the research contract had entered the scene by 1915 and this led to a cultural schism between 'gentlemen scientists' and 'mere mechanics' or what the Mathematician G.H. Hardy referred to as 'High' and 'Low' Science.

This broad situation continued during the three decades following 1915, and by 1964 (when the term 'science policy' was first used at the OECD) government analysts who were interested in understanding the mechanism through which the myriad benefits of research flowed into industry and the economy developed a series of linear models. Their interest was to formalize the 'trickle down' flow into a 'stream' of benefits in such a way that governments could deploy a variety of instruments and interventions to strengthen the national performance in S&T. This in many ways carried within it the debate started during the 1940s between the republic of science school associated with Michael Polanyi and the more planned 'social function of science' school associated with J.D. Bernal. Such interventions were to include grants, scholarships and other mechanisms geared towards increasing the supply of science and scientists in the belief that increasing the flow would increase the benefits, but still only through the trickled efforts of largely unfettered researchers.

In the years following, three variations of the linear model emerged. The first (as we have already seen) was the 'science push' model in which scientists working in universities would produce results anywhere in the world. These would be published in peer reviewed conferences or disseminated publically at conferences, read and understood by scientists or engineers working in industry, selectively applied to particular private sector problems of production or process, and commercialized (either as a product or as an improved product).

A second variation is the 'technology pull' model in which the research problem originates in the firm, becomes known or is somehow passed on to the researcher who in turn passes the solution (possibly on contract basis) back up the chain to the marketplace. In both variations, analysts assumed that there was a role for government to play through support of the research system. (The final variation of the linear model is the 'market pull' model, a variation in which government does not play much of a role, and in which private sector issues such as productivity and profitability are the primary focus.)

In each of these variations it is the researcher and the research that continues to be pivotal. Unfortunately, any case study application of the linear model illustrates that it is not a useful or accurate representation. Indeed, as both John Ziman and Rosenberg and Kline have forcefully argued, the process of research-intensive innovation is much more complex than any linear model can possibly admit. However, as Nathan Rosenberg has said, the simplicity of the model is so alluring that 'it is dead but it won't lie down'.

A number of critiques of these linear models can, of course, be made. Besides their oversimplification of a complex process they stagger because they place undue importance on the researcher and on research results. In so doing they blur the multifaceted types of motivations that drive an individual researcher or research lab, they hermetically and artificially seal the university from industry and government, they misappreciate the differences between public science and private sector requirements, they are unabashedly committed to the supply-side of science, they promote or reify a false dichotomy between science technology and between research elites and popular culture, and so on. A vast improvement can be found by re-balancing the supply-demand equation and by focusing on the socio-economic goal of S&T, namely innovation.

INNOVATION SYSTEMS IN TRANSITION (STEP 3)

Innovation in its baldest sense can be thought of as being anything new. More usefully, however, it is the use of new knowledge (that is, knowledge that is new to an organization) to offer a new product or service. In a technical setting, it is invention plus commercialization.

The process of innovation cannot be separated from the strategic context of an organization or from its competitive environment.[14] The new knowledge can be technical or social-strategic (as in the knowledge of a market) in nature. Technical knowledge is knowledge of components, linkages between components, research methods and techniques that go into a product or service, and so on. Socio-strategic knowledge (e.g. of a market) can include knowledge of distribution channels, product applications, customer needs, preferences and expectations, and so on. Even from this cryptic sketch of static elements, it is immediately clear that by focusing on innovation rather than on research one can begin to admit greater diversity, complexity, and hence realism to the equation. In so doing, a significant re-orientation of political-economic expectations for the research system on the part of policy makers can take place.

Joseph Schumpeter, in many ways the modern father of innovation economics, outlined five different orientations of innovation (product, process, market, material-factor of production and social organization) and privileged the entrepreneur rather than the individual researcher as being at the core of successful innovation. Moreover, by referring to 'entrepreneurs', Schumpeter was speaking more of a collection of qualities (comprehensive knowledge of the organization, its clients, its core competencies, its supply chain, the spark of creative potentialities that is unique to that organization, and so on) rather than to a specific individual within an organization or economy.

Add to this new nascent framework the new currency which dynamizes economic performance: 'knowledge'. In the linear formulation, noted above, the currency was undifferentiated: 'research'. However, research is a complex social activity made up of professional elite communities,[15] invisible colleges,[16] factors affecting productivity, time lags and 'place lags' between discoveries, a unique workplace (the equipped laboratory) as well as such immeasurables as creativity, intuition, surprises, and so on. By focusing on innovation and knowledge, however, one can vastly improve the appreciation of context, and institutional attributes required for good science and successful innovation.

By way of example, the neo-Schumpeterian literature of the past quarter century has illuminated the pathways of innovation with some precision. 'Knowledge' can be codified or tacit. Codified knowledge typically includes knowledge that can be written down and replicated elsewhere, as in patent applications, designs, blueprints, research papers, and so on. 'Tacit' knowledge includes experience, intuition and creativity. Michael Polanyi uses the examples of knowing how to ride a bicycle and how one recognizes the face of a friend.[17] This type of knowledge, which dominates human action, is essentially non-transferable (except perhaps in such guild-type activities that include years of apprenticeship) and typically only becomes passed on through human interaction, religion, tradition, and other cultural or ritual activities.

Moreover, in speaking of knowledge rather than only research, one can admit a variety of useful scintilators into the equation, such as skill and learning. Individuals and institutions alike have differing capabilities. A great engineer may not be a great accounting or salesman. A researcher may be a good diplomat or leader in a lab but may not necessarily be the best scientist. These represent various types of connaisseurship. As such, neo-Schumpeterians can speak of 'know-how' (technical knowledge), 'know-why' (fundamental research understanding), as well as 'know-who' and 'know-where' (network knowledge). A successful innovative organization represents a blend of knowledge types, and the goal of any such institution is not to simply innovate once (and continue living off of the proceeds of the 'one and only' innovation) but to learn how to innovate continuously; to produce a stream of innovative ideas. Over time, the type of knowledge and learning capability may shift within an institution, for example, from a research-driven capacity (as in an early IBM or Hewlett Packard) to a more market-oriented capacity as the industry, sector or setting matures. As with the new currency of 'knowledge', 'learning' (which is a process of adjustment and adaptation to both internal and external conditions) can take place in a variety of ways. Economists such as Ken Arrow[18] and Richard Nelson[19] can, therefore, speak of 'learning by doing', 'learning by using', and so on.

The implication of these re-framings is that economic performance (especially in the new knowledge-based economy) is not solely dependent on, or led by, one form of knowledge (research) but requires a variety of capabilities. In today's fast-paced globalized context, surprises, shocks and other disturbances can come from a variety of sources: research insights can come from other disciplines, industrial competition can come from firms in other sectors, and so on. Add to this the reasonable observation that no one institution can house all the knowledge and 'connaissance' needed to operate on a daily basis and one quickly comes to the conclusion that what is needed (if one can borrow the imagery of radio astronomy for a moment) is a large array telescope. Large MNEs, such as IBM and Seimans, have recognized this and have flattened their monolithic organizational structures into 'federations of firms', which are enabled by their head offices to make decisions (dealing with budget allocations, production, inventory, research, and so on) locally. This is in an effort to be faster, leaner and more responsive to local suppliers, labor forces, customers and communities. The research communities have long practised a form of this by having international networks of scholars in their fields, but universities themselves are now evolving in this direction as well. In order to provide custom training, research and education, many major universities are involved in university-industry partnerships. The President of the University of Michigan, for example, recently said that he considers himself to be 'the CEO of an international knowledge conglomerate, not a medieval university'. Thus we can begin to see, in this new formulation, a model of innovation that is decidedly more dynamic than earlier linear models.

Following the logic of the innovation system, a successful and effective research system in today's context can no longer conceive of itself in isolation from its national and regional context, it must see itself in terms of a partnership with other local institutions (financial institutions, business enterprises, schools and colleges, universities). It must see itself in terms of its commitment to local needs and community. Such a re-framing will allow linkages to be strengthened and local synergies to be achieved. This in turn will promote increased inward foreign direct investment, technology transfers which will enable and revitalize local industries, the development and anchoring of a technology-intensive and research-intensive skilled labor force, and the revitalization of the science system itself which, as was already noted at the outset, continues to enjoy a proud legacy.

TOWARDS A TRANSITIONAL INNOVATION SYSTEM

Many regions of the world are adjusting to rapid changes brought about through globalization, deep interdependencies, and competitive as well as social challenges. Science and technology are being seen by governments as providing the tools for adjustment. Many nations are adopting a system of innovation approach. In Canada, this has, since 1993, become the official language of its economic policy.[20] Throughout the APEC, regional science and technology ministers have signed an umbrella commitment to regional innovation systems at the Mexico Summitt in October 1998.[21] And in countries as diverse (industrially, culturally and historically) as South Africa and Chile, innovation linkages are seen as a way through which to nurture capabilities and engage the world economy, yet preserve cultural uniqueness of the area.[22] This framework holds considerable promise as well for the CEE governments.

In order to move in this direction towards a Transitional Innovation System however, policy makers and leaders of the Central and Eastern European countries need to directly address the challenge of innovation, and may perhaps find it useful to focus its efforts on the following areas:

Knowledge

The region needs to commit a itself to an appropriate level of R&D spending and the production of new knowledge in the universities, colleges and academies. This can lead to valuable indigenous knowledge but will also facilitate the identification, appropriation, application and diffusion of new knowledge produced elsewhere

Skills

Focusing on knowledge production and flows will have significant impacts on the skills profile of the region, and policy might fruitfully attend to the full spectrum of education and training.

Institutions

The national academies have a wide-ranging reputation for fostering scientific work, but whether they can be re-oriented to act as champions and network leaders is a matter for each constituency to consider.

Infrastructure

A knowledge infrastrucuture is a mandatory investment in attracting new technologies as well as new foreign direct investment This would range from telecommunications network, telephonic and internet infrastructure as well as refurbished physical infrastructure, such as schools, roads, and so on.

Technology Transfer

Policies that target and foster technology transfer (including regluatory regimes, taxation policy, intellectual property rights, and so on are a high area of priority attention.

Incentives

Policies that attract business investment from MNEs into local productive activities are to be encouraged. This can be enhanced by ensuring stable monetary actions.

Linkages

Given the geographic proximity of CEE economies as well as their structural similarities and sub-optimal capacity, linking research networks with business activities and educational facilities would expediate the development of a regional innovation system and transform the area into a learning region.

These brief points outline the path towards effective innovation strategies in interdependent states.

NOTES

1. Michael Polanyi, 'The Republic of Science', *Minerva*, 1, 1, 1962.
2. Ironically, perhaps, this requirement is somewhat reminiscent of Boris Hesen's 1931 London presentation on 'The Social and Economic Roots of Newton's *Principia*' or J.D. Bernal's *The Social Function of Science*, first published in 1939, which Hesen inspired and which fed the anti-collectivist reaction of Michael Polanyi, John Jewkes, Frederick von Hayek and the Mount Pellerin Society.
3. See Graham Vickery, 'The Globalization of Trade and Investment', in John de la Mothe and Gilles Paquet (eds), *Evolutionary Economics and the New International Political Economy*, Pinter, London, 1996; and Sylvia Ostry, *The New World Trading System*, Brookings, New York, 1997.
4. See Chris Freeman, 'Catching Up and Falling Behind: The Case of Latin America and East Asia', in John de la Mothe and Gilles Paquet (eds), *Evolutionary Economics and the New Political Economy*, Pinter, London, 1996.
5. See Norman Clark, *The Political Economy of Science and Technology*, Basil Blackwell, Oxford, 1984.
6. The source is OECD/DSTI/OLIS online.
7. Provazník *et.al.*, *op.cit.*, P. 25, 27 and 32.
8. See John de la Mothe and Gilles Paquet (eds), *Local and Regional Systems of Innovation*, Kluwer, Boston, 1998; Zoltan Acs (ed.), *Regional Innovation, Knowledge and Global Change*, Pinter, London, 1999.
9. See Robert Reich's 'Who Is Us?' thesis in his *The Work of Nations*, Alfred Knopf, New York, 1991.
10. See, for example, Sylvia Ostry and Richard Nelson, *Techno-Globalism and Techno-Nationalism*, Brookings, New York, 1996; Kenichi Ohmae, *The Borderless World*, Harper Collins, New York, 1991; Edward Luttwak, *Turbo-Capitalism*, Alfred Knopf, New York, in press; and Lester Thurow, *Head to Head: The Coming Economic Battle Among Japan, Europe and America*, Morrow, New York, 1992.
11. Patrice Higonnet, David S. Landes and Harvey Rososky (eds), *Favorites of Fortune: Technology, Growth and Economic development Since the Industrial Revolution*, Harvard University Press, Cambridge MA., 1991.
12. See Chris Freeman. 'Catching Up and Following Behind: the Case of Latin America and East Asia', in John de la Mothe and Gilles Paquet (eds), *Evolutionary Economics and the New International Political Economy*, Pinter, London, 1996.
13. Eugene Bertrand Skolnikoff, *The Elusive Transformation: Science, Technology and International Politics*, Princeton University Press, Princeton, 1994; and the New York Academy of Science, 'Scientific Cooperation and Conflict Resolution', January 28-30, 1998, New York City.
14. Michael Porter, *The Competitive Advantage of Nations*, Free Press, New York, 1990.
15. Robert Merton, *The Sociology of Science*, University of Chicago Press, Chicago, 1976.
16. Diana Crane, *Invisible Colleges*, University of Chicago Press, Chicago, 1972.
17. Michael Polanyi, *Personal Knowledge*, University of Chicago Press, Chicago, 1958.
18. See Ken Arrow, 'The Economic Implications of Learning By Doing', *Journal of Economic Studies*, 80, 1962.
19. Richard Nelson, *Understanding Technical Change as an Evolutionary Process*, Elsevier, Amsterdam, 1985.
20. See John de la Mothe, 'Canada and National Innovation Systems', in Government of Canada, *Science and Technology Resource Book, Volume II*, Ottawa, 1994; John de la Mothe, 'One Small Step in an Uncertain Direction: The Federal Science and Technology Review and Public Administration in Canada', *Canadian Public Administration*, Autumn, 1996.

21. See APEC, *Capturing Value Through Regional Innovation, Partnership and Cooperation*, S&T Ministerial, Mexico City, October 23, 1998.
22. See Government of South Africa *Science and Technology Green Paper*, Capetown, 1996; Paul Dufour, John de la Mothe and James Mullin, 'Using Science and Technology as Strategic Instruments in Canada's Foreign Relations with Latin America', *Canadian Foreign Policy*, 5, 2, Winter 1998.

10. Learning in Local Systems of Innovation

It has become widely recognized within the globalization debate that the innovative capacity of regions is of heightened importance for the wealth of nations. However, up until now, one of the major weaknesses of the very best work that has been done in the area of macro-innovation studies has been the emphasis on the various infrastructures (physical, human, communications, and so on) associated with national systems. These features are not unimportant, but they only provide a limited insight into the workings of innovation systems. Moreover, they tend to generate the false impression that 'systems' are co-terminous with the administrative contours of these infrastructures.

This often means that the existence of a local or regional system of innovation, when it is recognized, is inferred from the existence of these national infrastructures, and is in some way seen as being welded to them. And since national infrastructures are both more formalized and more celebrated than sub-national ones, this has led to a vast operation of co-relations between these national infrastructures and the presumed national systems of innovation.

From the point of view of a national statistical agency, for example, this sort of classification (based on administrative infrastructures) is understandably a useful first phase in data gathering. But it is no more sophisticated than the classification of animals according to the number of legs – a classification that was in good currency in biology a very long time ago. Clearly, such simplistic classifications are unlikely to throw much light on the complex process of innovation and wealth creation *per se*.

Yet, how can one hope to do better without a meaningful dynamic evolutionary image of the innovation process?

PROCESSES OVER STRUCTURES

Some attempts have been made at stylizing the *workings* of the innovation systems. For instance, Annalee Saxenian (1994) has insisted on the interactions between the structural features of corporate and industrial organization and local institutions and culture. A cognate effort has been undertaken by Richard Florida at the regional level. The Conseil de la science et de la technologie du Quebec (1997) has proposed a three-tiered image of the innovation system at the regional/national level: at its core is the innovating firm embedded in a proximate environment of alliances and networks, and in a broader environment providing the legal, regulatory, economic and public support infrastructures defining the rules of the game. The coalescence of the interactions between those three levels is seen as being at the core of the innovation system.

While Saxenian's and Florida's ethnographic works have proved helpful, this work remains on the whole largely descriptive. The major contribution of Saxenian, Florida, Phil Cooke, Zoltan Acs, and others have been to provide loose interpretative frameworks that emphasize structural features even though it puts at the center of the stage, and this is an important novelty, the nexus of interactions (at the local and regional levels) as the determining factor.

A framework that emphasizes process rather than structure focuses firmly on the process of innovation as its central concern. It recognizes that the innovation process is not linear but is network-shaped and dynamized in a fundamental way by a complex multilogue which weaves the various partners together. Moreover it regards as utopian the hopes that by manipulating structures one may transform the process. What is centrally important and what has more heuristic power is an understanding of the dynamics of the process. Finally, it emphasizes the interaction between three major dimensions (the cognitive space, the capabilities/absorptive capacity of firms, and the governance of the communities of practice) as playing key roles in the innovation process.

The basic features of this emphasis are set out in this chapter, and I suggest that it may well hold the key to the construction of a dynamic and evolutionary framework for the analysis of local and regional systems of innovation. The local milieu, rather than the regional/national structures, is principal. A subsidiary objective of this chapter is the identification of the crucial *process dimensions* of the interdependent innovation system and of the main *strategic externalities* generated by innovation races, for they will be of crucial importance in the construction of the next generation of statistical indicators which national statistical agencies and groups like the OECD and UNESCO so badly need.

Let us suggest a three-dimensional decoder of the learning process involved in generating new practical knowledge. First, we need to build on the fact that an innovation is first and foremost new practical knowledge. Consequently, what is required is a stylized view of the innovation process in *a cognitive space or zone*. A template was suggested a decade ago by John Ziman (1991). Ziman suggested 'some unpacking' of the traditional model of discovery and an exploration of the different knowledge domains in the cognitive space. Ziman focused on the cognitive roots of innovation and suggested that a neural net model of innovation was probably the most useful approach.

Ziman uses an old metaphor derived from the language of geography to define the cognitive space: it is used to identify transversal areas constructed from patterns of connections between different domains of the different layers of fields in the innovation process (sciences, technologies, marketing, and so on). Certain scientific ideas, practical techniques, and marketable commodities (each at different layers of the innovation process) are cognitively interconnected in the sense that they are related in a certain pattern of interdependence. This connectionist vision of the innovation process is very much like a neural network: what looks from the outside like a random set of connections is in fact a neural pattern capable of learning like a real neural net in the brain. The redundancy of connections allows information flows to circumvent a hole or a lesion. Indeed, the pattern of nodes and connections constitutes a system that is capable of experiencing learning as nodes or patterns of connections are modified.

The pattern of nodes and connections in this cognitive space need not be similar or identical as one looks from one system of innovation to another, for the ideas, techniques and commodities involved are not identical. The learning engine lies in the particular configuration or pattern of ideas, techniques and commodities *and* the specialized items of knowledge linking them. And the learning capability of this transversal network is its capacity to transform.

While the traditional view is that individual persons learn, what is suggested by more recent analyses is that the learning organization does not store its knowledge in separate heads but instead it stores it in the relationships that exist between stakeholders. It co-creates value by a dialogue of equals. What is required is a better understanding of that process. Already some progress has been made toward the development of cognitive economics but this remains to a great extent uncharted territory.

Second, this new practical knowledge is generated by organizations throughout the cognitive space, and these organizations are defined by their *capabilities/absorptive capacities*. One must therefore examine the factors defining the relative emphasis on exploration in search of the new and exploitation of the existing knowledge base that characterize the different communities of practice that make up these organizations.

In a rapidly evolving, surprise-generating context that is plagued with uncertainty and learning failures, the challenge is not simply to make the best use of existing resources and knowledge, to better *exploit* the available possibilities, but it is also to *explore* new possibilities and opportunities. The strategic choice strikes a balance between exploitation and exploration: undue emphasis on the exploitation of available knowledge may trap an organization in sub-optimal situations while undue emphasis on exploration may prevent an organization from gaining much from successful experimentation.

Organizations will be the locus of on-going conversations that will produce new knowledge and value-added through networking and partnering. The main challenge then is to determine what is the best organization of knowledge production if the objective is to generate learning and innovation.

This will depend greatly on a balance between commonality and diversity of knowledge, between coherence and mutual learning, between exploitation and exploration. Ethnographic work on the daily life of organizations suggests that these features are not captured in the formal characteristics of organizations. Practice differs significantly from job descriptions or rules and procedures. The corporate culture embodies a communal interpretation that may have little to do with the documentation available. Corporate culture embodies generally unwritten principles meant to generate a relatively high level of coordination at low costs by bestowing identity and membership.

This corporate culture is nested at the organization level, through the central features of work practice: stories of flexible generality about events of practice that act as repositories of accumulated wisdom, the evolution of these stories constituting collective learning of an evolving way to interpret conflicting and confusing data but also an on-going social construction of a community of interpretation.

Third, one must identify the features of the broader social process within which the organization is nested to ascertain the extent to which the workings of the innovation system depend on features of the *governance of the communities of practice* (proximity, trust, solidaristic values, and so on).

Actual practice in the workplace has a communal base. Learning also has a communal base. It is not about transmission of abstract knowledge from someone's head to another's. It is about learning to 'function in a community', about the 'embodied ability to behave as community members', about 'becoming a practitioner'. Learning is *legitimate peripheral participation* and it is fostered by facilitating access to, and membership of, the community of practice of interest.

Trust is at the core of both the fabric of the communities of practice and of their communal base. Trust is a way to transform 'laborers into members', to convert an employment contract into a membership contract. The 'concept of membership, when made real, would replace the sense of belonging to a place with a sense of belonging to a community' (Handy 1995). Belonging is one of the most powerful agents of mobilization. So what is required is an important 'moral' component to the new employment contract, *a new refurbished moral contract* that is not mainly contractual but mainly moral: 'a network of civic engagement ... which can serve as a cultural template for future collaboration ... broaden the participants' sense of self ... enhancing the participants "taste" for collective benefits' (Putnam 1995).

But a situation in which such a membership contract would become hegemonic would risk degenerating into a situation in which a dominant macro-culture would prevail. If such were the case, in the long run, such homogeneous and coherent culture would cease to be innovative. Innovation requires a certain diversity of knowledge and stems from the interplay of separate communities, from the interplay between the core community and the emergent communities at the periphery (the suppliers and the customers of a firm, for instance), from the organization and the environment it actively interacts with. Exploration calls for diversity, for separate stories to be in good currency. It happens at the interface between the organization and its environment and depends on the capacity for the non-canonical to prevail on the canonical.

It is therefore in the structure of the communities of practice that one must seek the levers that are likely to foster both learning and innovation by intervening with the work place. When the gap between the canonical and the actual practices widens too much, the only way to promote the growth of knowledge is to legitimize and support a number of enacting activities that may be disruptive, to foster a reconception of the organization as a community of communities and promote the view that communities of practice must be allowed to take some distance from the received wisdom.

The very coherence that makes learning easier is likely to make innovation more difficult. The central challenge, for the promotion of the growth of knowledge, is to find the requisite degree of dissonance that is necessary for a system to become innovative, and to identify the most effective schemes of decomposition of large organizations into quasi-isolated sub-systems likely to provoke the emergence of a workable degree of inconsistency and therefore of innovation.

The differences in the way the sub-organizations search for knowledge increase the scope of the search. So, as these differences are legitimized and the different ways of searching for new knowledge have the maximum opportunity to rub against one another (as in industrial districts or more closely interconnected communities of practice), innovation will ensue.

In an economy dynamized by information flows, knowledge, competence and capabilities, and the communities of practices, the new relevant units of analysis have to be those that serve as the basis to understand and nurture innovation. Focusing either on the firm or on the national economy would appear to be equally misguided. Under the microscope, too much in a firm is idiosyncratic and white noise is bound to run high. Under the national macroscope, much of the innovation and restructuring going on is bound to be missed. One may therefore argue that the most useful perspective point is the Schumpeterian/Dahmenian perspective focusing on development blocks, sub-national fora, and so on where the learning is really occurring.

In an evolutionary model, the process of learning and discovery is coupled with the interactive mechanism with the context or environment through which selection occurs. This interactive mechanism 'both provide[s] the source of differential fitness – firms whose R&D turn up more profitable processes of production or products will grow relative to their competitors – and also tend to bind them together as a community' (Dosi and Nelson 1994: 162).

It is very important to realize that social proximity is bound to play a fundamental role on both sides of the equation. Both on the organization side and on the forum/environment side, proximity breeds interaction and socio-economic learning. Moreover these interactive mechanisms are fueled by dynamic increasing returns to agglomeration. In most cases, these agglomeration economies are bounded, and therefore do not give rise to monopoly by a single region or location, but they generate increasing returns snowballing.

Nelson and Winter have suggested that at the core of the processes of innovation, learning and discovery, and of the processes of diffusion of technical and organizational innovations, is the notion of 'selection environment' which is defined as the context that 'determines how relative use of different technologies changes over time' (1977: 61). This context is shaped by market and non-market components, conventions, socio-cultural factors, and by the broader institutional structure. This selection environment constitutes the relevant *milieu* (internal and external, broader or narrower) in explaining the innovative capacity of a sector/region.

At the core of the dynamic milieu and of the innovation network are a number of intermingled dimensions (economic, historical, cognitive and normative) but they all depend to a certain degree on *trust and confidence,* and therefore on a host of cultural and sociological factors that have a tendency to be found mainly in localized networks and to be more likely to emerge from a background of shared experiences, regional loyalties, and so on. This is social capital in Coleman's sense and such social and cultural capital plays a central role in both the dynamics and the capacity to learn and transform of meso-systems.

The innovation process depends as much on the features of a selection environment as on the internal milieu.

First, innovation is all about continuous learning and learning does not occur in a socio-cultural vacuum, either within the organization or in the environment. An innovation network is more likely to blossom in a restricted localized milieu where all the socio-cultural characteristics of a dynamic milieu are likely to be found. Moreover, it is most unlikely that this sort of milieu will correspond to a national territory. Therefore, if one is to identify *dynamic milieus* as likely systems on which one might work to stimulate innovation, they are likely to be local or regional systems of innovation.

Second, some geo-technical forces would appear to generate meso-level units where learning proceeds faster and better. As Storper argues,

in technologically dynamic production complexes ... there is a strong reason for the existence of regional clusters or agglomerations. Agglomeration appears to be a principal geographical form in which the trade-off between lock-in, technological flexibility (and the search for quasi-rents), and cost minimization can be most effectively managed because it facilitates efficient operations of a cooperative production network. Agglomeration in these cases is not simply the result of standard localization economies (which are based on the notion of allocative efficiency in minimizing costs), but of Schumpeterian efficiencies.

Third, the deconstruction of national economies, the widespread devolution of central government powers, the rise of region-states and the growth of the new tribalism would tend to provide a greater potential for dynamism at the meso level. But Storper has argued that 'codes, channels of interaction, and ways of organizing and coordinating behaviors' are what makes learning possible (p. 85). He feels that the confluence of issues (learning, networks, lock-in, conventions and types of knowledge) must be rooted in political-economic cultures, rules and institutions and that in many countries these are highly differentiated at the regional level. Therefore one region may trigger technological learning and innovation networks in one sub-national area much faster than in others.

Canada, the USA and Mexico are such countries where one may reasonably detect a mosaic of political-economic cultures, rules and conventions with differential innovative potential. Consequently, one may say that there is a genuine 'territorialization of learning' in such a Schumpeterian world.

ORGANIZATIONAL LEARNING, PROXIMITIES AND COORDINATION

At the core of the innovation system are three profoundly intertwined processes: an adaptive and cumulative learning process, a system of interactions among proximate agents and groups, and a dynamic coordination process built on the other two. Together, they constitute the dynamics of the meso-innovation system.

Adaptive and Cumulative Learning

Learning is not sheer adaptation. Adaptation is a process of adjustment to new circumstances on an *ad hoc* basis. Whatever new routine has evolved in this manner may be easily forgotten. Learning is quite different. It is a cumulative process through which new knowledge, however trivially different from what was already in store, gets embedded in new rules, conventions, routines and filters. Indeed, learning is not restricted to a simple modification of routines and rules, it may also trigger a transformation of the representations, objectives, norms and strategies. But learning requires a reasonably well-defined internal environment, acting as a sensitive surface, for without it the new experiences would not be registered or represented as new, and would not call for adjustment in the organizational pattern.

Routines, rooted in context and history, are embedded in a pattern of rationales, rules, conventions and institutions that provide the process of decision-making and learning with unity and stability. In this world, the meaningful units of analysis are the parallel patterns of belief systems and mental representations *and* techno-organizational conventions and rules in which the process is nested.

For any agent or group, the environment is apprehended as a representation. And within a well-coordinated organization, there is much common representation. But there may be differences among the representations of different members. This is a source of learning since the organization may exploit such differences and diversity as a source of knowledge. A common representation may well be an amalgam or a synthesis of these partial representations, for organizational learning amounts to a reconfiguration of collective representation.

At any time, these representations and rules may be more or less fitting, that is, they may be more or less effective socio-technical armistices between the evolving physical environment and the evolving values and plans of agents and groups. The degree of fitness is not invariant as circumstances change: it is rooted in the probability of survival and in the capacity to develop the requisite competences and capabilities to survive.

Given the ever imperfect nature of mental representations, of conventions and of rules, and the mistake-ridden learning processes, the modification of both representations and rules constitutes the way in which the socio-economy evolves, transforms and learns. This learning may be more or less effective, depending on the nature of the challenges generated by the environment, and the nature of the competences, readinesses and reactive capacities of agents and organizations. For instance, the pattern of representations and rules may easily accommodate minor variations in the environment and adapt quickly to these new circumstances. However, it may be capable of only limited learning within a narrow band of circumstances. In the face of radical changes in the environment that call for a dramatic reframing of representations, rules and conventions, it may mainly generate a great deal of cognitive dissonance and dynamic conservatism, and be incapable of learning.

Indeed, as Nelson and Winter have shown (1982), organizations tend to stick to their usual routine as long as performance remains above certain target levels. It is only when performance indicators fall below such levels that the organization searches for better alternatives. This balance between the exploitation of the available knowledge and the exploration and search for new knowledge and new possibilities, underlined by March (1991), is closely related to the mechanisms of selection and mutation: a procedure or routine that performs well being adopted by the system (that is, a higher probability of survival being bestowed on it) in the case of selection, while some misfit between routines and the changing milieu may lead to a mutation in the routine or procedure.

Evolution emerges from this process of mutual learning between agents and organizations, in the form of the parallel and interactive processes of selection and mutation. This learning may be faster or slower depending on the nature of the organization. For instance, hierarchical organizations may be able to filter out new local events and prevent learning of certain sorts: the design of organizations most efficient for knowledge exploitation purposes may lead to learning disabilities in exploration, to organizations that have lesser exploratory competences.

Toulmin (1981) has sorted change mechanisms into four categories. Calculative change is triggered by rational choice as employed by mainstream economic theory; homeostatic change occurs in response to stimuli in accordance with fixed rules, as in single-loop learning in an organization (using new means); development change is typified by life-cycle theories and might correspond to instances of double-loop learning (learning new goals), that is, to the restructuring of the selecting unit, its goals or mission; finally, populational change is triggered by changes in the environment and in the adoption of selective units (that is, a change in its probability of being adopted and nurtured by the environment) – natural selection.

Proximities

The notion of a learning economy and of innovation as a form of learning have helped to dramatically reframe our perspectives on economic progress. The emphasis has been shifted from the economy as an allocative mechanism to the economy as a learning process. This does not mean, however, that learning proceeds inevitably or that it proceeds with as much momentum as would be desired at all times. In the same manner that in the old economy there were allocative failures, in the new economy there are learning failures: the learning economy is often disconcerted.

This process of collective learning, based on conversations with the situation and on interactions among stakeholders, is of necessity *situated*, whether one is focusing on technological or organizational or institutional innovation. In each case, proximity of one sort or another is necessary for the conversation or interaction o proceed.

Proximity is not a unidimensional or solely spatial concept. Agents and groups may be proximate territorially, organizationally, institutionally, ideologically, and so on. Moreover, since everything happens in time and space, there may be a propensity to ascribe to geographical or historical linkages more causal importance than they really deserve for the simple reason that co-relations are more easily detectable in those dimensions. In fact, complementarities of knowledge, competences or capabilities, or organizational and technological complementary connections, may well be the causal factors through which to explain faster learning through dynamic external economies.

But learning remains a social cognitive process. Consequently, it requires some interaction and a major source of external benefits comes from the geographical closeness that generates not only maximal probability of contacts but also maximal probability of *learning by learning,* that is, of developing new capabilities not only through agglomeration economies but through a greater density of situated cognition-driving interactions. In that sense, it is much less the spatial interactions *per se* than the mix of situated culture and institutions that characterizes the context and facilitates communication, cumulative informative exchange and community learning.

This is what has led some analysts to insist on labeling those situated innovation systems as *territorialized* innovation systems: where the institutional density of the territory, its embedded loops of learning, and the sedimentation in the same space of multiplex institutionalized relationships (incorporated in cooperative projects, relational exchanges, and other initiatives and alliances) are welding the localized networks into a trustful community of practice.

Spatial contiguity may be important and even necessary for this sort of proximities and the sort of multiplex relationships that ensue to develop, but it is not sufficient. The fundamental fabric of this territorialized innovation system is the substantive logic of collective action that becomes instituted in the local culture and in the supportive collaborative framework, and underpins the different *readinesses* of the system to make the best use of the existing capabilities but also to make adjustment in those capabilities.

Coordination

The goodness of fit between the learning process, on the one hand, and the territorial and organizational clustering process that accompanies and underpins it, on the other, is a central feature of the governance of the learning economy. The territorialized system of innovation constitutes a way to bring about a certain framework that helps to coordinate the interdependent decisions of the various actors or groups. In that sense, territorialization provides some of the relevant coordinates and shapes *a world* of constraints that leads to a resolution of the indeterminacy generated by interdependence.

Indeed, one of the important limitations of conventional neo-classical economics is the presumption that the interaction among rational individuals is fully intermediated by market mechanisms. Kenneth Arrow (1974) has shown that it is unlikely, but the exact nature of the visible and invisible institutions necessary to complement the market in the coordination arrangements have not been specified in a general way. They are quite different depending on the contexts. For instance, they may differ widely from one region to the next, from one culture to the next, from one period to the next. Individual rationality and mercantile contracts are not sufficient for coordination to occur. There are various non-market mechanisms at work: organizations, institutions, standards, norms and rules that are necessary for coordination to materialize.

Schelling has examined the obstacles to coordination in his analysis of pure coordination games. The archetypal situation is portrayed in the case of car operators who have to coordinate their activity by choosing on which side of the road they will drive. It matters little whether they choose to drive on the right or the left hand side of the road, but one must choose. It is a case where two acceptable Nash equilibria exist. And the indeterminacy can only be resolved by some convention or rule. In practice, the indeterminacy is lifted as a result of some contextual information that constitutes common knowledge and helps generate a focal point on which the protagonists will agree.

In the case of firms, the solution to such problems is found in the corporate culture: the firm as a community of practice is also a community of interpretation and finds in the set of its common values the source of a choice among the many possible solutions. This means that the coordination solution emerges as a *collective cognitive benchmark* which depends on the identity of the individuals partaking in the interaction. It depends on common knowledge; it presupposes a certain common cognitive capital, a certain experiential community.

The cognitive processes that lead to the emergence of a focal point materialize in the form of conventions on the basis of some interactive rationality. These conventions emerge from the social setting in which the economic game is nested. Indeed, the sort of social learning involved depends on the embedding network and the social proximity it provides, for this is the basis for the community of interpretation. These features of the coordination mechanism emphasize the necessary incompleteness of the market mechanisms and the need for *complementary collective cognitive devices* to ensure effective coordination.

This is central in the process of innovation which is based on complex *intersubjective* and *intertemporal* complementarities among the stakeholders during the sequential process leading to an innovation has shown that, in this complex coordination game, the *territory* may well be the locus of coordination of knowledge production, the root of the convergence to the focal points. For Pecqueur, situated territorialization is not a matter of cost of transportation or spatial friction, but the basis of collective learning, a source of common knowledge, and a crucial component in the guidance toward focal points.

These three processes (learning, proximity and coordination) underpin the basic process of innovation. The local and regional systems of innovation are spatial configurations that have emerged as covenants of identity and as frameworks for belonging and learning. But territory does not become automatically a collective cognitive device. It becomes such only if it becomes the source of common ideas, a clan, a culture of shared values. Only in such a case can it become 'un guide de connaissance et de reconnaissance entre individus'.

Such a localized system of innovation is very fragile since it is based not on administrative structures but on *a frame of mind*, a common representation, a collective cognitive map that may well not be transferable from one generation to the next.

In some cases, the localized system of innovation can more easily develop permanent roots when it becomes based on a convention of quality pertaining to products or on some development of the territory as an effective learning world in the new cognitive division of labor. In such a world the logic of innovation and learning is fueled by proximity and generates a new form of dynamic coordination through relational exchange.

It should be clear that the transversal importance of trust in this dynamic is crucial. But it is also a constructed dimension of the system of coordination: proximity, learning and sustainable evolutionary coordination mechanisms generate a self-reinforcing dynamics of interdependence and trust that others like Herbert Simon have compared to some form of altruism (Simon 1993) and which lead to limited opportunism. This in turn lends support to a much more robust learning system as learning goes much beyond the accumulation and development of technological protocols and competences into the accumulation and development of knowledge about the organization of relations among partners, the transformation and reconfiguration of their representations, and even the redefinition of interests and objectives. In such cases, the local system of innovation becomes a *trust system*.

11. Constructing Advantage in Smaller Regions

Let us go to a small, regional, example – Scotland. Scotland is a small regional economy which is cultural, historically and economically very community based. It is deeply enmeshed, as are many other advanced small and medium-sized economies, in an important transformation as they develop and enter the global knowledge economy. Since 1997 (1997=100), Scotland's Gross Domestic Product has grown to 113.3. However, agriculture, forestry and fishing has rested at 99.3. Production is down to 96. Construction has grown, throughout various business and investment cycles, to 106.1 while services – largely in such knowledge-intensive activities as ICT – have impressively outpaced other sectors by an indexed growth of 122.1 (Q4, 2002).[1] GDP per head is currently $22,000US as compared with Canada which stands at $26,000US.

With a population of 5.5 million people, 30 percent are engaged in managerial or professional occupations. Yet it has a long-term unemployment rate of 18.5 percent. The distribution of population is highly variable, with as many as 3300 people per square km in Glasgow and only 8 in the Highland Council Area. And Scotland is losing an estimated 250,000 persons to employment-related emigration annually. Scotland has an international reputation for excellence in higher education[2] and since 1998 enrolments in ICT fields have increased by 45 percent. Scotland is home to 20 percent of UK biotech start-ups, and is the sixth largest equity market in Europe (managing about £350 billion in funds). But between biotech, optoelectronics, telecommunications and semiconductor fabrication, Scotland employs only 37,000 people (out of a labor force of 2.5 million).[3] Sixty-five percent of Scotland's exports flow into the European Union, but the top service exports arise from non-knowledge-intensive activities, such as tourism, (27 percent), oil and gas (23 percent), followed by banks, insurance, assurance and higher education (32 percent). Computer and software services account for 18 percent. Thirty eight percent of manufactured exports come from Scottish office machinery.[4] However non-Scottish firms – such as Cisco,

166

Motorola Lucent, IBM, Hewlett Packard and Compaq – dominate the Scottish technical sectors and manufacturing. They tend to be at the lower scale of production and towards the lesser value-added end of the R&D spectrum. Official Scottish documentation notes positively an ability to attract over 200 call centres, even though these have been shown to be highly mobile, low value-added, low paying and lacking in regional staying power.[5] Scottish productivity trails Finland, the Netherlands, Belgium, Germany, France and the United States. Its entrepreneurship index shows lower levels than the UK as a whole, and digital connections are two-thirds those of London.[6]

Thus it can be succinctly stated that Scotland faces a number of issues as it transforms into a knowledge economy. The central challenges are related to how Scotland can:

1. attract and retain talented labor,
2. optimize knowledge spill-overs and value creation, and
3. attract high value-added foreign direct investment.

All of these issues ask the question 'how can they construct community, and construct advantage?'

In order to achieve this, Scottish Executive (regional government) and Scottish Enterprise have designed a number of policies and programs. It has a series of complementary activities, such as *Scotland: A Global Connections Strategy* (2001), *A Smart, Successful Scotland* (2001) and *A Science Strategy for Scotland* (2002). These documents illustrate the progress that has been made since devolution.

However, all the news is not good news. For example, the science strategy bears a remarkable and undifferentiated resemblance to the science strategies of a number of countries, including Canada, South Africa, Finland, Denmark, the Netherlands and Australia. It lacks specificity to Scotland's unique capabilities, opportunities and challenges. It emphasizes schools and public awareness, but does not locate itself within the economic context of the entrepreneurial, innovative, knowledge-intensive future of Scotland. Direct comparisons are problematic in that independent data, for example, GERD/GDP, HQP/capita for Scotland are not yet available. Moreover, there seem to be major disconnections in the production and flow of value-added knowledge. For example Scottish universities, which are world renowned, also show a disinclination towards collaboration with local players, especially other Scottish universities. International bilateral relations seem to be greatly preferred over multi-lateral research with local industry. The data displayed in Figure 11.1 illustrate this tendency.

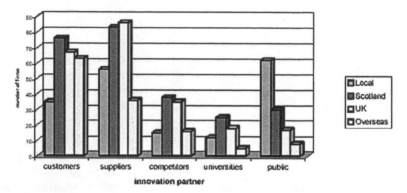

Figure 11.1

Scottish innovators rely more on distributed supply chains – notably distant final customers and on local suppliers for innovation, but not on local competitors, collaborators or universities. This eats away at efforts to construct community.

Put another way, the potential for building scale effects which are often required for competitive, world-playing (never mind world leading) research is largely missing. A similar tendency can be seen in the private sector, where pharmaceutical firms (for example) tend to situate themselves in stand-alone sites (not in science parks or knowledge communities) and deliberately separate research, development and design functions, only to distribute the value-added components abroad.

These types of examples, all gleaned from interviews with university officials, private sector executives and public servants in Scotland with the OECD Expert Panel, suggest that regions facing similar circumstances must adjust their longstanding commitment to a view of trade and production that is based on comparative advantage in which 'value-added' is defined in terms of 'what we have'. Nor can they, given a small domestic market base and population size, follow a strategy which centrally assumes scale and scope of either domestic consumer market or industrial capacity. Instead, they might well consider following a strategy of constructing advantage to maximize the impact of what they do as opposed to what they have.

A key factor we have identified as missing from the Scottish example is the notion of interactions.

INTERACTING COMMUNITIES

Much of the popular literature on the global economy has emphasized the growing importance of interdependencies between regions and the speed of interaction because of information and communication technologies. Indeed, many of the citizens of OECD countries are now 'on-line' both at work and at home.[7] They are connected. Scotland and Canada are both nations that claim policy and government program success in connecting their citizens to the internet. But connectivity in and of itself does not lead to regional economic development. National initiatives need careful integration with local networks adding another layer of complexity to our argument.

Some influential contributions to this debate have in fact suggested that the nation state is dead.[8] This is clearly a nonsense. We should acknowledge that governance is more complex, involving the play between local institutions (firms, colleges, universities, city halls, local councils), regional governments, national governance bodies (including NGOs) and multinational agencies such as the EU and the WTO. But governance now is also *more* important.[9] Traditional arguments about industrial policy and top-down government intervention in the market place are now moot. But new arguments about innovation policy through which local ingenuity, entrepreneurial vigor and appetites reach up and are met by regional and national government policies and programs which are adaptive enough to in essence become customized to local needs, is now the way forward. Why is this?

NOTES

1. www.scotland.gov.uk/stats/bulletin/00234-00.asp
2. In the last research assessment exercise, six Scottish departments received the highest '5-star' rating.

3.   This number is imprecise as the Knowledge Exchange also notes as an aside that the electronics industry employs 41,000 people but this figure does not jibe with the otherwise stated figures.
4.   Scottish Key Facts compiled by the Knowledge Exchange (Glasgow), 21-11-02.
5.   cf. Richard Nimijean, 'St. Johns New Brunswick as an Emerging Local System of Innovation', in John de la Mothe and Gilles Paquet (eds) (1998), *Local and Regional Systems of Innovation*, Boston, Kluwer.
6.   Spectrum International Benchmarking Study, 1999, cited in *A Smart, Successful Scotland* (2001).
7.   The antithesis of Timothy Leary's motto, 'turn on, tune in, drop out', it would seem.
8.   See for example Jean Marie Guehenno, *The End of the Nation State*, University of Minnesota Press, Minneapolis, 1995; or Kenichi Ohmae, *The Invisible Continent*, Harper Business Press, New York, 2000.
9.   John de la Mothe (ed.), *Science, Technology and Governance*, Continuum, London, 2002.

12. Constructing Advantage in Cities

As we have now seen, innovation is about handling complexity. It is fundamentally about interdependences, linkages, networks, partnerships, co-evolution and mutual adjustment. In international business studies, this set of facts is well known.

For Robert Putman, governance is about building a strong and active civil society.[1] In his excellent study of the political economy of Italy, *Making Democracy Work*,[2] he details how bakers or priests can have more political and business decision-making power than mayors. Yet a stable civil society is sustained. He also documents how macro-fiscal and monetary policies can actively hinder the growth of firms, ensuring an economy of small firms – thus, they think, protecting Italy's rich culture – and inadvertently promoting the shifting of Italian multinational industrial investment and activity over the borders, to France and Switzerland and further afield.

For Richard Florida,[3] the importance of place in a knowledge-driven economy is key. Constructing communities involves developing an organizational ethos that now signifies successful firms, cities and regions. Florida refers to this clutch of ideas as 'the rise of the creative class'. On the surface of course, this basic presentation may seem facile and non-operational from an urban planning, mayoral and managerial perspective. However, if one were to look, even at the most elemental of ingredients, involved in creative knowledge-intensive communities, then we could boil it down to the availability of infrastructure (both physical and smart – that is connectivity), leadership, capital and people. Urban planners, in Florida's world, might observe that quality of life, as represented by bike paths, a clean and recreational environment, safety, orchestras and other cultural venues – including blues and jazz clubs, good schools, cinemas, a vibrant downtown, and so on, which all are attractive to highly educated workers.

Florida and Putman both understand that communities are based on adaptive relationships,[4] networks and mutual interests.

171

In a networked economy, private ownership gives way to social space. Jeremy Rifkin refers to this as 'the age of access'.[5] In a broad sense, one could differentiate between differing types of networks.

Rifkin likes to point to supplier networks in which organizations sub-contract for a range of inputs; to producer networks in which organizations pool their production facilities, financial resources and human resources; to customer networks in which manufacturers, distributors, marketing channels, value-added re-sellers and end users work together; standard coalitions in which as many organizations as possible establish standards of practice around the industry leaders; and technology cooperation networks in which valuable knowledge and technical expertise is shared.[6]

Using these ideas, this chapter will sketch out some recent work on cities, the interactions between cities, and the governance of innovation in some smaller nations as they try to create communities in their quest to construct advantage around science, technology and knowledge.

THE CASE OF SOME CANADIAN CITIES

Cities of course are at the heart of economic growth in any country. In 2001, the Canadian Advanced Technology Alliance (CATA) launched a series of TechAction Town Hall meetings. This was in partnership with KPMG and other industry sponsors. It looks likely that this initiative will be extended in Raleigh-Durham (North Carolina), Tucson (Arizona) and Austin (Texas) in 2005.

The TechAction Town Hall meetings, held across Canada, involved executive community stakeholders who gathered to voice their concerns and pool their ideas about how to stimulate innovation and knowledge-based industrial growth. The goal of this series was to create a community based consensual for specific actions to grow the community's use of high technology in the near future. The TechAction Town Hall meetings had two components

1. An extensive survey of city executives and leaders, and
2. the business and community leadership surveys which were used to create an 'Action Blueprint' to advance community growth:

Here is a summary of some outcomes at the local level.

Calgary, Alberta

Calgary is an oil town with high-tech capabilities. It has a fine university, and along with the University of Alberta in Edmonton, has developed considerable skills in oil and mineral-related areas such as Geographic Positioning Systems (GPS). Having established an advanced technology centre, Calgary is confident in its capacity to innovate and that it will play a vital role in a national effort to improve innovation. Access to capital remains an issue. Calgary, however, possesses well-educated human resources, an adequate technical infrastructure and highly skilled leadership. Calgary's challenge is to put in place the financial measures to sustain its momentum in the coming decade.

According to Calgary's leaders, 'Action Blueprint' should be undertaken to overcome their challenges in the five areas measured in the survey:

- People: improve and focus management skill training around local areas of advantage
- Infrastructure: improve the marketing of Calgary's infrastructure and location advantages
- Capital: have government encourage venture capitalists to treat high tech in the same way as oil and gas
- Leadership: support and adjust taxes for early-stage business growth
- Innovation: provide more streamlined access to innovation programs

Halifax, Nova Scotia

Overall, technology business leaders are positive about the quality of life, social infrastructure and the education system in Halifax. Access to venture capital and interest from venture capital firms are seen as barriers to growth. The outlook, however, remains positive regarding regional innovation potential. Local leaders expect that a mix of government and public/private sector partnerships will help ensure that the required infrastructure is in place to support this anticipated success.

Action Blueprint:

- People: tie education more closely to employment needs
- Infrastructure: create a clear vision of our technology future
- Capital: create an angel investment community
- Leadership: move from silo mentality to a common branding for the community

Ottawa, Ontario – Canada's Capital

Ottawa scores high in all growth components needed for the advanced technology sectors. Access to capital, skilled human resources, technical infrastructure and leadership are already at hand. Ottawa is also rated positively for quality of life and social infrastructure. Local firms, however, tend to raid fellow companies rather than rely on colleges and universities for new recruits. Ottawa's challenge today is to put in place the measures to sustain its momentum in the coming decade
Action Blueprint:

- People: increase collaboration between industry and universities
- Infrastructure: reinstate support for broadband
- Capital: encourage investment related to the New Economy
- Leadership: create a benchmarking system to give foresight against the global best

Vancouver, British Columbia

Almost 90 percent of the Vancouver executives reported that they live and work in a vibrant and sustainable community, albeit due principally to neo-Ricardian comparative advantage, based on tourism, a deep harbor and natural resources. Although access to capital is an issue, more than half of Vancouver's business leaders are confident that the city is a global innovation leader, but based on what? Respondents advised the government to adopt an internationally competitive tax regime as its priority to ensure future innovation strength. Vancouver's greatest challenge today is to obtain capital for its continuing expansion.

Action Blueprint:

- People: identify Vancouver's priorities, and develop cross-disciplinary studies at universities
- Infrastructure: create physical and specialized infrastructure to energize specific clusters
- Capital: establish a method to allow individuals to share company risk, and reflect it in tax exemptions

- Leadership: create industry forums to encourage leadership and vision

In conclusion, understanding the strengths and challenges facing these cities – and creating an Action Plan to resolve them – is the most important single task facing communities today. Cities drive economic growth, in every advanced economy. While we often speak of growth in terms of national statistics, growth is in fact a local phenomenon.

Canadian cities contain 95 percent of all the businesses in the country. In today's global 'smart' economy, it is more important than ever that our cities be given the best possible foundation to invent, grow and generate the tax base on which all our social programs and our structure as a nation depend.

Let us move to another level, that of smaller regions or nation states.

NOTES

1. Robert D. Putman, 'Bowling Alone: America's Declining Social Captial', *Journal of Democracy*, January 1995, p. 65. This valid line of argument is less successfully amplified in his *Bowling Alone: The Collapse and Revival of American Community*, Touchstone, New York, 2000.
2. Robert D. Putman, Robert Leonardi and Raffaella Y. Nanetti, *Making Democracy Work*, Princeton University Press, Princeton, 1993.
3. Richard Florida, *The Rise of the Creative Class: And How It's Transforming Work, Leisure, Community and Everyday Life*, Basic Books, New York, 2002.
4. See John de la Mothe and Gilles Paquet (eds), *Local and Regional Systems of Innovation*, Kluwer, Boston, 1997; John de la Mothe and Albert N. Link (eds), *Networks, Alliances and Partnerships in the Innovation Process*, Kluwer, Boston, 2002.
5. Jeremy Rifkin, *The Age of Access: The New Culture of Hypercapitalism Where All of Life is a Paid-For Experience*, Tarcher Putman, New York, 2000.
6. *Ibid.,* P.19-20.

13. Lessons From Cities and Smaller Nations

Economic growth is local. National aggregate statistics notwithstanding, the causes – and benefits – of sustainable economic development are embedded in local institutions and people. In other words, if the OECD estimates that a country will experience growth of, say, 4 percent next year, no one expects this growth to be evenly distributed across every region. Growth is therefore 'lumpy'. Foreign investments, industrial concentration and talent agglomerate in areas that have prepared and culturally conducive institutions. We have seen this repeatedly in empirical studies, from comparisons of Route 128, Silicon Valley and science parks to numerous assessments of clusters and cities such as Dresden, Ottawa, Singapore and Austin.[1]

LOCATION

In all of these studies, the readiness of local and regional economies has proven to be decisive. The role of robust and active governance – a matching of 'top-down' policy making and program design with 'bottom up' leadership and action – is key. Governance is no longer about picking winners but is one of backing leaders. Of course, on one level, this simple observation is not surprising given Marshall's work, a century ago, on industrial districts. In this important and well known work, the decision to locate a firm, to start a firm, the demand for and supply of skilled labor, the draw on local and foreign investment capital, the inculcation of entrepreneurial drive, and so on, all relating to traditional factors of production, were seen as key. This is still true. Manufacturing and primary services still matter. Indeed, these combinations of factors of production allowed trade patterns, based on local advantages such as natural resources, to be well understood. 'Value-added' was based on what was 'at hand' (an abundance of wood, marine life, coal, climate, and so on). Much of this, which can be noted

177

here for its emphasis in terms of improvements of manufacture, improvements of technical skills, the development of local value chains, market access and trade profiles, can be linked with the work of the great Scottish political economist, Adam Smith.

FACTORS OF PRODUCTION

But what has dramatically changed since the time of Smith and his 'invisible hand', has been a global and critical shift in the factors of production. No longer do we rely, either analytically or in terms of strategy, decision and policy, on simple capital and labor $(Q=f(KL)$ equilibria. Instead, knowledge is now added to the equation. Growth accounting has, since Solow, made knowledge and technology *en*dogenous, not only in the eyes of economists but in the minds of policy makers.[2] Why is this so?

KNOWLEDGE

Knowledge is largely a public good. Unlike physical resources, it can be used and re-used over time without losing value. Intellectual property can be transferred locally and internationally without ownership being lost. Uncertainty is high in its production (that is, research), but this drops rapidly as it is imitated and diffused. Of course, firms pursue strategies of being world leaders, close followers, or imitators; each carries with it a variety of risk and investment requirements, particularly across industries. This in itself has significant implications for firms and regions. Traditional views of comparative advantage can be overturned by the governance of knowledge and innovation as can sources of advantage based on scale and size of domestic market.

Today, customization, niche production, knowledge and networks deliver *increasing* returns. The factors of production have changed and the contexts of smaller economies differ. In the cases of the Nordics, Scotland and Canada, for example, proximity to the former Soviet Union, the United States, the United Kingdom or the European Union most assuredly have had an important impact on industrial performance and structure. The cases of Australia, South Africa, Singapore and Taiwan, for example, differ again, but not because of their immediate proximity to large markets but more because of colonial histories. All are small or medium-sized economies, lacking scale or scope in the traditional sense. But all are competitive in the global economy based on innovation and knowledge-intensive activities. Thus the question remains on the front burner of decision makers: 'given an uneven playing field in comparative terms and a deficiency of scale and scope, how can we build advantage in the new economy?'

CONSTRUCTING COMMUNITY AND ADVANTAGE

Evidence shows that successful cities and regions understand that multiple levels of policy makers need to ask a series of ongoing questions. These could be stylized in the most simple of ways.

Q1: Why are people 'here' and why would people come and stay?

In Canada's eastern maritimes, the social demographic shows the highest number of universities per capita, the highest educated population and the highest aggregate level of unemployment in the country. This is because, while people are born in Nova Scotia, New Brunswick and Prince Edward Island, they move to Toronto or New York for graduate school and only return to the maritimes for retirement after a successful career elsewhere. From an economic development and innovation perspective, cultural charm and familial ties are therefore not enough. They *will* come however *if* there is opportunity for business development, risk capital and market access. Quality of life of course *does* matter, but for many people this means: is a place safe, can I run (ski, bike, walk), can I get to work easily and inexpensively (this is an issue for Londoners), and so on. But from a talent/investment/growth point of view, this is a subsidiary issue.

Q2: Why is investment drawn into a region?

Responses to this question would include: access to smart people; access to infrastructure; access to leveraged funds; access to new and adaptive technologies; footholds into new and potential markets; and a complementary regulatory regime. Moreover, branding efforts often ring hollow for investors. Where is 'silicon glen' in Scotland or why say 'the tartan tiger'? Incidentally, Canada, Wales and Ireland have also used the 'Tiger' metaphor despite the fact that no one has ever seen a tiger in any of these locales and even Dylan Thomas lamented about a 'Wales without wolves'.[3] No one is looking for a tiger. They are looking to invest in entrepreneurial opportunity, in locations that can grow smart firms, employ smart people, and to penetrate world markets. Regional and small national governments often fall into hyperbole. This actually deflects investment, perhaps attracting 'vulture capital' instead of *venture* capital. Gerhard Mencsh clearly understood this when he wrote his book on *Stalemate in Technology* in 1978.[4]

Q3: What should public decision makers do?

- Recognize, deeply, the nature of innovation. Many do not. Underneath the obvious factors of production, innovation is based on risk, uncertainty, expertise and networks. Sustainable communities are built on local networks and a spirit of collaboration. Public decision makers can play a critical role in this.
- Engage local industries, university instructors, higher education leaders, not-for-profit organizations and youth groups.

How can these two basic proposals be conceptualized and achieved? One of course could easily fall into the thoughtful area of Schumpeter or Hayek. But *practically* we can say, 'let's look at our city, our region, our future, and our potential as a community'. OK. We may wish to draw a diagram such as Figure 13.1.

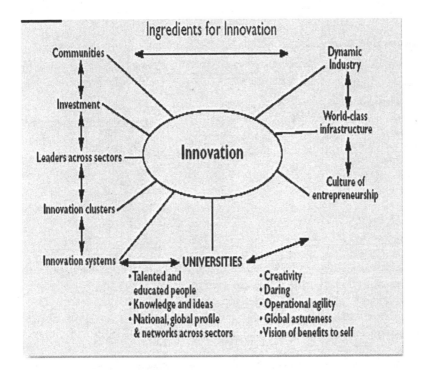

Figure 13.1
Source: Heather Munroe-Bloom, University of Toronto

What does this show? Not much maybe, but it does make us alive to the fact that creating communities and economic advantage is a 'full contact sport' and not a dry policy-making exercise. For innovation and growth to occur, a region or a city needs collaborative relationships. Otherwise why stay, why commit, why invest? This simple figure actually *challenges* leaders and decision makers at every level.

One can see how this has been recently adopted, albeit not perfectly, by the City of Ottawa (Figure 13.2).

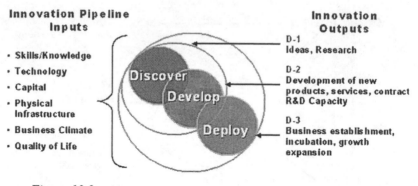

Figure 13.2
Source: City of Ottawa, 2002

Thus we can draw some issues for regions and smaller states and point to some lessons from Canadian cities that are trying to develop.

A 'smart' region needs leadership from all local actors, firms, universities, government and non-governmental organizations. This requires engagement, vision and debate in order to see your community as viable and vibrant in the global economy.

The innovative community also needs physical infrastructure, including airports, good roads, local amenities and institutions that offer support for investors and skilled people. Investment today is *not* going into New Haven even though it has Yale University and it is close to New York City. This is because the city has not dealt with the crime rate, has not dealt with revitalizing the downtown core through renovation, and only one airline goes into Tweed International Airport so it is hard to get to. Instead, Newark is getting tremendous investment and inflow of talent because of its ease of access, proximity to New York (20 minutes), good schools (Rutgers and Princeton are near), and so on.

COORDINATION BETWEEN NATIONAL AND REGIONAL ACTORS

An important element on constructing communities is one we alluded to earlier; linking regional actors with national policy institutions and frameworks which are becoming an increasingly strong force in research and innovation. However, regions and smaller nations differ enormously. This can be seen in Table 13.1.

This indicates that there are only two countries with a strong interaction between the national and regional level: Sweden and the UK. In Sweden the entry of the county as a regional actor is quite new, and at the same time these counties have few powers and little funding. The picture in the UK is more complicated with some regions having had a strong independent position (Scotland and Wales) in innovation, whereas the English regional policies such as the recent Yorkshire Forward initiative are newcomers to this field.

In 1998, the Swedish government introduced a new regional industrial policy. Based on the prevailing conditions of each individual region, the aim of the policy is to stimulate sustainable economic development that will spawn more companies and help existing enterprises expand. At the same time, regional 'growth agreements' were also introduced to facilitate implementation of the new policy.

Table 13.1

	Co-ordination - national and regional
Canada	• Strong State involvement in knowledge production, but concentrated in Ontario, B.C. and Quebec • Little co-ordination between federal and regional policies
Denmark	• Activities of regional actors dispersed over counties and local communities and often sub-critical (small budgets) • National level attempts to help co-ordinate within and between counties
Finland	• R&D heavily concentrated in few areas (Helsinki, Tampere, Olou) • Activities of regional actors dispersed over counties and local communities and often sub-critical (small budgets) • ST&I responsibilities very centralized at national level
Ireland	• ST&I responsibilities very centralized at national level and implemented by regionally allocated agencies
Sweden	• Strong co-ordination of national and regional research and innovation strategies • Regional performance contracts
United Kingdom	• The Regional Development Agencies are a relatively new actor with increasing innovation budgets

	<ul><li>Aimed to deliver research and innovation services from DTI</li><li>Strong interaction with DTI</li><li>In Wales and Scotland strong Development Agencies who work quite independently</li></ul>

A growth agreement must be primarily based on a fundamental analysis of the business development prerequisites in the region. Based on the analysis, a development program is formulated aimed at utilizing the identified opportunities and satisfying the need for measures to promote business sector growth.

According to the Swedish Ministry of Industry, the encouragement of a cross-sectoral approach to regional growth and development means that multi-sectoral collaboration should also be intensified between the various Swedish ministries. For this reason a special committee consisting primarily of the state secretaries from various ministries has been set up. Most of the ministries are represented on this committee, which has the overall responsibility for co-ordinating issues relating to growth and employment policies within the government offices.

When the new UK government came into office in 1997, it was committed to create a new level of regional administration across England. This was to both an attempt to emulate the economic success achieved in Wales and Scotland and provide some psychological balance to offset the creation of the regional assemblies in Northern Ireland, Scotland and Wales. The new regional development agencies (RDAs) were given an economic development brief by London. Over time, the RDAs have seen their 'innovation' budget grow. A series of national innovation funds (Competitiveness Development Fund, Innovation Clusters Fund, Regional Innovation Fund) has been launched, each one larger than the last, and each one more open in terms of the conditions set by the Treasury and DTI (the source of the funding).

As the RDA innovation budgets have increased, so the central DTI budget has been squeezed to the point that its enterprise budget (£330 million) is almost entirely expended through regional delivery channels. In practice, central government expects a growing share of innovation support activities to be determined and delivered locally (most RDAs now have a Science Council).

The Innovation Liaison group meets quarterly, is coordinated by the DTI and involves officials from London and the regional government offices in discussing policy needs and instruments (to minimize overlaps and underlaps) and has been opened up to the RDAs. This has proved popular and there is talk of strengthening the mechanism through the creation of a high-level steering group with its own budget.

SOME OBSERVATIONS FOR INNOVATION STRATEGY AND GLOBAL BUSINESS

Rather than develop a formal conclusion to this chapter it is perhaps more appropriate to briefly summarize the argument and make some observations on the implications of our analysis for strategy makers in firms.

At a very basic level, economic growth is lumpy and occurs within countries and regions but is actually centered on cities and regions. 'Smart' cities, that is, those with good infrastructure, smart people and capital, are capable of generating significant economic growth while traditional sources of competitive advantage, based on national sources of comparative advantage or on scale benefits, disappear as the global economy shifts.

Policy makers and strategists should turn their attentions towards constructing sources of advantage. The process envisaged, and the basis of the questions posed in this chapter, are focused not only on a policy debate between regional city and national governance systems, itself quite a distinctive idea, but also with other interested stakeholders; most notably with sources of inward direct investment, that is, firms and their managers.

NOTES

1. See Saskia Sassen, *Cities in a World Economy*, Pine Forge (Sage), Beverly Hills, 2000.
2. No longer is technology seen as $\overline{T}$ as being equally accessible over time and space, to all 'rationale actors' who possess 'perfect information'. See any of the textbooks on macroeconomics by N. Gregory Mankiew.
3. Politicians have recently referred to Canada as the Northern Tiger, Wales as the Welsh Tiger and Ireland as the Celtic Tiger. Even India is having trouble holding on to its real tigers!
4. Gerhard Mencsh, *Stalemate in Technology*, Ballinger, New York, 1978.

PART THREE

Cultures of the New Economy

14. Innovation, Globalization and the Challenges to Science and Technology Policy

INTRODUCTION

In the past decades, the character of both the world economy and the world order – from the fall of communism to Iraq – has changed dramatically. Science and technology have become deeply implicated in the move towards an increasingly 'globalized,' open and knowledge-based economy. In so doing, they have continued an ascendancy that began over five decades ago.

There is little dispute over the importance of science, technology and innovation in shaping the competitiveness of firms and the wealth of nations. There is widespread agreement that both will be critical to our understanding of emerging security and trans-boundary environmental issues. However, these economic and geopolitical changes are creating a context that is fast-paced, deeply interactive and interdependent, and thus are making many traditional policy responses – and assumptions – inadequate. Science and technology policy is under increasing pressure to organize, manage and direct an ever expanding and complex enterprise.

This chapter outlines some of these more important shifts and suggests some considerations for the future of science and technology policy.

EMERGING CHALLENGES

Innovation policy is a practical activity concerned with developing, managing and supporting the capabilities of countries to advance and apply knowledge. The dynamics of how best to do this are vexing. By the mid-1960s, this policy arena was considered to be a legitimate concern for governments, and during the postwar period, the relationship between science and the state became ever closer. Publicly-funded research budgets expanded rapidly in the widespread belief that the same approach to scientific research that had delivered nuclear weapons, antibiotics and jet aircraft would advance other national interests. In international relations, a healthy science system was seen as a hallmark of national prestige and cultural achievement. Encouraged by such statements as Vannevar Bush's *Science: The Endless Frontier* and Harold Wilson's speech on the 'White Heat of Technological Revolution,' an extensive research infrastructure was built for the advancement of knowledge and the protection of the public interest. This ranged from the development of well-funded and well-equipped university systems, government laboratories and other technical institutes to the creation of such agencies as the National Science Foundation (NSF), the National Aeronautics and Space Administration (NASA), and the British Atomic Energy Authority.

This expansion was common in a great number of countries. In Canada, Australia and Great Britain, for example, the number of universities, polytechnics and colleges grew rapidly; in Switzerland, international facilities for physics and energy research, like the Centre European de Recherche Nucleaire (CERN), were thought to be model agencies, soon to be replicated elsewhere; in France, its *grands projets* strategy for dealing with energy, nuclear power and transportation was developed.

Public expenditures on science and technology grew enormously; they now exceed \$250 billion annually. The Group of Seven (G7) nations now employ more than three million professionally-trained scientists and engineers. The scientific communities publish more than twenty thousand scientific papers daily, and the number of authors per paper is growing. These multi-authored papers reflect the rise of research teams – not individuals – as the norm; new kinds of collaboration between institutes, disciplines and nations are increasingly common. The concomitant rise of very expensive, collaborative, mega-science proposals to governments (outside the normal framework of research council applications) has increased, particularly since the late 1980s.

These, ranging from centralized facilities like the Sudbury Neutrino Observatory to distributed research platforms like the geophysics program of Lithoprobe and shared facilities such as the Canada-France telescope in Hawaii, suggest how various these institutions can be. Today there is considerable discussion about mega-visions – such as the Moon/Mars project and the closing of Hubble – and the more distributed issues such as stem cells.

New science and technology-based industries – from electronics, telecommunications and aeronautics to biopharmaceuticals – provide a vast number of jobs and are regarded by many to be the backbone of economic growth.

The system that delivered these benefits focused on institution building, individual researchers, disciplinary research and research grants. But, as Nathan Rosenberg has intimated, the linear model of innovation that science and technology policy has long assumed – which saw the links between research and growth as a relay race where participants pass the baton from one to the other – is 'dead, but it won't lie down.' Today's challenges are formidable and stem from a number of shifts both in the nature of the research enterprise and in the nature of its socioeconomic context.

These can be sketched briefly (1) The nature of science is changing: science is growing at an increased pace; the 'line' between science and technology has become blurred; and scientific and technological research is becoming transdisciplinary, increasingly transnational, and team-based. (2) The nature of economic activity is changing: science and technology are becoming increasingly relevant in such areas as trade, investment, foreign relations and regional development, as well as in a host of social and environmental areas. (3) The management of science and technology is changing: the costs of doing scientific and technological research are changing; governments are trying to reorganize their research funding, evaluation and foresight activities in order to position themselves competitively and to anticipate impacts; and governments are being forced to downsize public expenditures on higher education and science and technology while maintaining the enterprise's public prestige. The consequences of these shifts for the practice of science and technology policy are serious and must be considered.

THE SCIENCE-TECHNOLOGY-ECONOMY NEXUS

Many policy analysts and politicians today equate science and technology with innovation. However, innovation is a complex activity in which science and technology are only partial inputs. As Joseph Schumpeter noted long ago, innovation – upon which economic growth depends – cannot only be found in research and development (R&D). It can also, and more importantly, be found in the development of new products and new industrial processes (both of which may involve formal research) and in the search for new raw materials or new markets. And it can include social reorganization in the ways in which firms arrange their research, development, design, production, management and marketing functions. These are principally the domain of private firms, but public policy can influence innovation through the provision of a stable macroeconomic environment through tax regimes, monetary policy, trade policy, regulatory frameworks and standards, and intellectual property rights. Understanding how each of these affects a nation's scientific, technological and educational capabilities is in any government's best interest.

The boundaries between science and technology policy and the more traditional economic, industrial, trade and foreign policies are shifting. Indeed, throughout the 1980s, the term 'industrial policy' was something of a taboo in the United States, the United Kingdom and Canada, although with the new Paul Martin government in Canada it seems to have returned. The idea of government intervention in the economy seemed, at the time, to be anathema to healthy, sustainable economic growth. But, as Sylvia Ostry and Richard Nelson have recently noted, many influential people continue to argue that government should not be supporting the development of technology, but that this should he left up to business alone. However, high technology industries have, from their beginnings, been complex structures in which public institutions such as universities, and private for-profit ones such as business firms, have interacted.

This is a fundamental point. High technology industries in North America, Europe and Asia have developed because of government involvement. The style and extent of involvement have varied, but government-business-university interaction has always played a critical role.

In a sense, then, governments have been instrumental in shifting the industrial profiles of countries away from low knowledge or low value-added occupations, and in so doing have helped improve standards of living. Moreover, government sponsorship of research, training and education has been a major boon to the development of new jobs and industries.

In the so-called 'new growth theory' or 'strategic trade theory,' these factors are central. Innovation and the science-technology-economy nexus are broken down into their constituent parts: the 'black box' of technical change is seen as a series of dynamic processes that rely on both institutions (firms, universities, government departments) and knowledge. Analysts have been able to explain the innovative behavior of firms and regions by pointing to the combination of organizational histories and routines, the available know-how, research and skill sets, and the cultural and financial qualities offered by the local environments.

It is now widely accepted that any national science and technology policy must follow from the premise that firms – not governments – create wealth through science and technology. It is also acknowledged that public investments in science and technology have an indirect effect on economic development. These basic parameters apply across all countries, but the manner in which they are translated into policies and programs is mitigated by the organizational structures that exist within each country.

NATIONAL SYSTEMS, DIFFERENCES AND INTERDEPENDENCE

Science and technology infrastructures and policies differ across countries and regions. These differences, which Henry Ergas defined as being either 'mission oriented' or 'diffusion oriented', form the basis of competition and comparative advantage. Until recently, for example, countries like the United States, Sweden, the United Kingdom and France spent a considerable amount of their R&D dollars on military, space and energy missions whereas countries like the Netherlands, Denmark, Sweden, Finland, Australia and Canada focused their efforts on technology diffusion and knowledge transfer. The different approaches taken by countries can also be discussed in terms of 'supply and demand'. In this formulation, 'supply' is concerned with the provision of new ideas, new skills and trained personnel. The 'demand side' is more focused on getting new ideas, research results and technologies into practice. Which approach a country will take is based on its national capabilities and resources. Italy, for example, is a member of the G7 but it does not have the resources necessary to match Germany, Japan, or the United States in science and technology. It therefore follows an 'adopt and adapt' strategy, which promotes flows of foreign technologies into the country while ensuring research exchanges with (in particular) Europe and the United States. It also ensures that its membership in geopolitical 'clubs' allows access to new knowledge and technologies. A third way of classifying approaches is to group nations according to their science and technology expenditures. Thus, if one were to take R&D expenditures as being synonymous with technological advance, there would clearly be six leaders: the United States, Germany, Japan, Sweden, Switzerland and Israel. The first three countries have industry-financed R&D output ratios of around 1.8 percent and gross expenditures on R&D (GERD) as a percentage of the gross domestic product (GDP) of more than 2.5 percent. The leading group is followed by Austria, Italy, the Netherlands and Canada. Such taxonomies work well as a first approximation, but they can be misleading when questions of efficiency and quality arise.

A fourth, and more promising, framework, the 'national system of innovation' (NSI), has recently emerged from the Organization for Economic Cooperation and Development (OECD) and the work of B.Ä. Lundvall. It deals not with aggregate expenditures but with the interactions between organizations (user-producer linkages), networking, and the role of various institutions (government agencies, universities, and financial institutions).

In this framework governments are seen as 'guiding' or 'framework institu-tions' while universities are seen as training grounds and custodians of scientific knowledge. The policy and strategy goal of an NSI is to produce scientific and technological knowledge within national borders for consumption and the construction of competitive advantage. In this scheme, the majority of innovating units are corporations, but governments provide R&D funds, promote the training of scientific and technical personnel through research grants and scholarships, foster the development of 'smart infra-structure' (i.e., the information superhighway), negotiate the international 'rules of the game' (vis-a-vis national security, transboundary environmental conventions, trade, intellectual property rights and antitrust laws) and articulate national goals. The quality and quantity of these inputs decisively determines the characteristics, strengths and weaknesses of an NSL. The debates surrounding science and technology policy – like those concerning economic growth – have typically focused on a select 'club' of NSIs: advanced nations that have been shaped largely by the experiences of the Cold War.

However, with the end of a bipolar world, the relative decline of American hegemony, and the rapid rise in the number of nation-states, there are several factors besides economic performance that make size an important limiting factor in the scientific and technological strength of countries. Small countries tend to have limited domestic markets. This means that firms in small countries must export to foreign markets in order to gain economies of scale. They may also be heavily influenced in terms of trade or procurement policy by being in close proximity to a major power: the United States in the case of Canada; Germany in the case of Austria; or the former Soviet Union in the case of Sweden.

Increasingly, they also need to justify heavy expenditures on R&D, for as technology increases the sophistication of products and processes, so the scientific, technological and industrial resources and skills development become more costly and complex. Small countries tend to have less money, proportionally, to spend on R&D. They also have fewer research personnel per capita, and there is a considerable tendency for researchers from small countries to emigrate. Moreover, small countries have problems in concentrating R&D efforts. They need to fund across the full spectrum of scientific, engineering and technological research for educational purposes and in order to be as open as possible to new developments, but in so doing they often fail to define their own technological niche areas, buying into, or falling behind, the research agendas of larger countries. As a result, technologically advanced small countries generally adopt a specialization strategy. They tend to seek market niches, while the industries they support are those in which they already have strong niultitechnology corporations. (In the case of Canada, for example, these would include Bell Northern Research, Northern Telecom and Alcan.) Thus, while there may be a consensus across a wide number of countries on the importance of investing in science and technology and while the major problems of organizing a 'knowledge infrastructure' may be quite similar across the more advanced nations, policies may in fact be quite different.

As small, open economies begin to organize themselves or collectively join various science and technology 'clubs', their power to set market and research agendas rises. This is particularly notable in the case of the non-advanced small economies as they join a 'race' to find strategic cooperation partners, attract foreign investment and emulate the patterns of other countries to develop core technologies: the new science and technology agenda of the Organization of American States (OAS) involves cooperation between Latin America, Canada and the United States; Israel and its neighbors are engaged in joint technology transfer programs to strengthen the research infrastructure of the region; and post-apartheid South Africa has moved toward establishing researcher exchange programs with Canada and the Netherlands.

New world economic divisions are also emerging. As the European Commission warned in November 1994, these are different from the traditional East/West and North-South splits with which we have lived for four decades. Today we see the same dichotomies around discussions of the Free Trade Area of the Americas (FTAA). Now nations are divided between those that are 'catching up' and those that are gradually being excluded. But as can be seen in a previous chapter, catching up and falling behind are not the only options. Leaping ahead is an options as well, as we've seen with Singapore, Taiwan and other non-viable states (in Ricardian terms).

The general impression that there is a process of 'catching up' is broadly confirmed by science and technology indicators. If one examines the GERD/GDP ratios of countries in the period from 1981 to 2003, one finds a convergence of R&D intensity among the European Union (EU), the European Free Trade Agreement (EFTA) and the North American Free Trade Agreement (NAFTA) countries, and Japan. And, taking as a measure the scientific output in peer-reviewed journals over the same period, there is a stabilization taking place across fields. There has been a dramatic increase in the world share of publications produced by Spain, South Korea, Taiwan, Singapore and China, although their impact is still low. Each of these countries has essentially gone from zero representation in world scientific publishing to between 1 and 4 percent of the world total, beginning to rival the output of countries like Australia and Canada, What these indicators show is that in key areas of research – namely computing, engineering, mathematics, biochemistry and material science (i.e., areas upon which critical technologies and competitive advantages are built) – these nontraditional players are deliberately and successfully constructing a credible research base.

The excluded group is comprised of some one hundred nations, mostly in Africa and South America, and represents less than 1 percent of the world scientific publications, R&D expenditures and patents. It also contains about 30 percent of the world's population. With this minimal level of involvement in the creation of scientific and technological knowledge, the prospects for economic growth are low.

A third group of countries exists within the penumbra of the excluded countries. These are small nations that have had the beginnings of a sophisticated research infrastructure but unfortunately are in the process of 'moving backwards', much to the consternation of their researchers. For example, in Ethiopia sixteen years ago, researchers at Addis Ababa University had access to twelve hundred journals, but the elimination of the foreign currency budget in 1989 forced the library to cancel 90 percent of its subscriptions. Library shelves now stand bare, and research instruments are aging rapidly.

INNOVATION AND TECHNO-GLOBALISM

International trade has been one of the main engines of economic growth in the postwar period. With the liberalization of trade, world trade flows increased by more than 500 percent between 1950 and 1975. This compares with an increase in world output of only 200 percent. Outpacing output growth as well were expenditures on R&D, which in 2003 reached $500 billion annually, However, more recently something of a reversal has occurred. Research and development spending has flattened and investment flows have taken over from trade as a prime mover for economic growth. International investment flows now regularly top $1500 billion daily. In the process, technology and production flows have seen a remarkable growth. This new internationalization has been called 'techno-globalism'.

The internationalization of R&D, knowledge production, and technology is part of a much wider trend towards industrial and economic integration. Because technological advantages are major components of the international strategies of firms and nations, it should not be surprising that there are likely to be differences between the international distribution of R&D capabilities, and the pattern of commercialization, application and use of the results of technological advance. High technology industries accounted for 16 percent of OECD total manufacturing exports in 1970; in 1992 this figure had risen to 20 percent and stood at 26 percent in 2001. Within this group, there has been a considerable redistribution of export market shares, especially between the United States and Japan during the 1970-1992 period. Exports of medium technology industries remained constant in the 1970 – 1990 period, accounting for 43 percent of total manufacturing, and stood at 41 percent in 2002. Within this group, the United States and Japan experienced the largest changes in shares of motor vehicle exports, with the US share falling from over 18 percent in 1970 to 10 percent in 2001 while Japan's share nearly tripled to 22 percent. Low technology exports constitute a shrinking portion of the total OECD manufacturing exports, falling to 19 percent in 2001 from 22 percent in 1992. The US share of the total has increased from about 11 percent to 14 percent in 2001, while Japan's has fallen to 6 percent. The European countries decreased their shares from 26 percent in 1992 to 21 percent in 2001 (source: OECD STAN database, May 2003). The shift in knowledge production can also be seen in the activities of nontraditional players. Though starting from a very low base, growth rates in high technology exports from the Philippines, Venezuela, Malaysia, Singapore and Indonesia have all risen in value by more than 130 percent since 1986. China, over the same period, has achieved a growth rate of 1,700 percent and their pressure on the new economy is commented upon daily in the press.

The internationalization of production over the last three decades has led to a global diffusion of technologies and 'best practice' production techniques. But as firms have placed production facilities abroad, so too have they moved engineering, maintenance and R&D facilities. Important differences can exist between home user and foreign user requirements: foreign regulations, standards and procurement specifications can vary, as well as local customs and tastes. These factors have led many multinational firms to become involved in offshore R&D and technical design. Canada, the United States, France and Japan have the highest distribution of foreign industrial laboratories; the number of Japanese R&D facilities in Europe has risen from 77 in 1990 to 400 in 2000. International technology transfer among the more advanced economics is on the increase, and, since the 1970s, trade in high technology goods and services has increased dramatically, diffusing technologies throughout developing and newly-industrializing countries. The flow of researchers between countries has also increased markedly. Traditionally, this has been the most important mechanism of international technology transfer: skills move with people. Today, knowledge crosses borders in the form of patents, published articles, blueprints and manuals. In addition, advances in telecommunications have made it uneconomic to move people when information can be transported electronically. Nonetheless, an important part of knowledge and knowledge transfer is tacit (in the form of memory, experience, etc.) and therefore cannot be easily accessed or learned except through direct contact. Science and technology also crosses borders through international technical alliances, strategic alliances and joint ventures between multinational firms, The 1991 R&D collaboration between Motorola (US) and Northern Telecom to develop interfaces and compatibilities between Motorola's cellular telephones and Northern Telecom's central switching systems is one example. The 1992 research agreement between IBM, Siemens and Toshiba to create a new generation of memory chips is another. Similar agreements can be seen in the March 2005 announcement between IBM, Sony and Hewlett Packard of 'The Cell', an ultra-fast next generation chip. In information technologies, biotechnologies, and new materials, US-Japan agreements and US-Europe agreements represent approximately 40 percent of all alliances.

Disputes between nations over unfair subsidization and protectionism are destined to increase around technology and research-related questions. As a result, countries will shift their conceptions of national security away from military concerns and towards economic interests. Given the current environment post 9-11, the military-industrial complex has morphed into a style of dual-use technology development and appropriations. As technology, investment and trade become increasingly tied, and as the number of nations increases, pressures will continue to mount on the abilities of the diplomatic corps of nations – particularly science attaches and trade commissioners – to anticipate and evaluate such issues.

WHAT DOES TECHNO-GLOBALISM MEAN FOR INNOVATION AND INTERDEPENDENCE?

In recent years debates about science and technology within the OECD countries that had been building since the 1960s were brought to a head. In 1992, all candidates for the American presidency called attention to the profound changes that were taking place in the spheres of the economy, security and the environment, and made particular reference to the interdependencies that were emerging between nations. In February 1993, the Clinton administration issued a technology policy that focused on industrial technology development and world markets. In May of that year, the British government published *Realizing Our Potential*, a White Paper that called for national priority setting in science and technology and the establishment of a Foresight Steering Committee. In June 1993 the Dutch government released its policy statement on the issue, entitled *Competing with Technology*. In 1994, the Canadian government announced a maim- science and technology review that would look at duplication, coordination and changing institutional mandates within its science-based departments and national laboratories, and at the views and priorities of the Canadian public and its industrial leadership.

In 1995, the Australian government followed suit, releasing a series of reports from the Office of the Chief Scientist on national goals and priority setting in science and technology as well as on the future national requirements for science and technology. The issue of science and technology had seemed to have gained government attention. But by 2003 candidates' speeches focused on social security, security and other social issues, all of which implied science and technology, but the innovation system had taken largely a back-budget seat. Policy statements, governmental reorganizations of their science systems and their science advisory apparatus, and extensive public scrutiny of expenditures all point to the fact that something of a consensus has been reached on the importance of science and technology. This recognition no longer centers around culture and prestige, but now almost uniformly focuses on wealth creation, social development and border security.

The principal concern throughout the OECD is still with budgets. As one veteran of Washington politics put it, 'the budget is policy'. This is a 'hard realist's' perspective, but after two decades of almost unbridled growth budgets are being constrained. In Canada, cuts were *de rigeur* in the science and tech-nology budget in 1995/1996 and it was hardly visible in 2005. In Europe, science and technology budgets are being heavily constrained as governments seek to reduce public deficits and public spending. Think of the the cancellation of the Super Conducting Supercollider (SSC) in the United States and the repeated redesigns of and soon to be defunct International Space Station are both visible examples of these pressures.

The late Harvey Brooks has pointed out that no one speaks of priority setting and evaluation when funds are plentiful. But today's period of fiscal restraint is forcing governments to justify expenditures, evaluate critically between competing proposals and research areas, and identify technology areas that are critical or strategic to the nation's interests and industrial strengths. This process has led many nations to leverage funds from nonpublic sources through university-industry programs, the design of research consortia, networks and 'centers of excellence', matching industry contributions to university research, the promotion of international cooperation between researchers, and so on. It has also led to the criteria of utility and industrial application taking a stronger position over scientific merit, and it has forced governments to factor in the intentions of foreign governments to participate in projects before deciding whether to fund mega-science proposals. All of this has shifted the nature of research activity.

Over the past decades, there has been a convergence by governments on the distribution of funds across broad socio-economic objectives. These include a decrease in the share of public funds allocated to energy and defense research, a strengthening of the objectives of social welfare (including health, education and the environment), and a commitment to strengthening the science base. But in the process, the nature of science and technology policy has been altered as well.

Decision-making processes have become focused on short-term, 'value for money' concerns. Some governments have reduced science and technology expenditures across the board so that the onus is now on science-based departments, national laboratories and universities to 'do more with less'. Still other debates are concerned with whether the social sciences should be funded with public monies or whether technology foresight and technology assessment capabilities are worthwhile activities. There are also indications that governments are increasingly willing to look at the social effects of research and development. This will not be confined to issues of biodiversity or climate change but, because of the expanding sites of knowledge production, will involve consultation with citizen groups and international organizations. To some degree, this has been more a feature of the American system than of others. The US National Science and Technology Council, for example, has noted in its international science and technology strategic planning document that such issues as population stabilization, food security and nutrition, and challenges of (re)emerging infectious diseases will require considerable international effort in the coming years. Science and technology policy will be improved by augmenting the advisory structures of governments. This is partly because a plurality of institutions tends to strengthen democratic decision-making. But it is also because as science and technology become increasingly implicated in a vast array of issues, broad-based advice will increasingly be required.

CONCLUSIONS

The challenges and pressures facing science and technology policy today cover a complex range of factors that both international research communities and national governments will have to face in the decades ahead. They are at the heart of international trade relations, foreign policy, economic strategy, and social interests. Despite the best efforts by such institutions as the EIJ, the OECD and the NSF, the data that is available to measure science performance, technology developments and innovation are thin. Yet their collection and analysis needs to he supported. There may be a danger as well that too much science policy can be counterproductive! The growing policy convergence among countries and the desire to 'do more with less' may actually impede the performance of the research system. But the need for technology assessment, research evaluation, and science and technology foresight activities will only increase as knowledge-based activities continue to become central to public policy concerns, and as policy makers require a more articulate appreciation of the complex linkages, dynamics and impacts that are brought on by research systems. These activities also need to be supported. Broad consensus is emerging across governments on the importance of science and technology; national and public debates regarding science and technology are common and frequent. Governments are seeking ways to set priorities and adapt to change without damaging the research enterprise. And the challenges of techno-globalism will increasingly bring the need for cooperation, collaboration and an aggressive recognition of innovation and its interdependence.

15. Innovation, Science and Priorities in Open Societies

Now here I come to a bit of a disjuncture. Until now I have spoken about themes and evidence surrounding innovation and interdependence. But I believe both are deeply embedded culturally and historically. With your permission, kind reader, I will swing in that direction, because science, technology, discovery and innovation are electric. Let me begin with my kind friend. The late Harvey Brooks of Harvard University once commented that priority setting in science is especially difficult in times of cost cutting. Many lab managers know that this is true. Since the 1980s, many countries have become engaged in public policy exercises aimed at reducing the overall size of government and the size of deficits. The language that governments have used has varied, but has included such phrases as 'breaking through bureaucracy', 'right sizing', 'value for money', and so on. In these processes to re-balance the public books, public science has not been spared, though private science has indeed grown. Thus as government budgets declined, choices – priorities – needed to be made. The growth of science has been quite impressive across the OECD countries, but the share of public support for science has been steadily dropping. As a result, the private sector has become the main funder and performer of science thus posing important questions about the role of government policies and priority setting in intellectual property rights, standards, university research, technology transfer, and so on.

The effects of this restructuring are particularly strong in smaller and transitional economies. This is because they tend to have fewer researchers per capita and fewer absolute dollars to spend, while concomitantly needed to increase their exposure to world science and technology in order to stay at or near best practice. But their researchers need not only to carry out research but also must be good enough to recognize relevant science carried out elsewhere and import it. Thus problems of knowledge transfer and knowledge diffusion are of paramount importance in questions of priority setting and capacity building.

Unfortunately, in the restructuring process, the natural (if reactionary) response is to view the situation in terms of the ideological or political bias of the ruling party. Seen in this characteristic way, 'conservative policies' are thought of as tending to prefer free market operations, minimal government intervention and as having preference for trickle down economics, whereas 'liberal policies' are thought to prefer redistributive income schemes and some form of central planning. In point of fact, there is no liberal and conservative science policy. In our globalized interdependent world economy, we are well beyond left and right. 'The Third Way' that we find in Britain and America instead displays a clear practical amalgam of interests[1] and, as we search for a new social contract between science, government and society we find that we are operating in a new social context for science, one that is typified by a context of open societies, not endless frontiers.

INNOVATION, SCIENCE AND OPEN SOCIETIES

It is important to recognize the socio-political embeddedness of innovation and science. The term 'open society' was first introduced to the English speaking world in 1935 by Henri Bergson.[2] In his formulation, the open society stood as a paradigm of development for the community of man, something that resonates at this end-of-century meeting joint meeting of UNESCO and ICSU. To Bergson, all politics which we have known until now have been conducted on the premises of the closed society. To a large number of English speaking readers however, it was the Austrian philosopher of science, Sir Karl Popper, who is most identified with the phrase. Again, like Bergson, Popper emerges from the pages of *The Open Society and its Enemies* (1945) as being a deeply humanitarian man, and his conception of the open society has more deep similarities with that of Bergson than is general recognized.[3] But in both cases, readers are invariably left to ask 'what is the open society open to?'. It is of course recognized that Popper was writing at a time of great darkness in terms of the threat of totalitarian regimes[4] and centrally planned policies.[5] But this still does not lead us to a clarification.

This problem has continued to plague us today. Indeed, as Lord Dahrendorf has deftly put it

> Some concepts have an annoying quality. They are, and potentially are, attractive, but they are so loose, so baggy, that many [writers] are tempted to stuff their own

preferences into them until their original definitor gets confused and eventually lost. Our public discourse at this time provides illustrations ... Moderisation. The Third Way[6]... New Labor ... The open society has come to be a concept of this kind.[7]

And yet, major figures such as George Soros have chosen to annoint their philanthropic organizations with the open society moniker.[8]

Nonetheless, if one can let go of the hermeneutic difficulties, we can use the concept *lightly* to illuminate certain characteristics of 'the open society' which are of use in outlining the contours and tensions currently associated with scientific priority setting in small economies.

It may be something of a convenience, but I find it interesting that a clutch of ideas developed around the mid-century by a loose group of Austro-Hungarians, several of whom knew each other, can be so deployed.[9] (It is also fitting this this brief connection be at least noted given that this meeting is itself being held in Budapest.)

If we are indeed looking to flesh out the idea of an open society within the contemporary context of a knowledge-based economy or an information society,[10] and therefore at the role of science and technology *in situ*, then we must embrace an understanding of how knowledge production is best achieved.

To approach such an understanding, one could do worse than to point to (for the purposes of this brief note), and to immerse in, the observations of the 'invisible college' to focus on the importance of creativity and insight in science.

CREATIVITY AND INSIGHT

All of the invisible college – F.A. Hayek, Michael Polanyi, Peter Drucker, Joseph Schumpeter, and even Arthur Koestler (once he had given up his political writings) – feature a deep understanding of the fact that human knowledge and especially science is dependent on creativity, insight and judgement. But this still leaves problems of organization in the sense of priority setting.

COORDINATION AND SPONTANEOUS ORDER

To Hayek, the optimal coordination function for human knowledge can be best described in terms of 'spontaneous order'. He starts with the socio-political importance of knowledge in terms of the way we organize our societies, in oblique reference to the open society.'The enemies of liberty have always based their arguments on the contention that order in human affairs that some should give orders and others obey.'[11]

Of course, this is a seed of totalitarianism in which science withers and it too is a descriptor of top-down management styles in large organizations which often lead to organizational osteoporosis. But as Hayek rightly points out, much of the problem of organizational efficiency (including political system efficiency) stems from the problem of being

> unable to conceive of an effective coordination of human activities with deliberate organization by a commanding intelligence. One of the achievements of economic theory has been to explain how such mutual adjustment of the spontaneous activities of individuals is brought about by the market, provided that there is a known de-limitation of the sphere of control of each individual.[12]

Hayek goes on to say that an understanding of the mechanisms of mutual adjustment of individuals in a market economy is perhaps the most important part of the core knowledge we need to enter into the making of general rules.

The orderliness of human action in that we can carry out a reliable, consistent plan 'relies at almost every stage on the expectation of certain contributions from his fellows.'[13]

> That there is some kind of order, consistency, and constancy in social life is obvious. If there were not, none of us would be able to go about his affairs. *This orderliness cannot be the result of a unified direction* if we want individuals to adjust their actions to the particular circumstances largely known only to them and never known in their totality to any one mind. (emphasis added)[14]

In other words, (and for our purposes) science involves creativity, insight, as well as surprises and therefore advances cannot be known, planned or dictated top-down. He went on to note that order is guided by foresight (anticipation), by "people who make effective use of their knowledge" and who can "foresee with a high degree of confidence what collaboration they can expect from others".

NETWORKS OF EXPLORERS

On this point, Hayek relied on Michael Polanyi, recognizing that mutual adjustment in a complex, knowledge intensive field can only be the result of the spontaneous formation of 'a polycentric order'. Thus 'when order is achieved among human beings by allowing them to intereact with each other on their own initiative ... we have a system of spontaneous order.'[15] Here we have clearly both a political statement and a statement on the natural organization of science and scientists.

Such a social observation is predicated on two elements, first that knowledge is personal and second that largely it is tacit. Polanyi developed the thesis that 'into all acts of judgement [including scientific research and discovery] there enters, and must enter, a personal decision which cannot be accounted for.'[16] This emphasis on personal knowledge is not only a statement of commitment to a neo-liberal (in the British sense)[17] stand for the individual but is also meant to correct the positivistic view that scientific knowledge is objective and to attack the centralist planning appetites of J.D. Bernal and others.[18] 'Comprehension is neither an arbitrary act nor a passive experience'. It is 'a responsible act'.

As to Polanyi's major comment that 'we know far more than we can say'[19], tacit knowledge – contemporary research has shown – not only plays a key role of psychological importance but also animates vividly the innovation process as it *actually* takes place (i.e. not following the wooden linear models formulations) complete with technology transfer, diffusion, incremental innovation, and so on.

Another major element of Polanyi's contribution to the open society discussion is his application of Hayek's notion of spontaneous order, coupled with his own experience as a chemist. He did this to scope out a view of the scientific community based on a 'Republic of Science'[20] in which individual researchers chose the research problem of their own choice, guided tacitly by the avenues of work being carried out worldwide in their own field. He described both the practice and the motivation of science in terms of belonging to a 'Society of Explorers'. Not only does this framework draw on the insights of the Austro-Hungarians but it also previews the frameworks used today throughout the OECD vis-á-vis. expert networks, epistemic communities, etc.

THE ENTREPRENEUR AND CREATIVE DESTRUCTION

It is fine and well to point to creativity, insight, tacit knowledge and spontaneous order as central elements and core organizational conditions of an open society which is occupied with science. But it does not animate it. This can begin to be done through two elements, the entrepreneur and creative destruction. Both have been detailed by Peter Drucker and especially by Joesph Schumpeter.

Although Schumpeter was not the first to discuss the entrepreneur,[21] it was he who was best able to market the ideas and place them in a wider economic framework. As Schumpeter understood well, and as we have briefly suggested here, innovation is not simply a function of economic life but is equally reliant on social life as well. After an extensive treatment of the traditionally considered factors of production (land, labor and capital), Schumpter's argument deflates the view that capital is in itself productive (in that a capitalist or owner of capital does not profit from the possession of capital and merely accrues interest in a passive way). Instead he expresses a view that it is a political feature – power over the production equipment – which is not a factor of production in itself but is the basis for the energy behind capitalism. Thus replacing capital with the entrepreneur as the third factor of production, Schumpeter brings creativity coupled with ownership into the labor process. The entrepreneur is not like the ordinary manager. The production process and the means of production have no leaders in Schumpeter's view. Only the consumer can lead and the managers exist to interpret their needs. But since the consumers cannot by themselves articulate and implement the satiation of their needs, this is left up to the entrepreneur to be a determining force, as the only agent of economic change. While the entrepreneur creates new products and improves the production process with new innovations, these same improvements oust old products and processes from the marketplace, often with great social consequences. This process Schumpeter called 'creative destruction'.

Together these ideas contribute important dynamics to what an open society looks like. There is no getting around the fact that none of the scholars noted would agree with each other on all (or many) points. After all, for example, *au font* Hayek was an optimistic liberal, Popper was a social democrat, and Schumpeter was ultimately a pessimist. Moreover their points of departure were various. But the idea of an open society does indeed fuel both cultural ideas of innovation *and* interdependence, that is, the human quest for competition in which we seek together.

NOTES

1.   Anthony Giddens, *The Third Way: The Renewal of Social Democracy*, Polity, Oxford, 1998; Will Hutton, *The State We're In*, Jonathan Cape, London, 1995; John

Plender, *A Stake in the Future: The Stakeholding Solution*, Nicholas Brealey, London, 1997.

2. Henri Bergson, *Les deux sources de la morale et de la religion*, Felix Alcan, Paris, 1932 (translated by R.A. Andra in 1935 as *Two Sources of Morality and Religion*, Holt, New York).
3. There are of course numerous important differences, and Popper does trace the origins of the open society to the ancient Greeks.
4. Popper called this book 'his war effort'.
5. For an excellent review of the debate over central planning, see Daniel Ritschel, *The Politics of Planning: The Debate on Economic Planning in Britain in the 1930s*, Oxford Historical Monographs, Oxford University Press (The Clarendon Press), 1997.
6. One could add 'the civil society'. See John Keane, *Civil Society: Old Images, New Visions*, Polity, Oxford, 1999.
7. Ralf Dahrendorf, 'Three Problems of the Open Society', Karl Popper Lecture, London School of Economics and Political Science, London, December 3 1998, p.1 of mimeo.
8. Soros' organization is called The Open Society Institute. There also exists the Offene Gesellschaften and the Societá Aperta. I am grateful to Lord Dahrendorf for bringing these latter organizations to my attention. Personal communication, January 20 1999.
9. This should hardly be surprising given the widely recognized talents in the arts and sciences displayed by those from Vienna and Budapest and born between 1890 and 1920. See Laura Fermi, *Illustrious Immigrants: the Intellectual Migration from Europe, 1930-41*, University of Chicago Press, Chicago, 1968.
10. I myself dislike these terms and, if anything, prefer something like 'the innovative society' given that information is not knowledge or wisdom (so the social glue of society – such as trust and other forms of social capital – is lost) and every economy is knowledge-based and always has been, as Karl Polanyi has pointed out in his *Great Transformation.*
11. F.A. Hayek, *The Constitution of Liberty*, University of Chicago Press, Chicago, 1960, p.159.
12. *Ibid*
13. *Ibid.* p.160
14. *Ibid.*
15. *Ibid.*
16. Michael Polanyi, 'The Unaccountable Element of Science', *Philosophy*, 37, 139, January, 1962, p. 1.
17. On this distinction, see Robert Devigne, *Recasting Conservatism: Oakeshott, Strauss and the Response to Postmodernism*, Yale University Press, New Haven, 1994.
18. See Gary Werskey, *The Visible College: A Collective Biography of British Scientists and Socialists of the 1930s*, Allen Lane, London, 1978.
19. See his *The Tacit Dimension*, Doubleday Anchor, New York, 1967.
20. Michael Polanyi, 'The Republic of Science', *Minerva*, *1*, 1, 1962.
21. G. Gross (1884), V. Mataja (1884), J.B. Say (1803), and even Walras were, according to most histories of innovation, ahead of Schumpeter on this matter. Indeed it is a notion that populated the Austrian School of Economics.

16. Innovation and Interdependence in the New Republic of Knowledge

Alain Touraine, in his recent book *Beyond Neoliberalism,* asks the question 'is our society still capable of using its ideas [and] hopes to act upon itself? Attempts are being made on all sides to convince us that this question has to be answered in the negative'.[1] In many ways, this observation bears directly on policy, and to some small degree he is right. International industrial consultants, like Kennichi Ohmae, would have us believe that national governments and their policies no longer matter. Domestic political critics, like Barzelay and Armajani, would have us believe that government and their policies stand in the way of individuals realizing their full potential as *homo_economicus*, that governments have taken on too big a role in the everyday activities of their citizens and institutions. And post-modern revisionists, interested more in book sales than policy, have propagated the idea that utopia, history, politics, democracy, science, knowledge – and by extension, policy – have all 'ended'. They have not.

CHALLENGING POLICY CONTEXTS

But this is not to say that policy makers are not being challenged. There are at least four macro challenges, all focally engaged with knowledge, in which policy is inexorably enmeshed.

For example, the myriad processes and histories that have resulted in the popular short-hand called '*globalization*' has increased both the interdependency between nations as well as the pace of information, technology, and other knowledge flows. This has been accelerated by the internationalization of research and development in the private sectors, and an increase in the number of science and technology performers or service providers. At the same time, international cooperation in science between governments on a range of issues has also increased. Globalization has thus resulted in increased competitive, and cooperative, pressures. And it has critically decreased response times available to business and governments. In short, it can be said that science and technology-intensive challenges to our economy, our environment, our security – and thus to our policy making capacities – will only increase in scale and in scope. Institutions will be challenged dramatically. The new policy context is perhaps best typified by an increase in complexity and diversity.

A second related challenge stems from *how well nations produce, use and share knowledge.* 'Knowledge' refers not only to research and development in the natural sciences and engineering, but also to related scientific activities (surveys, statistics, mapping, etc.) as well as a full range of technical, managerial and social skills and cultural contexts. The way in which institutions can identify, appropriate, apply and disseminate knowledge is by acting as part of an innovation system.

The third, related, policy challenge stems from *innovation systems* – a framework, interestingly, that has been adopted by policy makers in small and medium economies such as Canada, Ireland, Australia and Norway – and reflects an important shift in how the government is beginning to think about science in the context of policy. This approach allows for a reframing of how science and technology provide useful knowledge. Further, it moves away from the highly stylized (and unrealistic) linear models of innovation in which businesses, universities and government were seen to have a clear and separate social division of labor in performing and funding science and technology, and in which R&D reliably led to technological progress and commercialization. An 'innovation system' approach allows instead for a move toward more accurate depictions of how knowledge actually leads to growth, underpins our economic and social union, and how institutions adapt to rapidly changing circumstances. This embraces the reality that no institution – business, research facility or government agency – can 'know it all' or 'do it all'. This means understanding that the benefits of an innovation system emerge not only from more R&D but also from strong partnerships, networks and linkages, through improved information flows and communications within and across sectors, through better coordination mechanisms, and by bringing decision-making responsibilities down to the most appropriate (and most responsive) level in an organization.

A fourth policy challenge can be called the *governance challenge.* It is a challenge not of reacting and micro-social-engineering but of steering and positioning complex organizations in turbulent waters. It is a matter of leadership, of responsibility and of vision, not only on the part of the science-based departments and agencies but also on the part of government as a whole in dealing with its science. A requirement is for policy groups to become highly adaptive organizations, to shift as it were from being huge ocean liners to a well-organized team of speed boats. It requires becoming effective signal processors, organizations that incorporate learning, and intelligent strategists.

Taken together, the growth and interdependencies of knowledge and *globalization, knowledge,* the surprise-generating mechanisms of knowledge-based *innovation systems,* and the strategy and leadership challenges of the new *governance* create a complex context for today's science policy makers which can best be reflected in a republican form.[2]

TOWARDS THE NEW REPUBLIC OF KNOWLEDGE

In its pure form, the republican ideal of science policy pivoted on the commitment to the idea that science and policy is a public affair.[3] This view was best forwarded by Michael Polanyi. While Polanyi is most interpreted as being a conservative thinker in the ideological sense, what his writings on science policy in fact reveal is a direct recognition of the complexity of knowledge in a democracy. It is for this reason that he clearly identifies the importance of self-directing communities, communication and knowledge flows/transfer, cooperation, and spontaneous coordination. He eschews both the feasibility and the efficacy of centralized planning in matters relating to knowledge production. In part his objection is practical as well as political: it is impossible to predict or dictate future developments in areas in which creativity and intuition rule and it is undesirable to approach complexity with a centralized mind-set when robust systems require the capacity to adapt to rapid change. In a sense, Polanyi previewed the conditions within which policy makers must operate today. The vast flow and importance of knowledge in socio-economic life, the scale and scope of interdependencies typified by 'globalization', and the systemic challenge of innovation all together conspire to challenge the decision-making and policy-making capacities of institutions, both public and private. Polanyi too previewed, in a tacit way, the need for a new organizing framework for knowledge.[4]

THE NEED TO RE-THINK

In the spirit of Michael Polanyi, Michael Gibbons and his colleagues, in two separate but linked volumes,[5] has forwarded just such a convincing organizing framework both to counter the negative orientations alluded to by Alain Touraine and the contemporary drivers of complexity found in globalization and innovation. In the first volume they argue that science in knowledge-intensive societies can no longer be acutely attended to with simplistic reference to academic disciplines, homogeneity or institutional isolation.

'Disciplines', after all, are merely social constructs – conveniences which allow us to pursue problem sets with the tools and concepts available at that time. 'Disciplines' are not static but they are complex, vibrant and continually evolving socio-technical systems. Trans-disciplinarity has thus long been the common practice in research. They authors rightly embrace the still neglected idea that most of the problems we face today – from competitiveness and productivity to population health and security – *require* a blend of natural sciences and *les sciences humaines*.

Similarly the idea that institutions are isolated entities is silly, yet it is stubbornly adhered to by some. One need only look to multinational enterprises (MNEs) to counter such views. A typical MNE, for example, can employ tens of thousands of workers worldwide, have distributed supply-chains which involve dozens of other firms, may rely on university researchers and a variety of labs in multiple institutions for contract research, and must comply with regulatory regimes which are set by governments at a range of levels. Institutional *interdependency* is thus the norm, not isolation.

This basic observation lays the groundwork for the authors' fascinating preoccupation with context – knowledge in *the context* of application. Indeed, what the authors succeed in doing is to sketch the social *milieu* in which the demands of the modern environment for institutional flexibility, adaptability and responsiveness. We need attention to knowledge flows – not just inputs and outputs as in linear models of innovation – (e.g. systemic flows of knowledge production, identification, diffusion and application) which have also been identified in more spartan terms by evolutionary economists are embraced and forged into a more viable analytic form.

In their second volume, the authors draw the arguments up to discuss the implications of their thesis for re-thinking the emerging new relationship between science and society. In sum, the authors of these two volumes have succeeded in putting forth a major template for a broad re-thinking of science and its roles. Moreover, *The New Production of Knowledge* valuably lays the groundwork – picked up and extended in *Re-Thinking Science* – for a socially distributed system of knowledge, not just an economic production system for knowledge.

Herein lies, perhaps, the most intriguing opening for a re-think of policy. Gibbons and his colleagues stress the context of knowledge. In 'weak contexts', communications patterns are determined largely by institutions and those individuals who are aggregated within institutions. In contrast, 'strong contexts' are typified by an intense involvement in the planning, strategic, and decision-making phases of an institution. These basic features allow the authors to focus on the dynamics of public spaces (*fora*) and to discuss the potential for opening new 'spaces' in complex environments. This is probably one of the most difficult elements in organizational change, including the policy world, where the tendency towards centralization, territory and control is still strong. In a world of incessant competition and cooperation, 'trading zones' become important. A term coined by Peter Galison,[6] 'trading zones' as a concept is employed in *Re-Thinking Science* to indicate that 'in Mode-2 society new spaces are opening up where, because of intensified competition, greater experimentation with potential partners in knowledge production is under way. Entrepreneurial attitudes, including the crucial entrepreneurship needed to acquire resources necessary to carry out research, are rapidly developed' (p. 145). The authors then briefly suggest that trading zones may give rise to coordination mechanisms such as 'contact languages' and 'transaction spaces' in which 'all partners bring something that can be exchanged or negotiated and, second, that they also have the resources (scientific as well as material) to be able to take something from other participants' (p. 146). These ideas of trading and transactions, of spaces and zones, are pregnant with a possible re-think of policy within the new republic of knowledge, but they are not delivered. What is necessary to realize a Mode-2 framework for policy is an attention to go the next step, to look for institutional adjustment mechanisms that are complementary to evolutionary norms as well as the signature of 'learning' in the context of policy. If we can answer the question 'can policy organizations learn?' then we will have extended both the Polanyian schema and the Mode-2 framework *en route* to answering in the positive Touraine's opening question ('is our society still capable of using its ideas [and] hopes to act upon itself?').

CAN POLICY ORGANIZATIONS LEARN?

In the realm of innovation, policy is centrally concerned with stimulating, guiding and monitoring knowledge-based activities within a political jurisdiction, typically a nation or a region. The goals of innovation policy are economic, although they are widely stated in broad welfare terms (e.g. the advancement of knowledge, sustainable development, or social benefits). Its instruments are programs and institutions, as well as ideas. However, as a policy area, not only is it – like any other policy area – deeply knowledge and information intensive but its subject is itself knowledge. Hence, given the variance of knowledge between the spectrum of explicit and tacit knowledge, knowledge management in innovation policy is by definition a domain that is fraught with ambiguity, uncertainty, judgement, creativity and spontaneity.

Thus meeting the challenges of innovation policy in a dynamic knowledge economy will require substantial advances in our understanding of how our research, technological, innovation and policy systems interact. These systems include knowledge producers (such as laboratories), knowledge users and appliers (such as firms), knowledge regulators (such as food and drug inspection agencies, intellectual property agencies), knowledge diffusers (including such smart infrastructure as information highways), knowledge funders (such as granting agencies), and so on. Elements of the needed general frameworks have begun to emerge over the past decade through the broad view of evolutionary economics and organizational learning. Substantial new attention has also started to emerge on the front of social capital. Most of that progress, however, has been from a rather high level of analysis. But while much of the recent policy research has usefully begun to look at institutions, processes and practices, there continues to reside a residual quest for 'equilibrium' states. Generally missing are approaches that are intrigued by social dynamics that can complement or embrace emerging theories of endogenous growth and technical change, complexity and networks.

Policy is a process, not a product. Yet in traditional frameworks, the individual policy maker was seen as a rational actor who needed more and better information to make 'better' decisions. The decision maker was portrayed as a thoughtful, lone individual who could be convinced by evidence and who could make sound judgements based on the merits of 'state-of-the-art' knowledge. Knowledge therefore directly effected decisions, and decisions were policy. Yet, during the early modern work on innovation policy, there was little attention paid to understanding policy learning processes or the matter in which policy organizations produced, assimilated, used or transferred information.

Over time however, research into innovation policy and knowledge production has grown considerably and has resolutely affirmed that linear models of knowledge production or management are naïve at best. The incorporation of knowledge and learning into prescriptions, as well as assessments, of organizational change and performance have relegated static rational actor models to something of a more realistic position in popular and analytic thought. Besides re-conceptualizing and dynamizing the linear notions of knowledge acquisition and learning by policy organizations, institutional theorists have often tended to portray organizations as being deficient at probing, in a substantive way, the root causes of their policy problems. In Canada, for example, questions of productivity, brain drain, avenues to enter the G-5 in terms of R&D spending and performance, the structure of research advice, targeted R&D versus breadth in spending, the benefits of priority setting versus *laissez faire*, and so on all have a *déja vu* quality in that they are on the front policy burner today for innovation policy and knowledge and have been for more than forty years. Thus innovation policies are sometimes perceived as being limited, as a result of government 'tinkering at the margins', and as being largely reactive, when faced with a problem or crisis.

Such approaches to organizational learning and problem solving thus ensure the recurrence of similar problems in the future since root causes have neither been identified or squarely addressed. In other words, through such lenses, organizations are not seen as being good learners and therefore, by extension, are seen as being poor knowledge managers. The anecdotal reality is that too many policy organizations – including innovation policy organizations – leave knowledge management and the culture of learning as an *ad hoc* endeavor instead of an important and deliberate enterprise. This results in a residual build-up – and possible clash – of rules, policies, routines, traditions, cultural and territorial artefacts that affect (or distort) the decision-making process, the interactions between technological, innovation and policy systems, and ultimately constrain the policy maker. Furthermore, numerous groups within an organization often compete in the production and policy adoption of knowledge agendas, each with their own biases and objectives, and in so doing territorial imperatives can dominate these views and actions to the detriment of policy development.

Thus, as depicted by Chris Argyris,[7] policy organizations have great difficulty in learning and seldom question the underlying basis or the interaction of their own policy problems with other policy groups. Policy organizations have been depicted as lacking in innovative understanding or action and as being resistant to organizational change, implicitly choosing to stress conformity instead of creativity. Indeed, in today's demanding knowledge-based environment, policies and policy organizations are being pressed to be increasingly flexible and responsive. Some have challenged policy organizations to develop more adaptive structures for knowledge management.[8] For policy organizations to learn, they require the requisite skill and incentives to identify and acquire knowledge, to value and store it, to share or transfer it and so on. But policy organizations cannot acquire, digest and utilize all the knowledge that is available. As Ryecroft and Kash[9] point out, organizations must become adept at operating as a networked organization, trusting in tacit knowledge, facilitating interchanges with the external environment and other related institutions, and not isolating policy analysts or actors. Self-inspection has been spouted as one tool to correct organizational deficiencies. But organizational retreats and regular 'public consultations' – which are popular with some government agencies – can sometimes be seen by employees and stakeholders alike with suspicion or cynicism, as a way to reinforce polemic.

Argyris defines organizational learning in this context as 'a process of detecting and correcting error'. I would add the need for pro-activity, strategy communication and inclusion of the ranks and would ask at what point in the delivery of a policy (however defined) can 'an error' be either defined or detected. (In other words, benchmarking and evaluation needs to be an integral part of the policy design and development process.) In the day to day operation of innovation policy – as policy operatives know – this is far from obvious. But Argyris is right in the sense that policy learning is a process in which an organization continually attempts to become competent in taking action while at the same time reflecting on the action it takes in order to learn. The policy learning process, so enunciated, is thus an iterative process, guided by strategy and vision as well as an awareness of the constituent parts (competing and complementary interests, policies, programs and initiatives), and focused around the management of knowledge which is primed to address and anticipate innovation policy issues.

LEARNING IN INNOVATION POLICY MAKING

Of course, organizational learning is a special case of collective learning – one that is of particular relevance to the study of innovation policy, policy change and policy making in a Mode-2 Society. As noted above, classical perspectives on policy defer, not to the privileged place of scientific knowledge,[10] but to notions of power, interest and coalitions rather than to learning.

With the rise of formal policy studies and analysis over the past five decades, an excessive emphasis on 'expert' technical knowledge was promoted. Parsons and Clark[11] put it well. In a then-typical view, political leaders – in creating discrete policy decision which had well defined alternatives – realised that the increasing scientific and technical content of the decisions they were required to act on required outside advice. They turned to a professional cadre of analysts, who presented the relevant scientific and technical information. The decision-makers, now knowing the relevant consequences of whatever decision they might make, then performed the appropriate balancing of values and interests to arrive at a decision. Note that the analysts operated only in a technical arena and their only audience was the decision maker. (p. 16)

Clearly, this caricature is rooted in a hyper-rationalistic version of Operations Research and does not deal well with complexity or ambiguity while it limits itself to problems that have a technical 'fix'. Few real problems fit these parameters, certainly within the realm of innovation policy that – by definition – is complex, knowledge-intensive and ambiguous. Indeed, if such an apparent separation between the technical and the political is possible, then the tension between Democracy and Reason – of the sort described by John Dewey – would not arise. But without doubt it is, for most policy analysis, a caricature. In an ambiguous and messy decision environment where policy goals are multiple and contested (i.e., reality), decision makers often do not know what question they need to ask and what the unintended consequences of their decisions may be.[12]

But even with a more realistic view of the relationships between technological, innovation and policy systems, there is still much room for learning in the innovation policy processes. At a macro level, policy analysis and innovation policy frameworks often serve a longer term 'enlightenment function'. 'Innovation Systems' is a case in point. After being widely exposed at Niagara on the Lake in Ontario, Canada in a 1988 conference on *Economic Theory and Technical Change* (the book with that same title had been edited and published by Giovanni Dosi *et.al.*), Canadian science and technology policy analysts and senior civil servants actively participated in the OECD's Technology-Economy Program (TEP) (1988-1989) in which innovation systems thinking was propagated. This process culminated in Montreal with the final TEP conference which was attended by an array of senior Canadian policy advisors, such as Sylvia Ostry. By 1993, the election statement of the Liberal Party explicitly referred to Innovation Systems as its language and framework for policy, a lexicon that continues today in policy documents and government conferences.

But the permeation and adoption of language does not necessarily connote 'learning' in policy. Bureaucracies are quite adept at adopting prevalent policy language while continuing to protect their longstanding programs. An increasing

number of studies in policy change have focused on learning as a key – yet under-
addressed – issue.[13] The most common focus is on the learning of top individual
policy makers. Three characteristic biases in the cognitive processes of
organizational decision making can be suggested, namely 'grooved thinking',
'uncommitted thinking', and 'theoretical thinking'. These serve to restrict
organizational learning. Others[14] take a similarly atomistic approach to
organizational learning, focusing on the top decision maker and not on the
integration and co-ordination of policy streams or the organizational culture
which rewards or recognizes learning behavior. Such an orientation, which
innovation policy studies are beginning to address in the corporate setting, are
therefore promising and will be pursued.

Peter Haas is almost unique in policy research in that he takes more of a
community focus in his work on policy networks in knowledge-intensive areas.
His 'epistemic communities' are created and dissolved around specific policy
issues or crises – such as Mediterranean pollution control – as they arise, but
again he gives little illumination as to the learning or adaptive capacity of policy
organizations or as to whether policy learning is sustained or temporal.

RE-THINKING POLICY AS ADAPTIVE LEARNING STRATEGIES

The idea of adaptation is not only important in the context of knowledge, learning
and innovation policy, but it is also central to evolutionary economics. David
Perkins has usefully articulated three different strategies for adaptation that policy
organizations tend to follow.

'*Adaptation by revision* is a basic pattern of search through which humans
handle most immediate and accessible needs that require search at all. A longer
more descriptive phrase would be "adaptation by trial and informed revision".'(p.
164). The advantage of adaptation by revision is its directness and efficiency. But
Perkins points out that the one limitation of this strategy is its requirement of
embedded intelligence. A second limitation is that this behavior can be trapped by
'oases traps' – that is, by local maxima through its persistent efforts to revise and

adapt directly based on which it knows. Thus longer term optimization may not be achieved.

Unlike the 'adaptation by revision' strategy which has a somewhat Lamarckian quality, *'adaptation by selection'* follows a more Darwinian pattern.

> From an initial form, variations are generated by a specific mechanism. The variations are constrained within some range – breeding roses does not produce elephants ... But they are not constrained in ways that guarantee improvements in fitness over the initial form ... A process of testing ensues, yielding a selection of the more fit variants. Adaptation by selection occurs widely ... [It] is essentially the mechanism of trial and error or reinforcing learning ... Adaptation by selection has advantages and disadvantages ... On the downside, it is inefficient, investing in many trial variations. On the upside, the process need not embody much intelligence about the fitness landscape ... Thus adaptation by selection can escape ... oases traps." (p. 165)

Adaptation by coding is a strategy that combines the adaptations by revision and by selection. 'The general idea is that search involves adaptive forms on two levels that may be called the *code* and the *construction*. The code might be a sketch or blueprint, the construction a prototype built from them. The code might be the genome, the construction the organism. The code may determine the construction closely (a blueprint or genetic code) or only loosely constrain it (a sketch or rough idea)' (p. 166).

To the extent that innovation and innovation policy are seen as not being simply bodies of practice but also as bodies or cultures of understanding – of comprehending – the nature of the learning, evaluating, and of the selection processes, become increasingly complex. While the notion of 'selection' of 'fit' may speak well in terms of the user and the provider, the realm of policy – and innovation policy in particular – masks numerous levels of impact and interaction.

If the user community is diverse, or there are many different kinds of uses, selection may preserve a wide variety of ideas. On the other hand, the body of understanding that is the result of selection may be quite unified. If both aspects are recognized, it would seem that advances in innovation policy and organizational learning need to be understood as a co-evolutionary process.

But to operationalize these notions of organizational learning with an idea to better fathoming knowledge management in innovation policy, then the question of practice comes into view.[15] Like knowledge management itself, the concept of 'practice' is deeply elusive. What are practices? What is being referred to or

analytically captured? There are numerous approaches to this in order to round
out our review. Stephen Turner has usefully illuminated this. Philosophically, the
immediate review suggests a great deal of overlap: he refers us to Polanyi's 'tacit
knowledge', to Ryle's 'knowing how and knowing what', to Kuhn's 'paradigms',
to Wittgenstein's 'inherited background', to MacIntyre's and Gadamer's
'tradition', and so on. More sociologically and legalistically thinking – and
linking to Weber, Durkheim and Tonnies – we can highlight morally binding
customs (*Sitten*) and other related socially binding frameworks. But, from a more
evolutionary framework, and in a way that is clearly complementary to these
overlapping forays, the notion of embedded routines becomes important for
policy learning in a Mode-2 sense, keeping in mind that learning in this specific
class of institutions and practices requires sustainably-changed behavior.

CONCLUSIONS

We began this chapter with a question posed by Alain Touraine asking 'is our
society still capable of using its ideas [and] hopes to act upon itself?' Michael
Gibbons and his colleagues have provided a sustained re-thinking about the
nature of the production and use of knowledge in contemporary society. They
have gone a good way towards reframing the issues. Granted, the terms 'Mode 1
and Mode 2' are opaque and distant to most practitioners of science or policy.
Moreover, drawing this bipolar distinction in such a matter invites a
misinterpretation whereas most institutional behavior and experience lies
somewhere in between the two 'modes'. But, following intuitively a republican
reconstruction project of the sort suggested by Michael Polanyi, the authors have
pointed to the exit ramp for us to positively and constructively reconsider the
changing relationships between knowledge, freedom, politics and society. In an
effort to assist, this chapter has sketched some challenges facing policy makers as
a result of the new knowledge-based realities and has focused on institutional
learning, networks and adaptation. This is perhaps a next step. But in either case,
as Jean Jacques Salomon has put it, after years of epistemological hegemony –
today – when it comes to science and our conception of science – society has
definitely talked back.[16] In an innovative and interdependent world, let us hope
that policy responds.

NOTES

1. Alain Touraine, *Beyond Neoliberalism* (Polity, Oxford, 2001, 1).
2. Steve Fuller, *The Governance of Science* (Open University Press, Ballmoor, 2000).
3. This definition of the term 'Republican' is given by Sanford Lakoff, *Democracy: History, Theory, Practice* (Westview Press, Boulder, 1996). Note how starkly different it is from the ideological 'right-wing' attribute often associated with the rise of Reaganomics.
4. For a comprehensive collection of essays, see Majorie Grene (ed.), *Knowing and Being: Essays by Michael Polanyi* (Chicago University Press, Chicago, 1969).
5. Michael Gibbons, Camille Limoges, Helga Nowotny, Simon Schwartzman, Peter Scott and Martin Trow, *The New Production of Knowledge: The New Dynamics of Science and Research in Contemporary Societies* (Sage, London, 1994) and Helga Nowotny, Peter Scott and Michael Gibbons, *Re-Thinking Science: Knowledge and the Public in an Age of Uncertainty* (Polity, Oxford, 2001).
6. Peter Galison, *Image and Logic* (University of Chicago Press, Chicago, 1997).
7. Chris Argyris, *Reasoning, Learning and Action* (Josey-Bass, San Francisco, 1982).
8. John de la Mothe, 'Empowering Information and Networks Through Adaptive Public Policies' in John de la Mothe and Gilles Paquet (eds), *Information, Innovation and Impacts* (Kluwer, Boston, 2000).
9. Robert Ryecroft and Don Kash, *The Complexity Challenge* (Continuum, London, 2000).
10. Michael Mulkay, *Science and the Sociology of Knowledge* (Allen and Unwin, London, 1979).
11. Edward Parson and William Clark, *Sustainable Development and Social Learning*, Faculty Research Working Paper Series, John F. Kennedy School of Government, Harvard University, R93-47.
12. Robert Jervis, *System Effects: Complexity in Political and Social Life* (Princeton University Press, Princeton, 1997).
13. Robert Keohane and Joseph Nye, 'Power and Interdependence Re-visited', in *International Organization*, 1987 (4), 4.
14. cf. Robert Jervis, *Perception and Misperception in International Politics* (Princeton University Press, Princeton, 1976); Ernest Haas, *When Knowledge Is Power* (University of California Press, Berkeley, 1990).
15. Stephen Turner, *The Social Theory of Practices: Tradition, Tacit Knowledge and Presuppositions* (University of Chicago Press, Chicago, 1994).
16. Jean Jacques Salomon, 'Society Talks Back', *Nature*, 2001, 412, 585-586.

17. Conclusion: The Embedded Culture of Innovation

Now to conclude, please allow me to become a tad more literary, more contextual and more philosophical, because I find that creativity and connectedness are at the core of what makes us civil and human. This book of essays has been about innovation and interdependence. Technology and innovation have made us interdependent. Creativity and the quest for knowledge are embedded into our fabric, our spirit. They are inexorably enmeshed with the human condition. Creativity is central. But the routinization of creativity has made us forget. Let us remind ourselves.

In aerospace, we have recently celebrated the anniversary of our first powered flight at Kitty Hawk, North Carolina. Steve Fossett, sponsored largely by himself and Virgin, has circumnavigated the globe without re-fueling in March 2005. In biology, we are daily remembering our discovery, and the resultant issues, from rDNA. In cosmology, with the insights of Cassini, Hubble, the Rovers, and infrared/x-ray/and optical instruments, we are looking into time. As Mars with its retrograde orbit (which confounded astrolab designers) came the closest ever in 60,000 years in the summer of 2003, we look to the skies with wonder yet cannot forget or ponder the risk and safety of the Shuttle missions or Space Station. Nor can we not think about the June 2004 achievement of the first private flight into space. We created the Internet to share data, to connect and create the global village, only to get blasted by Blaster in the summer of 2003. We chinch on public goods, believing in some market or another, and then watch the local village re-emerge again in the face of heat records, no air conditioning, no lights, no water and half a continent (North America) plunged into darkness because of some techno-fetish design flaw. (Rave on John Donne, Rave on.)[1] An extensive list of wonders and worries can be compiled − two sides of the same coin. Liberty, opportunity and technology give us water, health, security, education, connection, cell phones, cable, entertainment, nutrition. But what this shows us is that on the grounds of everyday life, in our age of innovation, economic strategies

222

and regional interdependence, we must increasingly think of knowledge in broad swaths. Complexity and chaos are *de rigeur*. Whether or not one was at the June 1999 UNESCO World Conference on Science in which women's groups, developing regions and First Nation groups interacted strikingly and constructively with policy makers and researchers regarding the social function – and very nature – of knowledge, or whether one prefers to use as a touchstone the sub-texts of literature, music, multimedia and culture, alienation and authentic experience seem to be the chief incongruent categories through which we must sift to organize what we mean when we say 'progress' (no one speaks of utopia anymore) and 'modernism': that condition in which the shock of the new is perpetually mitigated by science and research (changing our conceptions of ourselves) and technology (changing our relationships with nature and each other). Despite the ensuing interpretive confusion, however, a surprisingly common and uncannily enduring assumption about the modern element in our knowledge culture has persisted for more than half a century. Well before Hugh Kenner, Harry Levin, or Irving Howe[2] were inclined to artificially seal off the period for the purposes of study, the work of critics as different as Leavis and Lukacs was already structured by a shared presupposition that 'the modern' acts out of the loss of something primary that it wishes to regain. Implicitly but constantly amongst critics of the earlier century, the growing authority of science and technology has fueled this sense of loss.

Lionel Trilling's crisp designation of the literary 'will to modernity' as the redemptive search for a realm 'beyond the reach of culture' remains as clear a definition as available on what is axiomatic in our cultural assumptions about the modern[3]. Despite subsequent vicissitudes of the aims and procedures of cultural criticism, this presupposition has remained tenaciously paradigmatic, even determining the otherwise antithetical projects of such revisionist historiographers of literature as Fredric Jameson who simultaneously maintain both our normative understanding of modernism and our desire to change it.

The ironies of Trilling's prose, however, suggest that cultural modernism is far different from our inherited sense of it. Precise to a fault, Trilling's diction calls attention to some unlikely contingencies that his otherwise classical arguments detonate. For Trilling, an exemplary High Modernist such as James Joyce stands as such because he fully represents 'this intense conviction of the existence of the self apart from culture'.[4] Yet, unavoidably, the sly protestations of Trilling's rhetoric brings another factor into play. If, indeed, it is culture that 'knows' then how can it know any realm other than, or 'beyond,' itself? The intuitive response lies torn between a happy denial of Milan Kundera's hypothesis that 'life is elsewhere' and the tired collapse into the Enlightenment's tarnished promise of progress. What does this paradox of liberation suggest for culture? What aesthetic or discursive horizon does it close off or otherwise demarcate? For Trilling, and for many cultural critics, the answer is plain: the exemplary 'will to modernity' – the need, in Trilling's words, 'to believe that there is some point at which it is possible to stand beyond the reach of culture'[5] – is an expression of the need to reject 'how entirely implicated in culture we all are'.[6]

What kind of culture do we have in a knowledge society? Mark Kingwell of the University of Toronto explores millennial angst and body piercing in the youth culture. David Noble of York University explores the contemporary links (and ruptures) between technology and religion. Thomas Homer Dixon, formerly of MIT but now at Toronto, contemplates the implications of 'ingenuity gaps', the innovative haves and have nots, of security and environment. David Victor of Stanford University and the Council of Foreign Relations worries about innovation and climate change. The work is impressive and the list could easily be expanded to include immigration, security, borders, sovereignty, nutrition, war, etc. The now famous Madonna-Spears kiss from the MTV awards can either be read as pure PR or as a return to the collapse of culture argument of the 1930s (*Barbarians at the Gate*). But for our purposes, within a fully modernist (i.e., trans-literary) context, in which science, technology and innovation are fully implicated (and indeed leading the charge), what are the sources of authority and rupture which dictate or otherwise influence the forms of cultural response open to us? To some degree, humanist critiques of the 'Innovative State' derive a measure of unity from the contextual mode of interpretation in so far as they insist on recognizing (and responding to) the all-embracing technological character of what the Frankfurt School would call the social life-world. A tacit assumption of the literary-historical approach is the idea that culture is cognitive and meaning-generating. This conception is very much like that held by Clifford Geertz and other symbolic anthropologists – and equally difficult to operationalise. As Geertz defines it, a culture 'consists of socially established structures of meaning'; these structures are conceptual frameworks or templates that enable members of the culture to interpret the signs and symbols, practices and events that constitute their direct experience, and thereby to participate in the unending argument about meanings, values, and purposes that help set up a society's course of change.

In practice, however, anthropologists, cultural theorists and literary critics need to deploy the concept of culture in significantly different ways. Anthropologists, perhaps because of their longstanding preoccupation with relatively small, homogenous, pre-industrial societies, have tended to emphasize the unifying aspects of culture, whereas cultural theorists and literary critics need to emphasize the dissonant and self-contradictory aspects. Many analysts try, with varying degrees of success, to mask this conflict, to pretend that it isn't there and that the literary process is a 'knowing and intimate' partner of science (i.e., sharing in its authority). Clearly, this runs counter to Trilling's insightful observation that the very form of modern culture's existence is struggle, or at least debate – it is nothing if not dialectic.

Of course, such an observation is familiar as modernity is widely understood to open a series of paradoxes which are important – at the level of subject, style and logic – to observers of the cultural scenes. After all, the literature of modernity is essentially a literature about transformations in the public world and in its associated consciousness. Science, technology and innovation are never far from the surface. As Andy Groves of Intel predicted, today's technologies will become embedded – as they have – into our human fabric. Even as you read this book, students at Caltech and MIT are designing technologies to wear and monitor. The actual date of the advent of 'the modern' varies in different accounts, as do the characteristics identified by various writers. Nearly all accounts, however, have in common their concern for the public worlds of work, rationalization, politics and city life. As such the literature of modernity coincides, in effect, with that well-documented process of the separation between the public and private realms, highlighted during the era of Thatcher and Reagan, thought of during the era of Hayek and Friedman, and resurrected by George W. Bush.

Within this context; if we take seriously Weber's notion of an expanding rationalization, of the advent of a totally administered world which spells the end of the individual, then we must consider technology and science, as they are now, as the deepest languages of politics, economy, advertising and desire. They condition the histories that confront us on every corner of the Metropolis and that constitute our horizon. In so doing they contain both a moment of danger and opportunity, and, as a result, may not force us to be free, but encourage us to perpetually rethink the relationship between technique and society. They offer what amounts to a frenzied drive to liberty through a seductively disguised promise of reconciliation between the private and public via an ongoing historical amnesia. They constantly revise our images of ourselves as makers of a history we pathologically cannot recall due, in part, to the looming presence of some questionable (but assured) future. Thus, they provide the perfect focus for a modernist literature as they establish the method, logic and rationale for the fulfilment of contemporary literature's deepest wish – the eclipse of culture.

As a result, the authority of science, technology and innovation, which express themselves in all domains, is accepted by literature, and emulated in culture. For example, in the age of transparent technology, modernist literature has evolved parallel technologies of its own, both difficult and obscure. 'Et ignotas animum dimittit in artes', the epigraph to *A Portrait of the Artist as a Young Man,* claims the sponsorship of the fabulous technologist and warns us against expecting such books as we've been used to. Arcane skills, 'ignotas artes', such as those that enabled the Wright Brothers to triumph at Kitty Hawk, just over 100 years ago, have gone into its fashioning. Their machine had nothing to hide – you could see every moving part, like Joyce's prose – and yet it challenged comprehension. They first flew it in December 1903 and by January 7, 1904 James Joyce had effectively adopted the persona of Daedalus. Like the technology of its time, literary modernism sought, as evidenced by books like *Ulysses* and poems like *The Cantos* by Ezra Pound, to share in technology's authority and to become deeply technological, deeply innovative. This was their strategy and their connection.

This occurred at all levels. The internal combustion engine altered our perceptions of rhythm; X-rays made plausible transparent planes of matter; the wireless superimposed the voices of twenty countries (*Finnegan's Wake*); and newsreel quick-cutting promoted *The Waste Land.* Words moved on wires. Distant voices sounded in our ears. And under the most rigorous scrutiny, the text itself began to dissolve. Thus research, technology and innovation increasingly redefined the role of words and ourselves in relation to the text, to nature and to each other. They simultaneously embodied and promoted an aesthetic and a world view. The 'gear and girder' technologies of the early twentieth century totally displaced the still dominant Romantic view of a holistic, spiritual world. This deconstruction was thrown into bitter re-investigation with the terror attacks of 9-11 and the symbolic collapse of finance, investment, progress, profession and security. No corner of life was left uninspected. When the twentieth century poet, William Carlos Williams, called the poem 'a machine made-of words,' he presumed a very different world from that of Henry David Thoreau who wrote in 1844 that 'poetry ... is a natural fruit'. This nineteenth century belief that nature, the human imagination and art were unitary, maternal and co-generative changed radically under the machine assumptions of the twentieth. It continues to change today in the twenty-first century world of iPod culture.

Although it was technology that was most visible to modernist literature, science – and particularly the early revolution in physics – was soon to be fully implicated in culture's attempt to co-opt technology and innovation and move beyond culture. By 1921, when Albert Einstein visited the United States, the physicist had become a folk hero somewhat like Bob Dylan in the 1960s – an enigmatic and illusive prophet – and the new physics was front page news. The models of science presented by Werner Heisenberg, Max Planck, Albert Einstein, and popularizers like Aldred North Whitehead and Bertrand Russell, were dramatically different from nineteenth century models of science and appealed directly to the modernist aesthetic.

Einstein's original formulation of the special theory of relativity from 1905 stated that whereas an event viewed from two separate moving observers may appear different to each, neither observer would be wrong or encounter contradictions if he or she used the same basic laws of physics. For example, the speed of light is a constant. This might lead to contradictions, since one person observing a light beam might be moving faster than another person observing the same light beam. What happened, according to Einstein, was that the nature of time and space is altered by motion while the laws of physics remain unchanged. Einstein's later work on general relativity then extended his ideas to cover curved time and gravitation.

Max Planck's work also concerned light and motion, but he concentrated on sub-atomic phenomena. In 1900, Planck discovered that electrons absorbed or emitted light in quantum units. He also found that there was a constant by which to measure the value of such energy exchanges. These findings required the abandonment of the notion of a continuum of energy; Einstein later showed that Planck's findings suggested that light was composed of particles and behaved, or could be treated, as a wave.

Werner Heisenberg's 1927 work on the uncertainty principle, building on the work of Planck and Einstein, proposed that the error in position measurement times the error in momentum measurement can never be less than one half of Planck's Constant – said another way, that the position and speed of an atomic particle cannot both be known.

The story goes on. The new physics broke down the framework of classical physics, suggesting that space and time were fluid, and that phenomena changed depending on how they were observed (light being sometimes a particle and sometimes a wave, for example). As the old edifice of certainty was eroded, most physicists agreed that the difficulty of defining light or measuring sub-atomic *wavicles* was not due to the failings of scientific instrumentation but to the actual, ambiguous nature of the physical universe, a universe of 'fuzzy' statistical probabilities. This can be seen in the past decade, for example, in the hunt for the Higgs Boson. This ambiguity appealed to, and under-scored, the ambiguities of the modern Metropolis.

If the new physics changed our ideas about the nature of the universe, popular and literary accounts often misrepresented the implications and meaning of the scientific findings. Consequently, in their zeal to be modern, science became related in literature to democracy, free will, Bergsonian philosophy, the uncertainty of life in the Metropolis, and to the literary experiments that toyed with perspective or emphasized motion.

Nevertheless, the original angst of the humanities concerning innovation – its need to move beyond culture, its desire to emulate and gain the authority of science and technology – remained. Pressured by a lagging readership for novels and poems, an unsympathetic press, and by such assertions as those made by Gertrude Stein's brother, Leo, that progress in the arts lagged behind 'scientific' progress[7] and by Lionel Trilling, who shrewdly noted that 'in an age *of* science, prestige is to be gained by approximating the methods of science,' literature insisted on carving out an identity that was expressly dependent on science and technology. Many writers, poets and critics tried to borrow the growing science-based prestige in order to declare a place of their own. Some also argued that, to be relevant, the arts had to address the issues of the practical and technological world which people lived in. At the same time, many also saw themselves as being defenders of literature and human values *against* the very scientific (machine) age from which they were trying to derive authority and popularity. Thus, there were contradictions in the positions taken by those who wanted to both use and resist the effects of science and technology.

Given such complicity and weight, then, what has become of the relationship between science, innovation and humanities? It is clear that there are influences, just as there are scars of rupture and envies of authority. But what is, or should be, the relationship?

In asking this question it should come as no surprise that a growing concern within cultural criticism focuses precisely on this question. Far more substantial than a simple reaction to the hegemonic frameworks of C.P. Snow's *Two Cultures* or Aldous Huxley's *Literature and Science*[8] in this area, this movement has become so widespread and formalized in recent years that the Modern Languages Association has sanctioned the establishment of a Society for Literature and Science. Nevertheless, there are problems.

Throwing around such comfortable but overwhelmingly complicated terms as 'science', 'innovation', 'literature', and 'culture' might well indicate a failure to appreciate the multiplicity of meanings that they imply and the complexity of activity that they mask. To say that science and literature are products of the same culture is to say little until all three terms are understood specifically.

The formula 'science and literature' which governed much heated debate in the late twentieth century announces, through the 'and,' a difference; the innocuous copula becomes more problematic than the difficult major terms. 'And' implies relationship of course, but (para)tactically refuses to define it. The 'and' also intimates the oddity of the relationship: what can the two have to do with each other?, while it insists on implying that the relationship matters.

Reading a strong thread in cultural studies, a shared conviction becomes clear that the relationship matters because, despite the enormity of the subject and the terms, the conjunction of the two sometimes radically separated worlds of discourse represented by science and literature can help to illuminate the other and to demystify each as they sit under cloaks of unmerited cultural authority. As such, it forces us to address issues which are of ultimate importance to the way our culture and our societies are currently being shaped. Surely this is a noble and scholarly pursuit, but how is it achieved?

The 'method' is to seek common ground between science and literature in their 'cultural and social histories, paying close attention to original texts. Any divorce between text and context is undesirable,'[9] however, with the transformation of science into a mere 'discourse' it becomes increasingly difficult to define precisely what science is as opposed to, say, literature and culture. Science is reduced to a two-dimensional text, devoid of social organization or epistemological energy. In so doing, it becomes irritatingly clear that the methods often used are such that while embodying the anxious desire of modern literature to stand beyond culture and to share the authority of science, technology, knowledge and innovation, what they do is hide within a strong but unenlightening context of 'Culture'. The result is not very satisfying or very helpful. If the first and primary lesson is that science, literature, innovation and interdependence are mutually embedded in culture, nourish and illuminate each other, then surely this does not get us very far. As noted historian and sociologist of science, Steven Shapin, complains: 'work is often thought to be completed when it can be concluded that 'science is not autonomous' or that science is an integral part of our culture', or even that there are interesting parallels or homologies between scientific thought and social structures'.[10] Clearly this is not enough, nor is it entirely honest. Yet this is the tenor of many analyses.

Far more satisfying are the works by scholars like Steinman and Tichi who make no excessive claims for the 'congruities between science and literature'. In *Made in America,* Lisa Steinman focuses on the developing poetry and poetics of

William Carlos Williams, Wallace Stevens and Marianne Moore, three poets who stayed in America at a time when exile was fashionable, and who concerned themselves with defining the place of poetry in the machine age. Her assessments of the influences on imagery and style in a period in which science and technology were unabashedly glorified open possibilities for further work and make for compelling reading. In the slightly less successful, but still worthwhile, *Shifting Gears,* Cecilia Tichi presents a richly illustrated exploration of the American era of gear-and-girder technology – from the automobile and harvesting machine to bridges and skyscrapers – in which she argues that the technology redefined the human role in relation to nature. It fostered a perception of the material world as a complex of component parts, such as meshing gears, rolling bearings, pushing pistons, in which prominent American writers (including Dos Passos and Williams) became 'designer-engineers' of the word, using their prefabricated, manufactured components in poems and prose. As designers they enacted, in style and structure, the new technological values. Finally, by far the most insightful and economic are those of Hugh Kenner and Leo Marx. In Kenner's *The Mechanic Muse*, he brings his usual wit and erudition to bear in a series of essays on the response of literary modernists to their changing technological environments. In creative examinations of such familiar figures as Pound, Joyce, Eliot and Beckett, Kenner looks at how inventions as various as the Lino-type, typewriter, subway, the computer and the Internet have altered the way the world was viewed and depicted. Everywhere, innovation and interdependence. In comparison, Marx's contribution is full of cheek, argument and brilliance as demonstrated in 'The Neo-Romantic Critique of Science,' 'The Machine in the Garden,' and 'American Literary Culture and the Fatalistic View of Technology'.

Clearly, the vast range of issues (remember as Popper said, in the beginning is always the issue, and for us the issue is the dynamic of innovation and interdependence) that are of concern to literary and cultural critics in the areas of knowledge and interaction are of importance. In an age that has not only gone post-literate[11] and 'post-modern'[12] but post-scientific as well – in the sense that the products, conceptions and activities of science are no longer heroic and visible, but pervasively embodied – critics, from the literary left or the technological right, can no longer casually prod the text of past experiments and hope to say something meaningful about the process of social change. The problem can no longer be solved, as Bertrand Russell once put it, 'by a community which use[s] machines without being enthusiastic about them'.[13] In our age of the cyber, in which we are all by definition interdependent, the relationship between science and humanity can only be usefully discussed by recognizing the nature of the environment. This is worth considering as we build a new social contract between innovation strategies and society, interdependent as they are. The issues of innovation and interdependence can no longer be left to experts. We are all involved. Innovation and interdependence. We are all embedded. Or as Walt Whitman once said: 'everywhere the electric!'[14]

NOTES

1. Thanks to Ivan Morrison for this.
2. Harry Levi, 'What Was Modernism?' *in Refraction,* New York: Oxford University Press, 1960; Irving Howe, 'The Culture of Modernism', in *Decline of the New,* New York: Horizon, 1970; Hugh Kenner, *The Pound Era,* New York: University of California Press, 1971.
3. Originally published by Lionel Trilling as *Freud and the Crisis of Our Culture,* Boston: Beacon, 1955.
4. Ibid., p. 102.
5. Ibid., p. 93.
6. Ibid., p. 91.
7. Leo Stein, 'American Optimism', in *The Seven Arts,* 1917.
8. C.P Snow, *The Two Cultures and the Scientific Revolution,* Cambridge University Press, 1960; Aldous Huxley, *Literature and Science,* London: Chatto and Windus, 1963.
9. Ludmilla Jordanova, 'Introduction', in *Languages of Nature: Critical Essays on Science and Literature,* New Brunswick: Rutgers University Press, 1986, p. 17. A typographical error on the cover casts doubt as to whether the book is subtitled 'science and literature' or 'science as literature'.
10. Steven Shapin, 'History of Science and Its Sociological Reconstruction', in *History of Science,* 20, 1982, p. 176.
11. B.W. Powe, *A Climate Charged,* Toronto: Mosaic, 1984.
12. Arthur Kroker and Marilouise Kroker (eds), *Body Invaders: Panic Sex in America,* Montreal: New World Perspectives, 1987.
13. Bertrand Russell, 'Things That Have Moulded Me', in *Dial,* 83, September 1927, p. 184.
14. Walt Whitman, *The Wanderers.*

Bibliography

Acs, Z. (1996), 'Innovation and Regional Clusters in the United States', in *Evolutionary Economics and the New International Political Economy*, (eds) by J. de la Mothe and G. Paquet, Pinter, London.

Acs Zoltan (ed.) (1999), *Regional Innovation, Knowledge and Global Change*, Cassell, London.

Acs, Zoltan (1999), *Innovation in Small and Medium Sized Firms*, MIT Press, Cambridge.

Acs Zoltan (ed.) (2001), *Regional Innovation, Knowledge and Global Change*, Continuum, London.

Acs, Z., J. de la Mothe and G. Paquet (1996), 'Local Systems of Innovation: In Search of an Enabling Strategy', in P. Howett, *The Implications of Knowledge-Based Growth for Micro-Economic Policies*, Calgary, pp. 339-360. University of Calgary Press.

Alcaly Roger (2003), *The New Economy: What It Is, How It Happened, and Why It Is Likely to Last*, Farrar, Strauss and Goroux, New York.

Amstrup, N. (1976), 'The Perennial Problem of Small States: A Survey of Research Efforts', Cooperation and Conflict, XI, p. 163.

Argyris, Chris (1982), *Reasoning, Learning and Action,* Josey-Bass, San Francisco.

Arrow, K. (1974), *The Limits of Organization,* New York, Norton.

Arthur, W.D. (1990), 'Silicon Valley's Locational Clusters: When Do Increasing Returns Imply Monopoly?' *Mathematical Social Sciences,* 19, pp. 235-251.

Barker, Kate, Philip Gummett, Deborah Cox and Rebecca Boden (1999), 'The Changing Central Government of Science and Technology', Draft Paper, NATO ARW, Manchester, England, June 1999.

Barzelay, M. and B.J. Armanjani (1992), *Breaking Through Bureaucracy: A New Vision of Managing Government,* University of California Press, Berkeley.

Bennis, W.G. (1971), 'Changing Organizations', in Horstein *et al., Social Interaction: A Behavioural Science Approach*, Free Press, New York.

Bernal, J.D. (1939), *The Social Function of Science*, George Routledge and Sons Ltd, London.

Best, Michael (1990), *The New Competition*, Harvard University Press, Cambridge MA.

Bhagwati, J. (1991), *The World Trading System at Risk,* Princeton University Press, Princeton.

Boswell, J. (1990), *Community and the Economy,* Routledge, London.

Bradley, S.P., J.A. Hausman and R.L. Nolan, (eds) (1994), *Globalization, Technology and Competition,* Harvard Business School Press, Cambridge, Mass.

Branscomb, Lewis (ed) (1993), *Empowering Technology,* MIT Press, Cambridge, Mass.

Brooks, Harvey (1968), *The Government of Science,* MIT Press, Cambridge, Mass.

Brown, J.S. and P. Duguid (1991), 'Organizational Learning and Communities in Practice: Toward a Unified View of Working, Learning and Innovating', *Organization Science,* 2, 2.1, 40-57.

Bush, Vannevar (1945), *Science: The Endless Frontier,* US Government Printing Office, Washington, DC.

Carlsson, Bo (2002), *Technological Systems in Biotechnology*, Kluwer Academic, Boston.

Casadio, Claudio and Graham Vickery (1996), 'The Globalization of Investment and Trade', in John de la Mothe and Gilles Paquet (eds), *Evolutionary Economics and the International Political Economy*, Pinter, London.

Cooke, Philip Patries Boekholt and Franz Tödtling (2001), *The Governance of Innovation in Europe*, Pinter, London.

Cunningham, Paul (ed.) (1999), *Science and Technology in the United Kingdom*, Cartermill, London.

Cunningham Paul and Brendan Barker (eds) (1992), *World Technology Policies,* Longman, London.

Dasgupta, P. and J. Stiglitz (1988), 'Learning-by-Doing, Market Structure and Industrial and Trade Policies', *Oxford Economic Papers,* 40 (June) 246-68.

David, Paul, David Mowery and W. Edward Steinmueller (1992), 'Analyzing the Economics Payoffs From Basic Research', *Economic Innovation and New Technology*, 2, 73-90.

de la Mothe, John (1989), 'Science and Technology Policy Under Free Trade', *Technology in Society*, 11, 2.

de la Mothe, John (1992), *C.P. Snow and the Struggle of Modernity*, University of Texas Press, Austin.

de la Mothe, John (1996), 'One Small Step in an Uncertain Direction: the Science and Technology Review and Public Administration in Canada', *Canadian Public Administration*, 39, 3, Autumn, 403-417.

de la Mothe John (ed.) (2001), *Science, Technology and Governance*, Continuum, London.

de la Mothe John and Louis Marc Ducharme (eds) (1990), *Science, Technology and Free Trade*, Pinter, London.

de la Mothe, John and Paul Dufour (1993), *Science and Technology in Canada*, Longman, London.

de la Mothe, John and Dominique Foray (eds) (2001), *Knowledge Management in the Innovation Process*, Kluwer Academic, Boston.

de la Mothe, John and Albert N. Link (eds) (2002), *Networks, Alliances and Partnerships in the Innovation Process*, Kluwer Academic, Boston.

de la Mothe, John and Jorge Niosi (eds) (2000), *The Social and Economic Dynamics of Biotechnology*, Kluwer Academic, Boston.

de la Mothe, John and Gilles Paquet (1994), 'The Technology-Trade Nexus: Liberalization, Warring Blocs or Negotiated Access?', *Technology in Society*, New York, 16 January 1994, 97-118.

de la Mothe, John and Gilles Paquet (eds) (1996), *Evolutionary Economics and the New International Political Economy*, Pinter, London.

de la Mothe, John and Gilles Paquet (eds) (1998), *Local and Regional Systems of Innovation*, Kluwer, Boston.

de la Mothe, John and Gilles Paquet (eds) (1999), *Information, Innovation and Impacts*, Kluwer Academic, Boston.

Dosi, Giovanni et al. (eds) (1988), *Economic Theory and Technological Change*, Pinter, London.

Dosi, G. and L. Marengo (1994), 'Some Elements of an Evolutionary Theory of Organizational Competences' in R.W. England (ed.), *Evolutionary Concepts in Contemporary Economics*, The University of Michigan Press, Ann Arbor, pp. 157-178.

Dosi, G. and R.R. Nelson (1994), 'An Introduction to Evolutionary Theories in Economics', *Journal of Evolutionary Economics*, 4, 3, 153-172.

Dosi, Giovanni, Keith Pavitt and Luc Soete (1990a), *The Economics of Technology and Trade*, Harvest, Brighton.

Dosi, G., K Pavitt and L. Soete (1990b), *The Economics of Technical Change and International Trade*, Harvester Wheatsheaf, Brighton.

Dosi, G., J. Zysman and L.D. Tyson (1990), 'Technology, Trade Policy and Schumpeterian Efficiencies', in J. de la Mothe and L.M. Ducharme (eds), *Science, Technology and Free Trade*, Pinter, London, pp. 19-38.

Douglas, Mary (1986), *How Institutions Thinks*, Penguin, London.

Dunning, John (1997), *Structural Change in the International Economy*, Routledge, London.

Edquist Charles (ed.) (1997), *Systems of Innovation: Technologies, Institutions and Organizations*, Pinter, London.

Ergas, Henry (1987), 'Does Technology Policy Matter?', in Harvey Brooks and Bruce R. Guile, *Technology and Global Industry*, National Academy of Engineering, Washington DC.

Fjalland, M. (1993) 'Trade, Investment and Technology: A Comparison of Ohmae, Ostry, Porter, Reich, Thurow, and Tyson', research mimeo, Programme of Research on International Management and Economy (PRIME), Faculty of Administration, University of Ottawa.

Florida, Richard (2002), *The Rise of the Creative Class*, Basic Books, New York.

Foray, D. and C. Freeman (eds) (1993), *Technology and the Wealth of Nations*, Pinter, London.

Freeman, Christopher (1981), *The Economics of Industrial Innovation*, MIT Press, Cambridge, Mass.

Freeman, C. (1988), 'Technology Gaps, International Trade and the Problems of

Smaller and Less Developed Economies', Chapter 3 in, *Small Countries Facing the Technological Revolution,* C. Freeman and B.A. Lundvell. (eds), Pinter, London.

Freeman, Christopher (1995), 'Japan: A New National System of Innovation', in Giovanni Dosi *et al.* (eds), *Technical Change and Economic Theory,* Pinter, London and 'The National System of Innovation in Historical Perspective', *Cambridge Journal of Economics,* 19, 1, 1995, 5-24.

Freeman, C. and B.A. Lundvall (eds) (1988), *Small Countries Facing the Technological Revolution,* Pinter, London.

Freeman Christopher and Luc Soete (eds) (1990), *New Explorations in the Economics of Technological Change,* Pinter, London.

Frisby, David (2001), *Cityscapes of Modernity,* Polity, Oxford.

Fujita, M., Paul Krugman and A.J. Venables (2001), *The Spatial Economy: Cities, Regions and International Trade,* MIT Press, Cambridge.

Fukuyama, Francis (1992), *The End of History and the Last Man,* Free Press, New York.

Fuller, Steve, (1993), *Philosophy, Rhetoric and the End of Knowledge,* University of Wisconsin Press, Minneapolis.

Fuller, Steve (2000), *The Governance of Science,* Open University Press, Ballmoor.

Galbraith, James K. (1991), 'A New Picture of the American Economy', *The American Prospect,* (Fall): 24-36.

Gellner, Ernest (1995), *Anthropology and Politics,* Cambridge University Press, Cambridge.

Georghiou, L. and J.S. Metcalfe (1990). 'Public Science, Intellectual Property Rights and Research Administration', in de la Mothe, J. and L.M. Ducharme (eds), *Science, Technology and Free Trade,* Pinter, London.

Gibbons, Michael (1999), 'Governments and the New Production of Knowledge', in John de la Mothe (ed.), *Science, Technology and Governance,* Cassell, London.

Gibbons, Michael, Camille Limoges, Helga Nowotny, Simon Schwartman, Peter Scott and Martin Trow (1994), *The New Production of Knowledge,* Sage, London.

Giddens, Anthony (1998), *The Third Way: The Renewal of Social Democracy,* Policy, Cambridge.

Gilpin, R. (1971), 'Science Policy for What?' paper presented at the Conference on Science Policy and Political Science, Science Council of Canada, Ottawa, March 18-19.

Gilpin Robert and Christopher Wright (eds) (1964), *Scientists and National Policy Making,* Columbia University Press, New York.

Godfrey John and Rob McLean (1999), *The Canada We Want: Competing Visions for the New Millennium,* Stoddart, Toronto.

Goldberg, V.P. (ed.) (1989), *Readings in the Economics of Contract Law,* Cambridge University Press, Cambridge.

Gummett Philip (ed.) (1996), *Globalization and Public Policy,* Edward Elgar, London.

Griliches, Z. (1994), 'Productivity, R&D and Data Constraints', *American Economic Review,* 84, 1, 1-23.

Gwynne, Robert Thomas Klak and Denis Shaw (2003), *Alternative Capitalisms,* Arnold, London.

Haas, S. (1995), 'Economies externes technologiques, apprentissage et rendements d'agglomeration', in N. Lazaric and J.M. Monnier (eds), pp. 180-205.

Handy, C. (1995), 'Trust and the Virtual Organization', *Harvard Business Review,* 73, 3.

Hart, David (1998), *Forged Consensus: Science, Technology and Economic Policy in the US, 1921-1953,*Princeton University Press, Princeton.

Heiduk, G. and K Yamamura (eds) (1990), *Technological Competition and Interdependence,* University of Washington Press, Seattle.

Hill, C. (1989), 'National Technology Strategies Under Free Trade: Some Implications of the US-Canada Free Trade Agreement', in John de la Mothe (ed.), *Technology in Society,* 11, 7, P. 161-180.

Hollingsworth, R. (1993), 'Variation among Nations in the Logic of Manufacturing Sectors and International Competitiveness', in D. Foray and C. Freeman (eds), *Technology and the Wealth of Nations,* Pinter, 301-321, London.

Horgan, John (1996), *The End of Science: Facing the Limits of Knowledge in the Twilight of the Scientific Age,* Addison Wesley, New York.

Jacoby, Russell (1999), *The End of Utopia: Politics and Culture in an Age of Apathy,* Basic, Boston.

Jervis, Robert (1997), *System Effects: Complexity in Political and Social Life,* Princeton University Press, Princeton.

Kennon, Patrick E. (1995), *The Twilight of Democracy,* Doubleday, New York.

King, Alexander (1968), *Science and Politics,* Oxford University Press, Oxford.

Kline, S.J., and N. Rosenberg (1986), 'An Overview of Innovation', in R. Landau and N. Rosenberg (eds), *The Positive Sum Strategy: Harnessing Technology for Economic Growth,* National Academy Press, Washington.

Kodama, Fumio (1991), *Analyzing Japanese High Technologies: The Techno-Paradigm Shift,* Pinter, London.

Kreps, D. (1990), 'Corporate Culture and Economic Theory', in J.E. Alt and K.A Shepsle (eds), *Perspectives on Positive Political Economy,* Cambridge University Press, Cambridge, pp. 90-143.

Krugman, Paul (1995), *Pop Internationalism,* MIT Press, Cambridge Mass.

Kuhn, Thomas (1962), *The Structure of Scientific Revolutions,* University of Chicago Press, Chicago.

Kuznets, S. (1971), *Economic Growth of Nations: Total Output and Production Structure,* MIT Press, Cambridge.

Lacroix R. and F. Martin (1988), 'Government and the Decentralization of R and D', *Research Policy,* 17, 363-373.

Lakatos Imre and Alan Musgrave (eds) (1970), *Criticism and the Growth of Knowledge,* Cambridge University Press, Cambridge.

Landes, David (1992), *Prometheus Unbound: Technological Change From 1750 to the Present,* Harvard University Press, Cambridge, Mass.

Langlois, R.N. (1992), 'Orders and Organizations: Toward an Austrian Theory of Social Institutions', in B.J. Caldwell and S. Boehm (eds), *Austrian Economics: Tensions and New Directions,* Kuwer Academic Publishers, Boston, pp. 165-183.

Langlois, R.N. and P.L. Robertson (1995), *Firms, Markets and Economic Change,* Routledge, London.

Lortie, P. (1989), 'Setting an Agenda for a Knowledge-Based Economy', notes for a Speech before the Empire Club of Canada, Toronto, November 2, 1980.

Lundvall B.Ä. (ed.) (1992), *National Systems of Innovation: Towards a Theory of Innovation and Interactive Learning,* Pinter, London.

Lundvall, B. and B. Johnson (1994), 'The Learning Economy', *Journal of Industry Studies,* 1, 23-42.

Maddox, J. and H. McGee (1994), 'Mexico's Bid to Join the World', *Nature,* 28 April, 789-804.

Magun S. and S. Rao (1989), 'The Competitive Position of Canada in High Technology Trade', presented at Canadian Economic Association meeting, Universite Laval, Quebec, June 2-4, 1989.

Maital, Shlomo (1995), 'Peace, Trade and Technology in the New Mideast', *Technology in Society,* New York, 17 February 1995, 143-157.

Mansfield Edwin *et al.* (1977), 'Social and Private Rates of Return From Industrial Innovation', *Quarterly Journal of Economics,* (91), 221-240.

March, J.G. (1991), 'Exploration and Exploitation in Organizational Learning', *Organization Science,* 2, 71-87.

Marengo, L. (1993), 'Knowledge Distribution and Coordination in Organizations: On Some Social Aspects of the Exploitation vs Exploration Trade-off', *Revue internationale de systemique,* 7, 5.

May, Robert M. (1998), 'The Scientific Investments of Nations', *Science,* 281, 3 July 1998.

McCain, R.A. (1992). *A Framework for Cognitive Economics.* Westport: Praeger.

McFetridge, D. (ed.) (1990), *Foreign Investment, Technology and Economic Growth,* University of Calgary, Calgary.

McFetridge, D. (1993), 'The Canadian System of Industrial Innovation', in *National Innovation Systems,* R. Nelson (ed.), Oxford University Press, New York.

Mowery D.C. and N. Rosenberg (1989), 'New Developments in US Technology Policy: Implications for Competitiveness and International Trade Policy', *California Management Review,* 32, 1 (Fall), 107-124.

Mulkay, Michael (1979), *Science and the Sociology of Knowledge,* Allen and Unwin, London.

Munchau, Wolfgang (2003), 'Bullying by Large Countries Could Split Europe,, *The Financial Times,* Monday, November 24 2003, p. 13.

Nelson Richard (ed.) (1993), *National Innovation Systems: A Comparative Study,* Oxford University Press, New York.

Nelson, R.R. and S.G. Winter (1977), 'In Search of A Useful Theory of Innovation', *Research Policy*, 6, 1, 36-76.

Nelson, R.R. and S.G. Winter (1982), *An Evolutionary Theory of Economic Change*, Harvard University Press, Cambridge.

Nichols, Rodney (1995), 'Policy Pyrotechnics and Science', *The Sciences* (March/April).

Noisi, J. (1991a), 'Canada's National System of Innovation', *Science and Public Policy*, 18, 2, 83-92.

Noisi, J., ed. (1991b), *Technology and National Competitiveness*, McGill-Queen's University Press, Montreal.

Noisi, J., P. Saviotti, B. Bellon and M. Crow (1993), 'National Systems of Innovation: In Search of a Workable Concept', *Technology in Society*, 15, 2, 207-227.

Nowotny, Helga, Peter Scott and Michael Gibbons (2001), *Re-Thinking Science: Knowledge and the Public in an Age of Uncertainty*, Polity, Oxford.

OECD (1991a), *OECD Proposed Guidelines for Collecting and Interpreting Technological Innovation Data (Oslo Manual)*, OECD, Paris

OECD (1991b), *Technology and Productivity: The Challenges of Economic Policy*, OECD, Paris.

OECD (1992), *Technology and the Economy: The Key Relationships*. DSTI/STP/TIP (94)3, OECD, Paris.

OECD (1994), *National Systems of Innovation: General Conceptual Framework*. DSTI/STP/TIP (94)4, OECD, Paris.

Ohmae, Kenichi (1990), *The Globalized World*, HarperCollins, New York.

Ohmae, Kenichi (1995), *The End of the Nation State*, Free Press, New York.

Orr, J. (1990), *Talking about Machines: An Ethnography of a Modern Job*, Unpublished Ph.D. Thesis, Cornell University.

Ostry, S. (1989), 'The Political Economy of Policy Making: Trade and Innovation Policies in the Triad', Draft paper, Council of Foreign Relations, October 1989.

Ostry, S. (1990), 'The Threat of In-Action', speech at the Centre for International Affairs, University of Toronto, February 1, 1990.

Ostry, Sylvia (1991), *Governments and Corporations in a Shrinking World*, Council on Foreign Relations, New York.

Parson, Edward and William Clark (1993), *Sustainable Development and Social Learning*, Faculty Research Working Paper Series, John F. Kennedy School of Government, Harvard University, R93-47.

Patel, P. and K Pavitt (1994), 'The Nature and Economic Impact of National Innovation Systems', *STI Review*, 14, OECD, Paris.

Patel P. and L. Soete (1988), 'Measuring the Economic Effects of Technology', *STI Review*, 121-166.

Pavitt, K (1992), 'The Internationalization of Technological Innovation', *Science and Public Policy*, 19, 2, 119-123.

Pavitt Keith (ed.) (1986), *Technological Innovation and Industrial Decline in Britain*, Macmillan, London.

Porter, M.E. (1990), *The Competitive Advantage of Nations*, Free Press, New

York.
Polanyi, Michael (1959a), *The Tacit Dimension*, Anchor, New York.
Polanyi, Michael (1959b), *Personal Knowledge*, University of Chicago Press, Chicago, 1959.
Popper, Karl (1963), *Conjectures and Refutations*, Allan Lane, London.
Powell, W.W. (1990), 'Neither Market Nor Hierarchy: Network Forms of Organization', in *Research in Organizational Behaviour*, 12, 2, $9^0 5$--336.
Putnam, R.D. (1995). 'Bowling Alone: America's Declining Social Capital', *Journal of Democracy*, 6, 1, 65-78
Rae, Douglas (2003), *The City: Urbanism and its End*, Yale University Press, New Haven.
Reich, R. (1989), 'The Quiet Path to Technology Preeminence', *Scientific American*, 261, 4 (October), 41-47.
Reich, R. (1990), *The Work of Nations*, Knopf, New York.
Richardson, G.B. (1972), 'The Organization of Industry', *Economic Journal*, 82, 883-896.
Romer, P.M. (1990), 'Endogenous Technological Change', *Journal of Political Economy*, 98, 1, 71-102.
Romer, P.M. (1993), 'Two Strategies for Economic Development: Using Ideas and Producing Ideas', *World Bank Economic Review* (Supplement).
Romer, P.M. (1994), 'New Goods, Old Theory and the Welfare Costs of Trade Restrictions', *Journal of Development Economics*, 43, (February), 5-3 8.
Romer, P.M. (1994), 'The Origins of Endogenous Growth', *Journal of Economic Perspectives*, 8, (Winter), 3-22.
Rosenfeld, S.A. (1990), 'Regional Development, European Style', *Issues in Science and Technology*, VI, 2 (Winter 1989-1990), 63-70.
Rosenberg, Nathan (1991), 'Critical Issues in Science Policy*', Science and Public Policy*, 18, 6, 335-346.
Rosenberg, Nathan and Larry Birdzell Jr. (1986), *How The West Grew Rich: The Economic Transformation of the Industrial World*, Norton, New York.
Rothwell R. and M. Dodgson (1990), 'Technology Policy in Europe', in J. de la Mothe and L.M. Ducharme, (eds), *Science, Technology and Free Trade*, Pinter, London.
Rycroft Robert and Don Kash (1999), *The Complexity Challenge*, Pinter, London.
Sabel Charles and Michael Piore (1990), *The Second Industrial Divide*, Harvard University Press, Cambridge Mass.
Savitch H.V. and Paul Kantor (1990), *Cities in the International Marketplace*, Princeton University Press, Princeton.
Saxenian, A. (1994), *Regional Advantage: Culture and Competition in Silicon Valley and Route 128*, Harvard University Press, Cambridge, Mass.
Schelling, T.C. (1960), *The Strategy of Conflict*, Oxford University Press, Oxford
Schumpeter, J. (1934), *The Theory ofEconomicDevelopment*, Harvard University Press, Cambridge, Mass.
Shils, Edward (ed) (1968), *Criteria for Scientific Choice: Public Policy and National Goals*, MIT Press, Cambridge, Mass.

Silverberg, G. and L. Soete (1994), *Economics of Growth and Technical Change*, Edward Elgar, London.

Simon, H.A. (1993), 'Altruism and Economics', *American Economic Review,* 83, 2, 156-161.

Spinosa, C. *et al* (1997), *Disclosing New Worlds*, The MIT Press, Cambridge, Mass.

Storper, M. and R. Salais (1997), *Worlds of Production*, Harvard University Press, Cambridge, Mass.

Sinclair, B. (1989), 'Canadian Technology: British Traditions and American Influences', *Technology and Culture*, 20, 108-123.

Soete, Luc (1991), *Technology and Economy in a Changing World*, OECD Background Paper, Paris.

Solow, R. (1994), 'Perspectives on Growth Theory', *Journal of EconomicPerspectives*, 8, (Winter), 45-54.

Storper, M. (1992), 'The Limits to Globalization: Technology Districts and International Trade', *Economic Geography,* 68.

Strange, Susan (1996), *The Retreat of the State*, Cambridge University Press, Cambridge.

Swann Brenda and Francis Aprahamian (eds) (1999), *J.D. Bernal: A Life in Science and Politics*, Verso, London.

Teece, David (1990), 'Capturing Value Through Corporate Technology Strategies', in John de la Mothe and Louis Marc Ducharme (eds), *Science, Technology and Free Trade*, Pinter, London.

Thorns, David (2002), *The Transformation of Cities*, Palgrave, London.

Turner, Stephen (1994), *The Social Theory of Practices: Tradition, Tacit Knowledge and Presuppositions,* University of Chicago Press, Chicago.

Tyson, Laura d'Andrea (1992), *Who's Bashing Whom?*, The Brookings Institute, Washington, DC.

Utterback, James (1995), *Mastering the Dynamics of Innovation*, Harvard Business School Press, Cambridge, Mass.

Walsh, V. (1988), 'Technology and the Competitiveness of Small Countries: A Review', in *Small Countries Facing the Technological Revolution,* C. Freeman and B. A. Lundvall (eds), Pinter, London.

Walsh, V. (1987), 'Technology, Competitiveness and the Special Problems of Small Countries', *STI Review*, 2 (September).

Werskey, Gary (1978), *The Visible College: A Collective Biography of British Scientists and Socialists in the 1930s*, Allen Lane, London.

Wikstrom, S. and R. Normann (1994), *Knowledge and Value,* Routledge, London.

Ziman, John (1987), *Science in a Steady State*, Technical Change Centre, London.

Ziman, John (1991), 'A Neural Network Model of Innovation', *Science and Public Policy,* (February), 65-75.

Zysman, John *(1987), Government, Markets and Growth*, Cornell University Press, Ithaca.

Index

Abramovitz, M. 6, 69, 71
Arrow, K. 2, 125, 138, 153
Athens 3
Bernal, J.D. 63, 94-97, 136, 190
Brooks, H. 96-97, 184, 186
Bush, V. 96, 175
Crick, F. 1
De Solla Price, D. 1
Drucker, P. 36, 188, 190
Dylan, B. 209
Einstein, A. 209-210
European Union (EU) 4-5, 44-45,
89-90, 99, 123, 133, 156, 159, 166,
180
Foreign Direct Investment (FDI) 2,
39-40, 51, 70, 77, 81, 118, 130,
139-140, 157
Freeman, C. 63, 67, 71, 97, 103,
122-123
Free Trade Area of the Americas
(FTA) 48, 89, 180
Gross Expenditures on Research
and Development (GERD)
5, 14-15, 50, 102, 105-106, 123, 131,
157, 178, 180,
Hayek, F.A. 35, 168, 188-189,
190-191, 208
Heisenberg, W. 209-210
Hewlett-Packard 4, 138, 156, 182
Huxley, A. 211
Infineon 4
Joyce, J. 206, 209, 213
Kendrick, J. 6
Krugman, P. 6, 63-64

Kuhn, T. 1, 203
Kundera, M. 206
Leontief, W. 6, 55, 88-89
Lipsey, R. 18
Lundvall, B.A. 103, 122, 124, 133,
178
Mankiew, N. G. 6
Marx, L. 212-213
Microsoft 4
MTV 207
North American Free Trade
Agreement (NAFTA) 48, 56-57, 62,
77, 89, 99, 133, 180
Organisation for Economic Co-
operation and Development (OECD)
7, 36, 38-39, 40-41, 44, 47-48, 55,
58, 62, 71, 77, 94, 96, 99, 103, 119-
120, 122, 126-127, 129, 132, 135,
144, 158-159, 165, 178, 181, 183,
185-186, 190, 201
Planck, M. 209-210
Polanyi, M. 2, 63, 95-97, 125, 133,
136, 138, 188-190, 195, 197, 203
Porter, M. 6, 15-16, 63, 89, 90
Pound, E. 209, 213
Schumpeter, J. 1, 34, 38, 118, 124,
137-138, 148-149, 168, 176, 188,
190-191
Seimens 2
SNC-Lavalin 2
Snow, C.P. 211
Solow, R. 6, 88-89, 166
Thoreau, H. D. 209
Trilling, L. 206-207, 210

Watson, J. 1
Whitehead, A. N. 33, 209
Whitman, W. 213
Williams, W. C. 209, 212
World Bank 10, 62, 89
World Economic Forum (WEF) 10, 13, 62, 89
World Trade Organization (WTO) 10, 62, 99, 133, 159